MW01135356

SPIRITUAL
WAYPOINTS

SPIRITUAL
WAYP⊖INTS

HELPING OTHERS NAVIGATE THE JOURNEY

Bob Whitesel

wesleyan
publishing
house

Indianapolis, Indiana

Copyright © 2010 by Bob Whitesel
Published by Wesleyan Publishing House
Indianapolis, Indiana 46250
Printed in the United States of America
ISBN: 978-0-89827-408-0

Library of Congress Cataloging-in-Publication Data

Whitesel, Bob.
 Spiritual waypoints : helping others navigate the journey / Bob Whitesel.
  p. cm.
 Includes bibliographical references (p.   ).
 ISBN 978-0-89827-408-0
 1. Evangelistic work. 2. Discipling (Christianity) I. Title.
 BV3790.W478 2010
 269'.2--dc22
                            2009048441

To Rebecca, Breanna, Mark, Cate, Kelly, Tory,
Kai, Corrie, Dave, Ashley, and C.J.
Your love and his bring life's waypoints into perspective.

Anyone who sets himself up as "religious" by talking a good
game is self-deceived. This kind of religion is hot air and only hot air.
Real religion, the kind that passes muster before God the Father,
is this: Reach out to the homeless and loveless in their plight,
and guard against corruption from the godless world.
—James 1:26–27 (MSG)

CONTENTS

ACKNOWLEDGEMENTS

To my friends, for candidly sharing personal stories about your spiritual journeys: The waypoints you have experienced have illuminated the road for others.

To my colleagues at Wesley Seminary at Indiana Wesleyan University, Fuller Theological Seminary, and GreatCommissionResearch.net, I thank you for your assistance in charting the journey. Special thanks to Henry Smith, Jim Fuller, Ken Schenck, Russ Gunsalus, Chip Arn, Gary McIntosh, Ed Stetzer, Ryan Bolger, Eddie Gibbs, Elmer Towns, Keith Drury, and Bob Logan.

To the team at Wesleyan Publishing House, for your dedication to accurately and completely charting the journey in this book and its companion volume *Waypoint: Navigating Your Spiritual Journey* (2010). A heartfelt thank you to Don Cady, Joe Jackson, Craig Bubeck, Kevin Scott, and Rachael Stevenson.

To my wonderful wife, Rebecca, and our growing family of Breanna, Mark, Cate, Kelly, Tory, Corrie, Dave, Ashley, and C.J. Your love, support, and fellowship on the journey have made all challenges and obstacles worth the effort.

And most of all, to my Lord Jesus. The light of your words corrects my course and illuminates my path.

With the right tools and the knowledge of your destination, it's virtually impossible to get lost. U.S. government satellites have created a Global Positioning System (GPS) that allows users of handheld GPS units to track their position within thirty feet. In addition, increasingly smaller GPS units now allow hikers, bikers, commuters, and tourists to individually track their journeys with remarkable precision.

When using a GPS unit, a location that a traveler wants to remember can be designated as a "waypoint." The GPS unit will assign a precise longitude and latitude coordinate to this waypoint. This location can then be shared so that others with GPS units can find the exact location too.

As an avid hiker, I find the capability to designate and share a waypoint as a useful metaphor for marking one's spiritual journey. When people on a spiritual journey encounter a special place on their route, they can designate it as a waypoint and share it with others. Through marking and sharing spiritual waypoints, fellow travelers can share the joys as well as note the similarities in their journeys.

Better yet, in the sport of "geo-caching," hikers post waypoints (in GPS coordinates) to lead other inquisitive trekkers to a hidden stash or "cache." While the stash may include any combination of valuable and odd paraphernalia, the enjoyment lies in the ability to follow waypoints to a treasure.

In similar fashion, the waypoints on our spiritual journey lead to a cache where immeasurable blessings await.

TOOLS FOR THE ROAD

In this book, you will encounter the spiritual waypoints of leading thinkers such as Sally Morgenthaler, Tony Campolo, Shane Claiborne, Dan Kimball, Len Sweet, and others. And you will most likely know many people who are on this spiritual quest. To help all travelers navigate the journey, I have this and a complementary book: *Waypoint: Navigating Your Spiritual Journey.* While *Spiritual Waypoints* is written primarily with experienced spiritual travelers (pastors and church leaders) in mind, the smaller and more accessible *Waypoint*, written as a self-help book, helps travelers understand their own spiritual quests.

But if you are a spiritual guide who is new to the idea of *Spiritual Waypoints*, you've come to the right place. Turn on your GPS and start moving. This book is your introduction and explanation of each of the spiritual waypoints that lie behind and ahead for you, and for those to whom you are ministering.

—Bob Whitesel, D.Min., Ph.D.
www.bobwhitesel.com

As a human race we are on a journey and we need to know the road.

—LESSLIE NEWBIGIN[1]

INTRODUCTION

The church world is disconnected, incomplete . . ." Thus began the last conversation I had with Doug. He and I had met as political activists before we both became disillusioned by our inability to bring about political change. Assassins' bullets had struck down our heroes: John F. Kennedy, Martin Luther King, Jr., and Bobby Kennedy. The resulting disillusionment had been spiritually crushing, and its aftermath had driven both of us to a new, more organic purpose. We wanted to work for the inner transformation of individuals— a process we both felt would only be achieved by introducing our friends to the One who had transformed us: Jesus Christ.

Both Doug and I underwent profound changes. Doug had formerly been deep into the drug culture, while political activism had been my obsession of choice. Yet both avenues seemed ineffective toward addressing the ecological and political polarizations our generation faced. In desperation perhaps, we had turned to the worldview of Christ, who we eventually came

Life seen as a journey, an ascent, a pilgrimage, a road, is an idea as old as man himself. One of the earliest titles for Christians at the time of the Acts was "the people of the way."

—ESTHER DE WAAL[2]

to know as Lord. We found a new life in His compassion, solace, perseverance, and transformative power that eradicated destructive habits and haunts, replacing them with an authenticity for which we had longed. In those early years of the 1970s, Doug and I became passionate about this new revolution. And we had been inseparable as friends . . . until one day.

Doug announced that he was leaving the church we attended, a large and fast-growing congregation on the edge of town. In justification Doug huffed,

"Their focus is too narrow, and you know that . . . [You] used to be the most passionate person I knew for helping the hurting and poor. And now you overlook all of that and just talk about evangelism. You've got evangelistic nearsightedness . . . you've left out half the job . . . you're trying to mend their souls before you've mended their lives."

At the time, I dismissed Doug's protestations because my heart was broken by the loss of my best and most stable friendship. Doug's last words were even less considered until years later, when my research into how the church must engage culture brought me full circle, back to reconsider Doug's painful critique.

I never saw Doug again, though I did hear of his ministry. He became a lay leader in a local Catholic parish, and eventually the director of the city's homeless shelter. I admired Doug, but I always wondered why our friendship had severed. In addition, Doug's criticism that my church world was disconnected and incomplete churned in the back of my mind until almost fifteen years later when I began investigating why people do not attend church and found that many shared Doug's viewpoint.

CHARTING A COURSE OUT OF THE FOG

As a church growth consultant, I utilize community interviews to sharpen my understanding of a client's community. In 1991, I began to ask non-churchgoers about their views on evangelism and social action. For almost two decades, their responses have increasingly mirrored Doug's concerns. In these interviews, I am observing a growing criticism that the evangelical church is fixated upon the conversion encounter, and not the process that leads up to it or follows it.

How could this happen? As a professor of church leadership and growth, I knew that church writers frequently focused on the need to minister to the whole person, first to their physical needs and then to their spiritual needs. Scholars like J. Gresham Machen painstakingly described how the New Testament church ministered to the needy.[3] Leaders such as Billy Graham taught that we are to take regeneration in one hand and a cup of cold water in the other.[4] Donald

McGavran, who many regard as the father of the church growth movement, warned that "today the sinfulness of the social order offends thoughtful Christians everywhere . . . The great inequalities of wealth and poverty among the haves and have-nots, and the revolting treatment meted out to oppressed minorities, are clearly contrary to the will of the God and Father of our Lord Jesus Christ."[5]

Arthur Glasser, dean of the Fuller School of World Mission even popularized the terms *cultural mandate* and *evangelistic mandate* for the twin thrusts of Christian engagement.[6] C. Peter Wagner suggested that church growth occurs when these two mandates are "balanced," describing the cultural mandate as "the distribution of wealth, the balance of nature, marriage and the family, human government, keeping the peace, cultural integrity, liberation of the oppressed—these and other global responsibilities rightly fall within the cultural mandate."[7] Lewis Drummond updated this idiom, stating that "in postmodern terms, we might say that Jesus came to bring equal access and opportunity to those in substandard living conditions, to give voice and identity to those other than the dominant social elite, and to alleviate the ravages of capitalistic imperialism and colonialist economic aggression."[8]

A decade earlier one writer had warned that separating the cultural and evangelistic mandates created a false dichotomy, for "true Christian compassion does not erect false dichotomies which separate body and soul . . . If I love my neighbor, I will want to see him fed, clothed, cured and well adjusted. I will want to see also that he is not going to hell, doomed to an eternity separated from God."[9] The Lausanne Committee for World Evangelism even described the balance of evangelistic and cultural mandates as analogous to "the relationship between two wings on a bird or two oars in a boat . . . being inseparable."[10]

Despite these affirmations, my interviews and recollections have led me to believe that most churches today sorely lack this balance. Donald Kraybill

Lewis Drummond [states], "in postmodern terms, we might say that Jesus came to bring equal access and opportunity to those in substandard living conditions, to give voice and identity to those other than the dominant social elite, and to alleviate the ravages of capitalistic imperialism and colonialist economic aggression."

argues that the church has created an "upside down kingdom" by uncoupling economic freedom from spiritual freedom.[11] Ron Sider regrets that much of the church has succumbed to "melodramatic pessimism," lamenting deplorable conditions but feeling helpless to change them.[12]

There is an historical explanation regarding how the church split into camps that either emphasize social action or evangelistic action. Though the reason is multifaceted and beyond the scope of this book, Roger Finke and Rodney Stark give a detailed overview of this rift while Wilbert Schenk tenders a useful three-page summary.[13] Regardless of the genesis, the divide exists. And if theologians, practitioners, and observers agree that a balance is warranted, then the question this book addresses should be how is that balance achieved? I will suggest that the journey the good news travels and the waypoints that mark the journey may be the procedural map that can pierce this fog of pessimism.

BALANCING MANDATES REQUIRES BUILDING BRIDGES

I recently investigated growing churches with leaders primarily under the age of thirty. I discovered that one of the primary characteristics of these churches is not only a desire to balance the cultural and evangelistic mandates, but also a success in doing so.[14] Each of these churches was succeeding at meeting first the physical needs and then the spiritual needs of its communities.

> By leaving the ghetto behind, the church has implied that its mission is meaningless to the poor, the hopeless and the wretched—except when an ocean separates the church from the ghetto.
>
> —DAVID MCKENNA

For example, one newly planted Southern Baptist congregation met in three rented nightclubs around Phoenix, Arizona. Attaining a critical mass of over 155 attendees, they set about to purchase office and ministry space. While many churches in such scenarios would purchase a worship facility in the suburbs, this congregation purchased a homeless shelter in downtown Phoenix. At each of the three weeknight locations, the pastor reminded the attendees that "this is not real church. Real church takes place on Sunday mornings at

Sunday brunch." By Sunday brunch, the pastor referred to a weekly Sunday morning meal the church provided for over three hundred homeless people. For this congregation, this was *real* church—a weekly encounter where Christians sat alongside struggling people helping them make a better life for themselves and ultimately a life-changing encounter. "We want people from the nightclubs to serve the urban people, and this is where 'the service' takes place" observed the pastor of The Bridge, Aaron Norwood.[15]

The Bridge builds connections to the needy, a metaphor at the center of Donald McGavran's imagery of the "bridges of God." McGavran noted, "Every human society is like a town on one side of a river over which at convenient places bridges have been built . . . people near the bridges are better connected than those far from them . . . good stewards of the grace of God should remember the bridges and stream across them. 'Find the bridges and use them.'"[16]

Building bridges to the needy is a task that many evangelical churches must undertake if they are to reacquaint themselves with the needs that cry out for a cultural mandate. I do not dispute that most churches have a compassion for the needy, but usually they envision this need as somewhere else and far removed. David McKenna warns that "by leaving the ghetto behind, the church has implied that its mission is meaningless to the poor, the hopeless and the wretched—except when an ocean separates the church from the ghetto."[17]

To cross even a local chasm, bridge building will be necessary. But bridge building, by its very nature, requires clear planning and patience to execute. A span is not erected overnight or without carefully crafted plans. And thus, purposeful yet unhurried planning and pace are characteristics of all bridge building.

BRIDGE BUILDING REQUIRES A PLAN

A helpful metaphor toward depicting this planned and purposeful process is that such bridge building can be thought of as a journey. A journey reminds us that outreach is a bridge-building process that requires time, patience, mapping, and perseverance.

Sociologists James Engel and Wilbert Norton depicted this journey as a process of deepening communication. They noted that it took place over time with a variety of adaptations, stating, "Jesus and His followers . . . always began with a keen understanding of the audience and then adapted the message to the other person without compromising God's Word. The pattern they followed is as pertinent today as it was two thousand years ago."[18]

Richard Peace, professor of evangelism and spiritual formation at Fuller Seminary, looked carefully at the twelve disciples in the New Testament and concluded that a step-by-step process unfolds through which the disciples eventually have a transforming experience.[19] Peace calls this "process evangelism," summing up:

> The Twelve came to faith over time via a series of incidents and encounters with, and experiences of, Jesus. Each such event assisted them to move from their initial assumptions about Jesus to a radically new understanding of who he actually was. In his Gospel, Mark invites his readers to make this same pilgrimage of discovery.[20]

Esther de Waal, in *The Celtic Way of Prayer: The Recovery of the Religious Imagination,* notes that the Christian life has always been viewed as a journey, stating,

> Life seen as a journey, an ascent, a pilgrimage, a road, is an idea as old as man himself. One of the earliest titles for Christians at the time of the Acts was "the people of the way." We see the individual Christian as a pilgrim on earth having here no abiding city; we speak of the Church, particularly since Vatican II, as a pilgrim church. But we cannot think of life as a journey without accepting that it must involve change and growth.[21]

Lesslie Newbigin sums this up nicely saying that "as a human race we are on a journey and we need to know the road. It is not true that all roads lead to the top of the same mountain. There are roads which lead over the precipice.

In Christ we have been shown the road . . . God has given us the route we must follow and the goal to which we must press forward."[22] Thus, the journey metaphor accommodates the imagery of planned, deliberate, and unfolding bridge-building across cultural chasms.

THE HOLISM OF A JOURNEY

A journey also denotes a flexible progression with varying scenarios, milestones, interruptions, and course corrections. The journey metaphor conjures up the image of strenuous assents, downhill traces, varying impediments, and careful mapping. Maps, sextants, and modern GPS devices attest to the desire of travelers to pinpoint where they may be on their journey. Thus, the use of the journey metaphor accentuates the importance of understanding place in relation to process. Wilbert Shenk emphasized that the "flaw" with most thinking about outreach is that the "parts rather than the whole" are emphasized.[23]

The metaphor of a journey can help overcome this flaw, by emphasizing the totality of the journey. In three separate books, Ryan Bolger,[24] Eddie Gibbs,[25] and I[26] have noted that younger generations seek holistic understandings of evangelism that do not separate the Great Commission (to make disciples of all people) from the Great Commandment (to love one's neighbor as oneself). Gibbs and Bolger suggest this be viewed as "different sides of the same coin," which is an attractive metaphor because only one substance is involved.[27] But coin imagery suggests that the coin at some point must be flipped over, and a new emphasis begins. The coin imagery in this author's mind, unfortunately separates into two phases the inseparable progression of a common and continual journey.

Author Brian McLaren appropriates the word *story* to describe this process, noting:

If you ask me about the gospel, I'll tell you as well as I can, the story of Jesus, the story leading up to Jesus, the story of what Jesus said and did, the story of what happened as a result, or what has been happening more recently today even. I'll invite you to become part of that story, challenging you to change your whole way of thinking (to repent) in light of it, in light of him. Yes, I'll want you to learn about God's grace, God's forgiveness, and about the gift of salvation.[28]

This is a more attractive metaphor. But still, a story is static, inflexible, and even when modernized—historically captive. It carries none of the dynamic, flexible, and indigenous attributes of the varying obstacles, excursions, accompaniments, and progressions encountered on a journey. Thus, the imagery of a journey better highlights continuity, commonality, and elasticity. And a journey is often a communal undertaking, and thus the journey metaphor accommodates the idea of accompaniment, companionship, and inter-reliance.

A JOURNEY OF BREAKING AND REFRESHING NEWS

The word *evangelism* is maligned today, often associated with churches that coerce or force conversion in a self-seeking or exploitive manner. Yet Jim Wallis, editor of *Sojourn Magazine*, argues that a response to bad religion should be better religion.[29] In similar fashion, the argument could be made that our response to bad evangelism should be better evangelism.

Such disparagement was not always the case. The word *evangelism* originally signified breaking and revitalizing news. Evangelism is an English translation of the Greek word *euangelion* (Matt. 24:14), which described the "good news" that Christ and his followers personified and preached.[30] Customarily an optimistic message brought by a courier, *euangelion* was a combination of the Greek words *good* (*eu*) and *messenger, angel*, or *herald* (*angelion*). For early hearers, "to evangelize" or "to bring good news" carried the connotation of great responsibility,

Evangelism is an English translation of the Greek word *euangelion* (Matt. 24:14), which described the "good news" that Christ and his followers personified and preached . . . For early hearers "to evangelize" or "to bring good news" carried the connotation of great responsibility, fantastic insights, with more news to follow.

fantastic insights, with more news to follow. Alan Richardson says, "For those who thus receive it the gospel is always 'new,' breaking in freshly upon them and convincing them afresh."[31]

Because evangelism is a process of bringing this refreshing and breaking news, it is logical that not all of that news could be communicated at one hearing. Because the news we carry is both deep and broad, it requires a journey of dialogue. And as with any subject, this news is best understood when the learning starts with the basics and then moves into more complex and complicated themes.

IS THE JOY IN THE TREKKING OR THE DESTINATION?

Some readers may wonder if merely heading out on this journey of good news might be sufficiently rewarding, feeling that the recompense is in the going. Robert Louis Stevenson once famously intoned, "I travel not to go any-where, but to go. I travel for travel's sake. The great affair is to move."[32] While a trek by itself can be a rewarding experience, the journey of which we speak is comprised, as Doug and I discovered, of life-changing renovations and eternal destinations. Such consequence indicates that simply enjoying the journey along an adventuresome route is not sufficient.

John Stott reminds us that there are spiritual triumphs on this journey, and their importance dwarfs even the excitement of the trek, writing:

Evangelism relates to people's eternal destiny, and in bringing them good news of salvation, Christians are doing what nobody else can do. Seldom if ever should we have to choose between satisfying physical hunger and spiritual hunger, or between healing bodies and saving souls, since an authentic love for our neighbor will lead us to serve him or her as a whole person. Nevertheless, if we must choose, then we have to say that the supreme and ultimate need of humankind is the saving grace of Jesus Christ, and that therefore a person's eternal, spiritual salvation is of greater importance than his or her temporal and material well being.[33]

21

Howard Snyder agrees with Stott, stating:

Evangelism is the first priority of the Church's ministry in the world [italics Snyder]. This is true for several reasons: the clear biblical mandate for evangelism; the centrality and necessity of personal conversion in God's plan; the reality of judgment; the fact that changed persons are necessary to change society; the fact that the Christian community exists and expands only as evangelism is carried out. The Church that fails to evangelize is both biblically unfaithful and strategically shortsighted.[34]

Wagner creates a good summation, stating, "When a person dies without hearing that 'God so loved the world that he sent his only begotten Son, that whosoever believes on him should not perish but have eternal life (John 3:16 RSV), it is too late. The best thing that could possibly happen to that person has been denied."[35]

Some rightly fear that prioritizing either one can undermine the other. Concern about this could be a reason for the evangelical church's nearsightedness. But Snyder reminds us that "an evangelism that focuses exclusively on souls or on an otherworldly transaction which makes no real difference here and how is unfaithful to the gospel."[36] As such, both the trek and its destination are important.

THE IMPORTANCE OF WAYPOINTS

When attempting to understand where travelers are on their journey and what obstacles lie ahead, the concept of a waypoint provides a helpful metaphor. As previously noted, a waypoint is a place on a trek that explains where the traveler is in relation to the overall route. As such, waypoints on the journey of evangelism can help travelers understand their location, progress, and direction.

Less flexible terms have abounded to mark this journey. Engel and Norton chose the concept of a scale.[37] Later their pioneering diagram would be called the Engel Scale.[38] Robert Clinton chose to depict the journey as a series of phases (see appendix).[39] Eschewing scales, Billy Graham pictured evangelism as steps.[40] Graham distilled the process into a series of just three steps, noting that "students of psychology have agreed that there are three steps in conversion: First, a sense of perplexity and uneasiness; second, a climax and turning point; and, third, a relaxation marked by rest and joy."[41]

There is nothing inherently wrong with such demarcations, and in fact they can explain sophisticated concepts via simple models.[42] But to many people today, they may appear mechanical, inflexible, or biased (toward either the cultural or evangelistic mandate). It may be that the very minimalism of these models is what clouds the finer points from being investigated or understood.

The problem may be that all of these earlier demarcations favor a quick telling and not an expanded narrative. Perhaps due to postmodern people who today eschew such mechanical processes, I have favored the image of a story or a journey. A scale, step, or phase reduces this important journey into a mechanistic procedure. And a scale, step, or phase seems subject to human manipulation, management, or control. Neither could be further from the truth. The journey is guided by the Holy Spirit[43] and represents an intersection of the supernatural and the natural.[44] No scale could ever hope to encompass or depict the manifold routes, obstacles, travel companions, or new vistas one will encounter on that route. Thus, exact and precise depiction of this process is not only impossible, but it rails against the creative Spirit of God and his individual interaction with each of his creatures.

Therefore, rather than futilely try to depict the mechanics, I have chosen to describe common occurrences that the traveler will encounter, which I will designate as *waypoints*. A *waypoint* is a position, not a phase or a frozen marker. It tells where a traveler is in relation to other features on the road. It gives an indication of a general position on a route or journey. And a waypoint can be different for each trekker. And though a waypoint will always occur, because the precise route of the journey varies each time, the waypoint will appear in a different place for each trekker, that is, indigenously and personally.

In addition, waypoints may not be spaced at even lengths. Rather, the purpose of a waypoint is to help travelers perceive where they are in relationship to the bigger picture of the journey. And waypoints allow the companions that will accompany a traveler to gauge where they may intersect the traveler on his or her journey. Waypoints give us a general idea of direction, position, and most importantly, the next waypoint.

THE FEATURES OF WAYPOINTS

Just as it is important for travelers to know where they are on this journey, it is likewise critical for organizations to know what waypoints they address best. The first question to ask is where on this journey is our church offering effective ministry?

	WAYPOINTS
16	No awareness of a supreme being
15	Awareness of a supreme being, no knowledge of the good news
14	Initial awareness of the good news
13	Awareness of the fundamentals of the good news
12	Grasp of the implications of the good news
11	Positive attitude toward the good news
10	Personal problem recognition
9	Decision to act
8	Repentance and faith in Christ
7	NEW BIRTH
6	Post-decision evaluation
5	Incorporation into the body
4	Spiritual foundations (conceptual and behavioral growth)
3	Inner-life growth (deepening communion with God)
2	Ministry emergence (spiritual gifts emerge)
1	Impact emergence (life influences others)
0	Convergence (experience, gifts, and influence converge into a life of integrity and inspiration)

FEATURE 1: CHURCHES SHOULD EXPAND OUTWARD FROM THEIR CURRENT WAYPOINTS TO COVER NEW WAYPOINTS

Let's look at an illustration of Grace Church. Grace Church is heavily involved in social action through a clothing shelf and food bank (the cultural mandate) and thus is probably ministering primarily at Waypoints 14 or 13. It might be too big of a leap for Grace Church to immediately commence ministry to travelers at Waypoints 9 or 8. The important intermediary—Waypoints of 12, 11, and 10—would be missing.

Here is how this misstep might occur at Grace Church. As noted, Grace Church has an effective ministry utilizing a clothing shelf and food bank (Waypoints 14 and 13). Some congregants feel that what is missing is a call to decision (Waypoint 9). Thus, a nationally known sports figure is invited to share at an event that is heavily publicized and attended. The sports figure calls for hearers to respond. Twenty-eight patrons of the clothing shelf or food bank respond with professions of new birth. The result one year later was that of these twenty-eight respondents, only four are continuing on their journey of Christian discipleship. While four are certainly worth any effort, one wonders what might have happened if Grace Church had covered the missing segments of the journey, Waypoints 12, 11, and 10.

In my experience, churches reach out more effectively when they move to cover the next adjacent waypoint and strengthen their ministry there. This eliminates the problem of creating gaps or disruptions in the traveler's journey. After increasing in effectiveness in the adjacent waypoint, the church can then proceed further outward to more waypoints, increasing the holism of its ministry.

Let us see how Grace Church could have done things differently by undertaking two exploratory steps and one result.

1. First, the leaders of Grace Church need to ask themselves, "Is there a nearby or associated church that is effectively doing ministry at either of the waypoints next to us?" If there is, then Grace Church should first contact them and explore partnering in ministry. Partnering, however, will depend upon theological and doctrinal differences or if the nearby ministry is reaching a different culture.[45] If a suitable ministry partner can be found, then a church can readily increase its span of ministry on the journey of evangelism.

2. However, if there is not a viable partner to increase Grace Church's ministry span, then the church should work from the waypoints they are effectively doing (Waypoints 14 and 13) *outward* to adjacent waypoints (Waypoints 15 or 12). From here this expansion would eventually increase to as much of the journey as feasible.

3. If Grace Church expands its ministry to first help those travelers at Waypoint 12 and then travelers at Waypoint 11, it is progressively helping travelers navigate a larger portion of their spiritual journey. Without intersecting bridges between waypoints, a traveler can become confused, disorientated, and even worse, lost.

FEATURE 2: FOCUSING ON ONE WAYPOINT CAN STAGNATE A CHURCH

There is danger for a church that becomes a specialist in only a few waypoints. Waypoints by their very nature indicate a point on the way. Thus stopping anywhere on the continuum becomes unnatural and worrisome. This can result in the nearsightedness of which my friend Doug spoke. Churches can get fixated on the few waypoints they are doing well and not see the needs of those travelers on other parts of the journey.[46]

> There is danger for a church that becomes a specialist in only a few waypoints. Waypoints by their very nature indicate a point on the way. Thus stopping anywhere on the continuum becomes unnatural and worrisome.

Some churches may be too small or even too successful to want to offer ministry at more than a couple waypoints. If that is the case, then, as noted earlier, partnerships can help churches build bridges to adjacent waypoints. Such collaboration will ensure that travelers can readily move to the next waypoint, even if it means going to a partner church.[47]

However, by emphasizing a journey with ongoing and long-term processes, a church is less likely to succumb to focusing on just a few waypoints.[48] And a journey metaphor reminds us that each new waypoint builds upon an earlier one. Because churches are communal expressions called out to demonstrate God's love and purposes, they should seek to help as many travelers as possible to travel as far along on their journeys as possible.[49]

FEATURE 3: COUNTING DOWNWARD EMPHASIZES CONVERGENCE

The reader might wonder why these waypoints count down (16–0), rather than up (0–16) to convergence. The countdown motif was utilized for several reasons:

First, counting upward would end at some arbitrary number for eternal convergence. The magnificence of eternity seems too grand to assign a number.

Second, if the numbers were assigned in an upward fashion from 1 to 16, then an unintended impression might be that a person at Waypoint 12 is superior to a person at Waypoint 3. While growing in Christ is redemptively lifting, maturity fosters humility, and thus assigning higher numbers for Christian maturity clouds our intentions.

Third, 0 for convergence carries the sense of the last waypoint of one journey and the stepping off into a new journey of timeless dimensions. Zero can thus be the launching place for another journey—otherworldly and eternal.

FEATURE 4: THERE IS BIBLICAL SUPPORT FOR AN ONGOING JOURNEY

As seen earlier, the Great Commission of Matthew 28:19–20 is the apex toward which the Great Commandment (Mark 12:31) aims and instructs.[50] Within the Great Commission are four verbs: *go, make* (disciples), *baptize*, and *teach*. Though in the English they appear identical, in the Greek only one of these verbs is the main verb, and the other three describe it (the other three are participles, that is, helping verbs that modify or explain the main verb).

Which, then, is the main verb, the one the other three are describing? The Greek language holds the answer, for the unique spelling of *matheteusate* indicates that "make disciples" is the main verb, and thus "to make disciples" is Jesus' choice for the goal of our going, baptizing, and teaching.

In our search for a culture-current metaphor, we see the image of a journey emerging, with traveling wayfarers moving forward to encounter new waypoints.

But what exactly is this disciple that we are commissioned to foster? *Matheteusate* is derived from the Greek word for "learner," and means "to make learners." McGavran stresses that *matheteusate* means "enroll in my [Jesus'] school."[51]

And yet, the Greek grammar holds more surprises. *Matheteusate* has a unique Greek spelling, indicating that it is in the imperative voice and the present perfect tense. These grammatical constructions tell us the following:

- The imperative voice indicates that to make learners is a crucial and urgent undertaking.
- The present tense denotes that making learners should be a current action.
- And the perfect tense carries the idea that making learners should be a continual and ongoing action.

Therefore, the present and ongoing imagery of a journey becomes a welcome metaphor.

In short, discipleship requires continued obedience over time . . . Thus becoming a disciple is a *process* beginning when one received Christ, continuing over a lifetime as one is conformed to His image (Phil. 1:6), and culminating in the glory at the end of the age. In this broader perspective, the Great Commission *never* is fulfilled but always is in the process of fulfillment.[52]

In our search for a culture-current metaphor, we see the image of a journey emerging, with traveling wayfarers moving forward to encounter new waypoints. For churches to focus too narrowly on a few waypoints slows and disconnects the process travelers will have to seek out new churches to help them travel on the next leg of their journey. Many wayfarers will find the change too awkward, and many will not make the leap at all.

In the following chapters, we will carefully examine each waypoint. In the process, we will encounter personal stories that illustrate each waypoint and learn what churches can do to help travelers negotiate each point on life's most important journey.

NO AWARENESS OF A
SUPREME BEING

Richard was not your typical new seminary student. A former electrical engineering major at Yale University, he enrolled at Fuller Theological Seminary in preparation for a career as a missionary. There Richard encountered four students who shared his passion to share the good news in relevant ways. Together they started an innovative missionary agency they called African Enterprise. And while working in South Africa, they developed a new form of media outreach that combined rock music, multiple slide images, and lighting effects into what they called a light show. The response was beyond their expectations as crowds jammed the University of Cape Town auditorium every night.

> I was at this time living, like so many . . . in a whirlwind of contradictions. I maintained that God did not exist. I was also very angry with God for not existing. I was equally angry with Him for creating a world.
>
> —C. S. LEWIS[1]

The message of the light and media show was twofold. The first half employed dark images and hard-edged rock music to underscore the lack of purpose, confusion, and pessimism that modern youth were experiencing. The second half was more hopeful, portraying the selfless and positive message of Christ's good news. This juxtaposition of hopelessness with the unconditional love of Christ made a journey-changing impression.

Many told Richard and his friends that the good news of the second half had changed their outlook and had given them hope. But Richard was not prepared when one student responded, "this has really changed my mind. I am president

of the atheist club of the University of Cape Town." The student's subsequent statement initially confounded Richard. "Because of this," the student continued,
"I am no longer an atheist, but now, I am an agnostic."

Richard knew that an agnostic has an awareness of a supreme being, while
an atheist claims no awareness of God. In other words, the good news of the
second half of the show had helped this traveler move from Waypoint 16 (no
awareness of a supreme being) to Waypoint 15 (awareness of a supreme
being). Yet initially, Richard's heart sank. Richard had been thinking that this
person was ready for the new birth experience (Waypoint 7) and that this
former atheist might give a testimony of his new birth at the following night's
presentation.

But then Richard's disappointment gave way to a more holistic understanding
of what God was doing. He recognized that this person was on a God-ward
journey, and the presentation helped this person move in a positive direction.
Richard began to pray for this young man for he knew the student's journey was
not finished. And Richard knew that he and his friends had helped this wayfarer
cross to another waypoint on his spiritual journey. "So my prayer was that other
people and other influences over time would help move him along his spiritual
journey until he committed his life to Christ," recalls Richard.

Richard later became professor of evangelism and spiritual formation at the
very seminary that had prepared him. And Richard Peace is known today for
his research and writings on the journey of evangelism.[2]

WAYPOINT CHARACTERISTICS

Today there is a growing skepticism regarding the value, purposes, and
civility of religion. Christopher Hitchens, as a leading spokesperson, says,
"the whole racket of American evangelism was just that: a heartless con run
by the second-string characters from Chaucer's 'Pardoner's Tale.' (You saps
keep the faith. We'll just keep the money.)"[3] And William Cavanaugh convincingly argues that, erroneous skepticism about what motivates Christians
is on the rise.[4]

In such a cynical environment, many are moving away from God on the journey of which we speak, perhaps from Waypoint 15 to Waypoint 16. In other words, many people are beginning to question their belief in a supreme being, and thus more people might be leaving Waypoint 15 (awareness of a supreme being) to regress to Waypoint 16 (no awareness of a supreme being). The 2008 American Religious Identification Survey (ARIS) appears to confirm this trend, stating that "the U.S. population continues to show signs of becoming less religious, with one out of every five Americans failing to indicate a religious identity in 2008. The 'Nones' (no stated religious preference, atheist, or agnostic) continue to grow."[5]

In this growing environment of doubt, the community of faith must increase its efforts to engage disbelief with two parallel thrusts. In this chapter, and each following chapter, we will look at actions churches can undertake to help travelers at each waypoint. But before we consider these actions, let us look at signs that can alert us that travelers are at Waypoint 16.

> "The U.S. population continues to show signs of becoming less religious, with one out of every five American failing to indicate a religious identity in 2008. The 'Nones' (no stated religious preference, atheist, or agnostic) continue to grow."
>
> —2008 AMERICAN RELIGIOUS IDENTIFICATION SURVEY

SIGNS OF TRAVELERS AT WAYPOINT 16

Wayfarers at this waypoint exhibit a host of characteristics. Three that are prevalent include the following:

The Unselfish Activist. Some travelers at Waypoint 16 may excessively fill their lives with good works, such as social action or scientific inquiry. Their purpose may be to live a good life by helping others or advancing knowledge. But they tend to overfill their lives, often resulting in academic or vocational obsession. Any obsession that robs a person of balance in his or her life, even religious mania, is unhealthy.[6] But here the obsession is so all-consuming that it leaves little time for family, friends, recreation, or relationships. This overemphasis can be a sign that a person is avoiding the supernatural by being preoccupied with the present.

The Confrontational Activist. This is a sudden and active zeal for defending one's belief that there is no God. Often these may be people who once claimed

an awareness of a supreme being, but through physical, intellectual, or emotional dichotomy have rejected their former belief of a supreme being.[7] These
travelers are a challenge to assist on their journey because they often possess
emotional baggage. A person who engages these wayfarers must be slow,
rational, understanding, and filled with grace.

The Self-Absorbed Artist. Though there are many signs a person is at Waypoint
16, the last of three recurrent behaviors is acute egoism. Egoism is different from
egotism, where the latter means a self-centeredness and selfishness. Instead,
egoism indicates that individuals see things only from their own viewpoint. They
may be passionate, caring, and loving, but they tend to look at the world only
from their view. Thus, they may unintentionally trample others' feelings or go in
directions that are good for them but not others. Egoism indicates seeing the
world from only their standpoint, and thus they are the center of their universe.
The idea of a supreme being may threaten their position, and thus they can repress
the thought. Because of this threat, they may bluntly react to religious messages
with severe contempt, antagonism, and even fury. However, because they are so
self-absorbed, they can develop their talents to amazing levels and thus are some
of the most creative artists of a generation.[8]

ACTIONS THAT HELP WAYPOINT 16 TRAVELERS

At Waypoint 16, a Christian must offer assistance to wayfarers via two avenues:
intellectual engagement and social modeling. Let us look at intellectual
engagement first.

ACTION 16.1: RELEASE YOUR ORGANIC INTELLECTUALS

Most faith communities are weak at explaining their belief in God to someone
who has rejected the very notion of God's existence. However, in such communities of faith, there are individuals who are skilled at intellectual analysis and
engagement. They are the ones who gleefully teach Sunday school and Bible studies,
for the mental stimulation of the task. The Bible mentions around two dozen gifts
of the Spirit (see Rom. 12:6–8; 1 Cor. 12:8–10, 28; Eph. 4:11), and these people

may have the gift of teaching (Rom. 12:8; 1 Cor. 12:28; Eph. 4:11–14; Acts 18:24–28). The gift of teaching has been described as an ability "to communicate information . . . in such a way that others learn."[9] Yet the gift of teaching is not the same as entertaining oratory or cheerleading for the phrase, "that others learn," reminds us that listeners will gain knowledge. Michael Griffiths says, "Traditionally too much Christian teaching is pulpit soliloquy and nobody ever checks up to see where anyone takes notice of whether teaching produces any action."[10]

In the field of political science, such gifted communicators are called "organic intellectuals," for they naturally understand people and are able to help the average person understand difficult concepts. Antonio Gramsci, the political activist who coined the term *organic intellectual*, emphasized they were not just academics but were playwrights, media professionals, novelists, and journalists.[11]

C. S. Lewis was an organic intellectual who is best known as an eloquent champion and writer on Christian themes. Yet in his memoir, *Surprised by Joy*, he tells how he began life as an atheist.[12] It was through intellectual analysis and mentorship (via Christian fantasy writer George MacDonald[13] and friends like J. R. R. Tolkien) that Lewis became a passionate advocate of Christian belief. His *Mere Christianity* has been heralded as "not the shouting, stomping, sweating, spitting televangelist fare so often parodied; Lewis employs logical arguments that are eloquently expressed."[14] While some of his writings were directed at mostly Christian audiences (for example, *The Screwtape Letters*, *The Problem of Pain*, *Letters to Malcolm: Chiefly on Prayer*), Lewis wrote many books for people without an awareness of the supreme being (for example, *God in the Dock* and *The Pilgrim's Regress*).[15]

"Traditionally too much Christian teaching is pulpit soliloquy and nobody ever checks up to see where anyone takes notice of whether teaching produces any action."

Lewis has also introduced countless young people to the rationale for Christ's sacrifice through the childhood eyes of Lucy, Edmund, Susan, and Peter as they witness the savage death and resurrection of the kindly yet kingly lion named Aslan. In a similar organic fashion, J. R. R. Tolkien's Lord of the Rings trilogy exemplifies to adolescent readers the nobility of sacrifice, obligation, lineage, and inter-reliance.

I knew one such organic intellectual named Linda. She has risen to the top of her profession: president and general manager of a large television station. Her gift was communication (after all, she was in the media business), and in her church she started a Bible study that grew rapidly due to her sharp intellect and easy-to-understand style. However, most of the attendees were Christians. Now, there is nothing wrong with such gatherings, but often we keep our best intellects ministering to Christians and do not release an equal number to engage our mission field.

If your church has leaders possessing organic gifts of teaching whereby they can readily and convincingly explain difficult concepts, it is time we send them out to start book studies, readings, and discussion groups with people who are, as C. S. Lewis once was, "very angry with God for not existing."[16] Libraries often host book studies and are looking for communicators. Service organizations have leadership training and seek gifted trainers. Poetry readings engage hearers with lyrically challenging ideas. These are all valid venues for a church's ministry. But remember, when leaving the confines of cloistered halls, all opinions are welcome and appreciated. Such external venues are not a time to stifle opposing viewpoints but to welcome them. The organic intellectual welcomes new ideas and appreciates the skillful and probing mind that fosters them. This is called fostering an ask-assertive environment, and we shall study it further in the following section.

ACTION 16.2: THE A, B, C, AND D OF SOCIAL MODELING

Social modeling is exactly what it asserts—modeling behavior that is interrelational and social. Here we are speaking about Christians modeling the positive attributes that Christ exhibited. The very word for Christian means "little Christs" and should remind us that when we use it, we are envoys and ambassadors of Christ.[17] Even detractors such as self-avowed atheist Christopher Hitchens acknowledges the power of social modeling, saying, "the good effects of Christianity are neither to be denied, nor lightly esteemed, though candidly I will admit that I think them overrated."[18] It is toward ensuring that such modeling is not overrated but authentically affirmed that the church must set her sights.

While social modeling can be helpful at all waypoints, it is especially important at Waypoint 16. At this waypoint, a person has no awareness that a supreme being exists, and thus social modeling can be the first encounter with Christlikeness. To be effective, social modeling has two premises.

First, social modeling must be based on a mutual relationship. This means that a two-way personal connection must be established before modeling has any power. Research has shown when outreach is conducted in an impersonal manner, it can create three to ten times as much negative responses as positive responses.[19]

Second, social modeling is only effective if the one modeling is admired; that is, it is based upon a positive and mutual relationship. The church that is reaching out at this waypoint will realize that its people must act in such a way that their lives attest to a belief in a God who is eternal, compassionate, loving, and just. Therefore, let us look at four things a church can undertake to redemptively exhibit social modeling.

Action A: Truth Telling. This means telling exactly the truth and not embellishing it. Communities of faith can become cultures of exaggeration and overstatement. Such amplification often occurs when attendance figures are bantered about or conversion statistics stated.[20] An organization can become so infected with exaggeration that budgets will be inflated beyond what is needed because amplification is expected. For example, truth telling is waning if a department always has to ask for two new employees to be assured they get one. The entire organization often mutates into an unhealthy environment of overstatement and hyperbole. To an outside world that is watching and having financial dealings with the church, it appears that we have no respect or concern about the retribution of a God who demands truth telling (see Matt. 5:37[21]). The result is that churches say they believe in God but by fudging on the truth give an impression to a watching world that his requirements and retributions do not really matter.

> Research has shown that when outreach is conducted in an impersonal manner, it can create three to ten times as much negative response as positive response.

Action B: Fair Dealing. This is when a church has two sets of standards dealing with Christians in a more honest and fair manner than they deal with people who are not.[22] By breaking contracts, not paying bills, finagling for the lowest price, and so forth, churches may feel they are stretching God's money at the expense of the ungodly. But in actuality, Christians are modeling a lack of fair dealing and equality. People observing this behavior may conclude that because Christians are a reflection of God, then God must be a deity that does not deal fairly.

Action C: An Ask-Assertive Environment. This is an environment where questions are not only welcomed but also encouraged. Churches that are reaching out to people who have little awareness of God will want to demonstrate God's approachability by being open themselves to questions and never offended. In a church, this environment may be manifested in questions arising from the floor during a sermon or on the street during the week. It was C. S. Lewis's questions peppering his conversations with friend and colleague J. R. R. Tolkien that led Lewis to Waypoint 7: new birth.[23] Yet in many churches questions, if allowed at all, are organized into tidy little segments after a long lecture. The lecture format of most church preaching keeps this practice entrenched. However, asking questions is encouraged in an ask-assertive environment. This is especially important because Christians model a supreme being who personally engages his creation from the garden of Eden (see Gen. 3:8–9) through to the new earth (see Rev. 21).

Action D: Imagery of Hope. This final action is exemplified by Richard's story at the beginning of this chapter. This story captures the image of utilizing organic intellectuals crafting an aesthetically pleasing and emotionally engaging media presentation of the hope and help that God offers a floundering world. Recall how the first half of Richard's presentation emphasized the lostness and estrangement of the youth culture. But then the second half lauded how God provides hope and meaning. This tension between despair and hope is reflected in the quote by C. S. Lewis on page 29. Lewis lamented, he was caught in "a whirlwind of contradictions. [He] maintained that God did not exist. [He] was also very angry with God for not existing. [He] was equally angry with [God] for creating a world."[24] Lewis was exasperated because the world needed hope, and he saw none coming until portrayed in the writings of fantasy writer George MacDonald. Whether the fantasies of MacDonald or the light and music presentation of Richard Peace, the imagery of hope can be so powerful and so needed that it will propel a traveler on a journey forward and God-ward.

INTERVIEW WITH RICHARD PEACE

Author and the Robert Boyd Munger Professor of
Evangelism and Spiritual Formation at Fuller Theological Seminary

Whitesel: You were in South Africa, engaged in an evangelistic ministry in the cities and at the universities. How did you feel when you realized the president of the atheist club said he was no longer an atheist but an agnostic?

Peace: At first my heart sank. I was thinking he was going to give his life to Christ right then and there, and then he could give his testimony the next night. But then I realized what actually happened was powerful. To be an atheist is a faith position, and he had just taken a bold step of faith in a new direction. His faith was moving in a God-ward direction.

Whitesel: What did you do next?

Peace: I prayed for him for I did not know where his journey would take him. So my prayer was that other people and other influences would over time help him move along his spiritual journey until he committed his life to Christ.

Whitesel: To most people, this is a different understanding of conversion. Most people think of conversion as something that takes place at just one point in a person's life.

Peace: I think we've limited our understanding of the unfolding process that conversion often takes. It takes time for people to come to the place where they can recognize who Jesus is and what he has done for them. We need to take seriously where a person is on his or her faith journey and then help that person take the next step in a God-ward direction.

Whitesel: But this requires a clearer understanding of where a person is on his or her journey. We cannot just assume everyone is at Waypoint 9, ready to accept Christ.

Peace: That's right. We must become spiritual diagnosticians. We must travel with them, understand their position on the journey and connect with them to help them on the next segment of the God-ward journey.

Whitesel: So, what can a person do to help others navigate these waypoints?

Peace: It is a matter of modeling godly behavior, building a relationship, and talking to people about spirituality. It is not about condemning them for where they are on their journey or using a canned witnessing plan.

Whitesel: Then our job is to build relationships and begin two-way dialogue if we are to help them navigate their journey?

Peace: Right. My job is to tell stories of how God loves us and wants a personal relationship with us that can only come from repentance and faith in Christ. This pattern of reaching out is conversational. The old pattern was confrontational. The new pattern says, "Here is my story, tell me yours—and here is God's story." It is more interesting when God is the evangelist.

Whitesel: Any final thoughts?

Peace: Yes, we have to let people be who they are and where they are in their spiritual journey. God leads the process. Therefore, a person reaching out should not be leading or manipulating the process. We must understand where they are, be with them there, and be sensitive to what they are wrestling with. Then we must model Christian love and share how our story intersects their story. We tend to rush straight to commitment to God. And if we do it too soon, it is counterproductive. It can turn people off to the wonderful good news.

QUESTIONS FOR GROUP OR PERSONAL STUDY

1. Who are the people in your congregation that are skilled at explaining difficult concepts? What Bible studies do they teach? How well are they attended?

   - Could these people be better utilized reaching out to people who have little or no knowledge of God?
   - What venues might be available (libraries, book studies, community forums, discussion groups, poetry readings, etc.) for such outreach?

2. Does your church have a problem with truth telling, often using amplification, overstatement, or exaggeration?

   - Do church leaders often exaggerate their budgetary needs because they expect their requests to be cut back?
   - What will you do to fix this?

3. Does your church have a problem with fair dealing? Do you treat Christians and members of your church better than others? Do you pay your bills on time? Are you generous with your secular vendors, neighbors?

   - What can be the results of modeling this social behavior?
   - What impression are we giving a watching world regarding the character of our God?

4. Are there examples where you as a church are living like there is no punishment for your wrongdoings? Has sin been permitted or glossed over, inadvertently giving the impression to a watching world that you do not believe in divine retribution?

5. Are there artists in song, sculpture, painting, drama, dance, or mixed media in your church who can put into artistic expression their encounters with a living God?

   - Are these artists just focused on ministering to predominantly Christian audiences?

   - Or are they encouraged to use their gifts to engage those struggling with disbelief?

6. Do you permit questions anytime and anyplace during the sermon? Too much dialogue in churches is one-sided with information being lectured to submissive and compliant audiences. Those who have no awareness of a supreme being or who have relinquished it need hospitable and receptive environments for their questions, concerns, and options. What will you do to foster an ask-assertive environment?

AWARENESS OF A
SUPREME BEING

This is how you love a town, Bob." So began Mike's story. "Today we call it 'Love Dayton' and it's what we have been doing for a long time— meeting people's needs right where they are. We provide recycled medical equipment to people unable to acquire the equipment themselves, sponsor Anna's Closet for gently used clothing, offer J. J.'s Furniture to pass along furniture to those in need, and host the Gateway Café to provide a full-course meal at no charge in conjunction with our Monday night food pantry. This is how the good news starts to grow in a town. We've tried programs like seeker services and the attractional model. But this is the soil out of which our church grows: serving the needy.

"You know what is the most remarkable thing," continued Mike, the pastor of this formerly small, rural Ohio church. "Many of the people who help us serve the needy are not yet Christians. But they resonate with our care for God's creation. They see their own passion for helping others reflected in us. That's how we introduce a lot of people to the good news. They join us in serving others and see that our love is authentic and relevant. They can't see God in your life unless they're traveling with you."

> Christ has no body now but yours. No hands, no feet on earth but yours. Yours are the eyes through which He looks compassion on this world. Christ has no body now on earth but yours.
>
> —Teresa of Avila[1]

WAYPOINT CHARACTERISTICS

Waypoint 15 signifies travelers who, while they are aware of a supreme being, have no knowledge of God's good news. As stated in the previous chapter, "the U.S. population continues to show signs of becoming less religious . . . The 'Nones' (no stated religious preference, atheist, or agnostic) continue to grow."[2] Almost 25 percent of North Americans may be at Waypoint 15 or higher. Let us visualize this growing segment on the map of our journey (Figure 15.1).

FIGURE 15.1

NORTH AMERICAN POPULATION & WAYPOINTS[3]

16	No awareness of a supreme being
15	Awareness of a supreme being, no knowledge of the good news

25 percent of North American population and growing

14	Initial awareness of the good news
13	Awareness of the fundamentals of the good news
12	Grasp of the implications of the good news
11	Positive attitude toward the good news
10	Personal problem recognition
9	Decision to act
8	Repentance and faith in Christ
7	**NEW BIRTH**
6	Post-decision evaluation
5	Incorporation into the body
4	Spiritual foundations (conceptual and behavioral growth)
3	Inner-life growth (deepening communion with God)
2	Ministry emergence (spiritual gifts emerge)
1	Impact emergence (life influences others)
0	Convergence (experience, gifts, and influence converge into a life of integrity and inspiration)

SIGNS OF TRAVELERS AT WAYPOINT 15

The needs of travelers at Waypoint 15 are best understood through the assessment grid of Abraham Maslow. A psychologist, Maslow was concerned that caregivers often misperceive needs, attempting to address higher needs that are not yet felt by the recipient. He suggested that the recipient may have basic needs that are unmet, and since these basic needs are not yet met, the recipient is not interested in the fulfillment of higher needs.

Figure 15.2 is a diagram of Maslow's Hierarchy of Needs. Let us look at a few levels, working upward from the basic needs at the bottom.

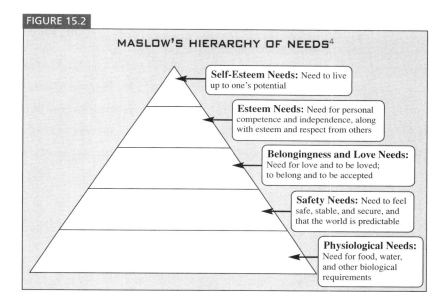

FIGURE 15.2

MASLOW'S HIERARCHY OF NEEDS[4]

Self-Esteem Needs: Need to live up to one's potential

Esteem Needs: Need for personal competence and independence, along with esteem and respect from others

Belongingness and Love Needs: Need for love and to be loved; to belong and to be accepted

Safety Needs: Need to feel safe, stable, and secure, and that the world is predictable

Physiological Needs: Need for food, water, and other biological requirements

Unmet Physiological Needs. These are travelers with needs for the basics of sustainable life such as food, water, and so forth. People who are without work, incapacitated by illness, emotionally or mentally abused, may be consumed by worry about how to meet these basic needs. For example, a need for food will supersede all higher needs. People at this stage may not care about housing, joining a faith community, or bettering themselves. They only want to have a sustainable and ongoing source for food and water. Churches can and should develop

MEETING PHYSICAL NEEDS

Examples of ministries churches can use to fulfill physiological needs include:

- Family emergency services
- Medical emergency assistance
- Food and domestic hunger ministries
- Housing and residential programs
- Hunger/housing loans and grants programs
- Disaster relief services
- Addiction and recovery counseling and support

ministries for people at this level of need though this will require extensive effort because these needs are pervasive and long-term.

Unmet Safety Needs. These are needs for long-term security and a sense that the future is now predictable. Once people feel they can meet their hunger and thirst needs, they turn their attention to their security needs, such as a place of their own, long-term employment, learning a job skill, and so forth.

Churches that only address short-term physiological needs will not fulfill long-term safety needs. Too often churches offer short-term places to stay, short-term food staples, and short-term loans. These offers will sound hollow and incomplete for travelers at this waypoint, because they are looking for assistance that will ensure long-term survival.

FIGURE 15.3

SELF-SUFFICIENCY

Examples of self-sufficiency and sustainable development programs:

- *Job Training.* A homeless person once told me, "I am at home on the streets . . . I've learned to survive and that's the only thing I'm good at." Helping such people acquire marketable skills is key toward helping them meet long-term needs for safety and security. Examples can include:
  - o Job skills evaluation and training
  - o Vocational rehabilitation
  - o Networking—community service work at the church can provide references for future employment
  - o Scholarships provided by the church call allow for training to improve employability
- *Job Placement.* Oftentimes a predictable future begins with dependable employment. Churches that help community residents attain secure and long-term employment will often help them meet long-term safety needs, including:
  - o Employment counseling and networking
  - o Career research
  - o Mentoring for application and résumé writing
  - o Personal hygiene, clothing, and conversational skills to help prepare for job interviews
  - o Networking the under- and unemployed with potential employers
  - o English as a second language (ESL) assistance
  - o Support for GED and equivalency education
- *Health Programs.* Insecurity about the future can arise from an illness with an uncertain or vague prognosis. Helping people at this stage means assisting them in finding adequate health care, information about their illness, and specialists in their malady. One church was located adjacent to a large hospital. When patients and family visited the church in search of solace, the church prayed for them. While this was an authentic and beneficial act, the patients often left with less inspiration than the parishioners. The church discovered that in addition to prayer, they could offer a patient advocacy ministry. Soon the advocacy ministry had fostered a connection and cooperation with the hospital. The church now not only offered prayer, but also patient help for those suffering from an unpredictable future.

Unmet Belongingness and Love Needs. These needs have to do with acceptance into a community of inter-reliance. At this waypoint, people realize that living in a symbiotic relationship with others will enhance their life. A person may join a faith community, volunteer for a ministry, or seek acceptance. It is at this point that Christians often exhibit their most energetic efforts. There is nothing wrong with this, for travelers at this stage want to belong and be accepted. But when churches focus only on incorporation, they appear manipulative and self-absorbed to people who have been struggling with safety or physiological needs.[5] Therefore churches must have a robust ministry to meet both physiological and safety needs before they can legitimately offer (and campaign for) assimilation.

At this stage of belongingness and love needs, recipients are also seeking unconditional acceptance and love. But because they may have an unstable and inconsistent background, they may have habits that test Christians' acceptance. Foul language, addictive habits, and ignorance of church traditions will often perturb Christians accustomed to a more genteel church environment. The church must not allow itself to be agitated because people are early in their God-ward journey. Instead, travelers need to feel a different love from the church than they have experienced in the secular realm. To demonstrate this, Christians must offer unselfish love. The Old Testament word for this love, *chesed*, conveys a "kindness, especially as extended to the lowly, needy and miserable."[6]

Churches often experiment with multiple ministry tactics until they find one that works. Such experimentation can have tragic results. No church should experiment on needy travelers.

Other levels of Maslow's needs will be explored in the appropriate chapters of this book. Thus, the reader may want to bookmark Figure 15.2 for future reference.

ACTIONS THAT HELP WAYPOINT 15 TRAVELERS

There are two missteps to which churches often succumb when helping Waypoint 15 travelers. The first is to implement a prefabricated approach by merely adopting ministries that other churches are using. Even the illustrations in this book are given as examples, not models. Effective ministry requires that each church grow a local and contextualized ministry to Waypoint 15 wayfarers. Actions 15.1 and 15.2 will examine how to address this.

Second, churches often experiment with multiple ministry tactics until they find one that works. Such experimentation can have tragic results. No church should experiment on needy travelers. This does not honor the *imageo Dei* in which all humankind was created (Gen. 1:26–27). Actions 15.3 and 15.4 will assist in ensuring this misstep does not occur.

Yet these actions should not be delayed. A church must embrace both urgency and preparation. The following four actions are designed to move the need-based process forward at a judicious pace. All four actions are required because of the breadth and depth of the needs. But any size church can undertake these, though in more limited fashion.

ACTION 15.1: RESEARCH NEEDS

The type of research conducted is important, for some types of research are more helpful than others. Primary research occurs when information is gathered firsthand. Secondary research is when someone gleans insights from another's research. Secondary research is helpful but often pales in potency to primary research where a researcher is personally immersed in a local mission field. How can a church gather firsthand information on the needs of its community? Let us look at three actions that can produce primary research.

Action A: Live among Them. To ascertain community needs, it helps to live among them, eating where they eat and shopping where they shop. In fact, one of ten major factors in halting church growth is when leaders become distanced from their constituency.[7] If this occurs, church leaders will only be guessing at community needs.

Action B: Meet with Them in Group Settings. Informal gatherings, focus groups, and town hall meetings are ways to connect with community residents. Often when people are interviewed one-on-one, they hold back their feelings. Research into group dynamics tells us that people will often expound more deeply and expressively in groups.[8] If the purpose is to ascertain needs, then understanding can be enhanced by group intensity. However, churches must be very careful to only solicit input and not to politic for the church's viewpoint. To do the latter will result in immediate distancing and suspicion.[9]

Action C: Don't Clone Another Church's Ministry. Unless necessary, don't merely duplicate ministry that other churches are utilizing. To do so will rob you of a locally developed and contextualized ministry. However, if your church is too small, it can partner to expand its ministry. Look for other churches that are reaching out at adjacent waypoints and partner with them.[10] Success often depends upon doctrinal and historical factors. But if the needs of a community can be met by collaborating with another ministry, then pursue this option.

ACTION 15.2: DESIGN YOUR MINISTRY FROM THE BOTTOM UP

As a consultant with church clients of all sizes, I have found that the most helpful ministries are those that emerge from a collaborative effort between church leaders and needy residents. There are two elements for designing a contextualized ministry.

Action A: Inclusion. Include non-churchgoers in the planning and design of your ministry. Many will reject this offer because they are not yet ready to volunteer, let alone advise. But those who are emerging out of lower need stages may be entering the belongingness and love level. Thus they will want to contribute and at least give their thoughts. Yet a natural inclination of Christian leaders is to reject such offers feeling that the emerging person needs more time to grow or gain more secondary knowledge (such as, book, theological, or doctrinal knowledge). But once travelers have had their physiological and safety needs met, they must be allowed to contribute, even minimally, to the ministry of a faith community. Churches can help wayfarers by inviting them to participate in the ministry planning process. This invitation must be extended much earlier and more earnestly that most churches realize.

> Churches can help wayfarers by inviting them to participate in the ministry planning process. This invitation must be extended earlier and more earnestly that most churches realize.

Action B: Allocate Sufficient Money. As noted in the previous chapter, churches customarily err on the side of either the cultural mandate (social action) or the evangelistic mandate. It was also shown that God's intention for his church is a more holistic approach where a church ministers at many waypoints rather than just in a narrow range. Narrow ministry becomes entrenched because churches tend to budget based upon history rather than forecasts. A church that understands it should reach out at early waypoints will also understand that it must allocate sufficient funds to do so. Churches must evaluate what percentages of its budgets are going to support the cultural mandate and the evangelistic mandate. And a plan can be brought about to create a balance, where roughly 50 percent of a church's budget goes to support the cultural mandate and 50 percent goes to support the evangelistic mandate. Regardless of intentions, these mandates will never be brought into parity until finances are allocated with equivalence.

ACTION 15.3: CONNECT YOUR MINISTRY TO THE COMMUNITY

For a community that has been established to communicate good news, communication is one the weakest skills in most churches. Many congregations design fantastic ministries only to have them marginally attended because residents do not know they are available. The following are three basic actions for successfully telling the community about ministries that can meet their needs.

Action A: Have a Trial Run. A church should initiate a trial run with little initial fanfare. This will give the church an opportunity to try out the ministry without being deluged by community needs. To communicate that you are hosting a trial run, use word-of-mouth communication.

Action B: Use Indigenous Communication Channels. Church leaders often do not understand how community residents communicate. In one church's community, fliers in self-serve laundromats communicated better than online advertising (few needy residents had regular or easy access to the Internet). Each community has developed different communication channels. If a church invites residents to participate in the planning process, then residents can share the veiled yet influential ways that news travels in their community.

Action C: Be a Good-Doer, Not a Do-Gooder. The difference between a do-gooder and a good-doer was revealed to me ten years ago. Dan was auditioning to be the drummer in a worship team I led. Though he was more than suitable for the task, I was confused because he looked familiar. "You visited me last Christmas," Dan responded, noticing my bewilderment, "Brought a lot of nice things for the kids." Each year our church visited needy residents, giving them gifts and singing carols. "You were nice enough to come," Dan would say to me later. Dan and I had become friends, and now our team was planning to visit needy households. "You go; I won't," Dan stated. "I want to be a good-doer, not a do-gooder." Further conversations with Dan revealed a difference between "do-gooders" and

> A church that brings food a couple times a year to a needy family does little to minister to their long-term physiological needs or safety needs. Such churches in Dan's mind were comprised of "do-gooders."

"good-doers." On the one hand, Dan saw do-gooders as people who go around doing limited and inconsistent good deeds. He perceived that they were doing good on a limited scale to relieve their conscience. Thus their good deeds were perceived as self-serving, insincere, and limited.

A church that brings food a couple times a year to a needy family does little to minister to their long-term physiological or safety needs. On the other hand, Dan saw "good-doers" as those who do good in a meaningful, relevant, and ongoing manner. And he was right. In hindsight, I had been striving to do good, not trying to do good better. Therefore, a church should connect with its community by offering ongoing ministry and not just holiday help.

ACTION 15.4: EVALUATE THE RESULTS

Donald McGavran called the church's aversion to analysis the "universal fog" that blinds the church to her mission and effectiveness.[11] McGavran preferred the term *effective evangelism* as the best way to describe what we should be measuring.[12] Effective evangelism has much to commend it. Evangelism, as noted in the introduction, means "good news" or a heralding of "unexpected joy." Thus, if we are embarking as fellow travelers and guides on this journey of good news, shouldn't we want to travel that route more effectively? And if so, how do we measure progress?

Some mistakenly perceive that counting attendance is the best way to evaluate effectiveness.[13] But there are four types of church growth mentioned in the Bible, and growth in attendance is cited as God's task—not the job of the church. In two previous books, I have looked at measuring these in detail, but let's briefly examine four types of church growth and a church growth metric that can measure each.[14]

The context is Acts 2:42–47. Here we find Luke's description of church growth that followed Peter's sermon on the day of Pentecost. Luke describes four types of growth.

Growth A: Growth in Maturity. In verse 42, Luke notes that the followers were growing in a passion for the apostles' teaching, fellowship, and prayer. Our first metric is to ascertain if, as a result of our need-based ministry, wayfarers are increasing in their participation in Bible study, fellowship, or the practice of prayer. One way to measure this is to determine if people are becoming increasingly involved in study groups, fellowship networks (that is, informal small groups), or joining with others for prayer. If these numbers are calculated as a percentage of overall attendance, growth in maturity may be estimated.

Some people mistakenly perceive that counting attendance is the best way to evaluate effectiveness. However, there are four types of church growth mentioned in the Bible, and growth in attendance is cited as God's task—not the job of the church.

Growth B: Growth in Unity. Verses 44–45 describe how the church grew in unity and trust. This is much harder to measure, because it requires subjective evaluation. But if people open up, much like Doug did about do-gooders, then these and similar actions can indicate that ministry is creating deeper and more honest levels of communication. Unity often results from deepening levels of communication.[15]

Growth C: Growth in Favor in the Community. In verse 47, Luke emphasizes that the church was increasingly "enjoying the favor of all the people." Here is a metric often overlooked, which asks, Is the community increasingly appreciative of the ministry the church is offering? Asking community residents for regular feedback is a way to accomplish this. One church crafted an online survey and gave away coupons for free coffee at a coffee shop to whoever completed the survey. This survey was not designed to augment the church database but was used only to ascertain if community residents felt the church was doing good better. Another church regularly polled socially sensitive community residents such as school principals, public leaders, community organizers, and businesspeople about how effective the church was in meeting community needs. The results were that these churches could gauge effective ministry by observing changes in community appreciation.

Growth D: Growth in More Christians. Luke concludes this passage about early church growth by reminding his readers that "the Lord added to their number daily those who were being saved" (v. 47). Luke was pointing out that because it was a supernatural intersection, it was God's task to bring people to and through the experience of salvation. But in the preceding verses, Luke emphasized that it was the church's role to grow people in the other three types of church growth: maturity, unity, and favor in the community.

Church growth metrics remind us that we are engaged in a task that is not about large cadres of attendees but about the inner growth of God's creation into: a deepening relationship with him, more unity among his children, and in such a way that a watching world rejoices.[16]

INTERVIEW WITH MIKE SLAUGHTER

*Author, advocate for Darfur, and lead pastor of Ginghamsburg
United Methodist Church, Tipp City, Ohio*

Whitesel: What is the Love Dayton Initiative all about?

Slaughter: It's all about loving a town by first meeting their physical needs and then meeting their spiritual needs. Too many churches focus on meeting just spiritual needs, and many people aren't ready to respond because they've got basic needs going unmet. Like you, we've found it useful to use a journey metaphor. Our ministry is called New Path. Its goals are to assist families and individuals in financial crisis. We do this by not only meeting immediate needs, but also by creating an environment that supports long-term stability, empowers individuals, and fosters transformation. But we need a lot of volunteers to do this. So we let people who aren't even sure who God is join us and volunteer.

Whitesel: Is there a danger inviting those who are not yet sure who God is to work alongside of you and represent your church?

Slaughter: I suppose there is. But people in need are very forgiving. They are just happy someone is helping them. And they can tell that people are at different places on their spiritual journey. I think we give needy people too little credit for discernment. It doesn't bother them. In fact, they can probably relate to them better.

Whitesel: It sounds like some people journey with you for some time before they reach the next waypoint.

Slaughter: Most people seem to need multiple experiences before they want to know more about the good news. They want to grasp the implications of the good news by seeing Christians live it. Working alongside of us lets them see this firsthand.

Whitesel: Can you give me an example?

Slaughter: Sure. Right now we have volunteers going to the Gulf of Mexico to help people recovering from recent hurricanes. Five of the people going are currently unemployed. They are working through some pretty big issues in their lives, but they still feel compassion to help others. They are not involved in the church worship services, but they are growing. As part of that growth we want them to see that serving others is what it means to follow Christ. They are finding their place on the journey through practical service. The Christian practice of good deeds sometimes precedes belief. And this helps them see the good in the good news.

Whitesel: You seem very passionate about this. From where does this passion come?

Slaughter: It's because we've got a lot of work to do. For example, our church has been very involved in helping the people of Darfur. The next thing you know, George Clooney blogged about us and said ours was a Christian response. Someone replied, "Christians care about genocide and Darfur?" That is mind blowing to me. Perception is reality. Bob, we've got a lot of work ahead of us if we are to change perceptions that the church only cares about salvation and not about the quality of people's lives too.

QUESTIONS FOR GROUP OR PERSONAL STUDY

1. Do people who are not Christians participate in your ministry to the needy? If so, what roles are they given? What roles are they not given? Are you exempting them from some roles because they are neophytes, not well known, or rough around the edges? Ask yourself the following questions and write out your reply:

   - Do you welcome people who are not Christians to be involved in planning your ministry to the needy?
   - What will you do in the next six months to involve people who are not Christians in the planning of ministry?

2. What ministries do you offer to meet physiological needs? List each and appraise if they are meeting long-term needs for food, water, and biological requirements, or if they are only meeting short-term needs. If they are meeting short-term needs, what will you do to adjust them to meet long-term needs?

3. What ministries do you offer to meet safety needs, that is, to meet the need to feel safe, stable, and secure? List and appraise each.

4. Do you have a balance between ministries that meet physiological needs and those that meet safety needs? Use Figure 15.4 to measure your balance between physiological and safety needs. If they are not balanced, what will you do to ensure that both needs are met and the route of the good news is unbroken?

FIGURE 15.4

Physiological Needs (Need for food, water, and other biological requirements)	*Safety Needs* (Need to feel safe, stable, and secure; and that the world is predictable)

• Family emergency services
  ○ Housing
  ○ Food/clothing
  ○ Counseling
• Medical emergency assistance
  ○ Financial help
  ○ Information
• Food and domestic hunger ministries
  ○ Food pantry
  ○ Meals
• Housing and residential programs
• Hunger/housing loans and grants programs
• Disaster relief services
  ○ Housing/food
  ○ Food/clothing
• Addiction and recovery counseling and support
  ○ Professional counseling
  ○ Mentoring
  ○ Friendship
	• Job placement
	  ○ Employment counseling
	  ○ Career research
	  ○ Application and résumé writing
	  ○ Preparation for job interviews
	  ○ Networking for under- and unemployed
	  ○ English as a second language (ESL) assistance
	  ○ GED education
	• Job training
	  ○ Skills training
	  ○ Vocational rehabilitation
	  ○ Learn new job skills
	  ○ References for future employment
	  ○ Scholarships
	• Health programs
	  ○ Patient advocacy
	  ○ Medical equipment

5. When have you been a do-gooder? And when have you been a good-doer? What will you do to enhance the latter and cancel out the former? List four ideas that you will undertake good-doing within the next year.

6. Read Acts 2:42–47. Describe each of the four types of church growth. How could you measure each in your local church? Put together a plan that can be implemented in the next six months to measure all four types of church growth.

INITIAL AWARENESS OF
THE GOOD NEWS

R on was intrigued by the young man's political connections in one of the world's most volatile countries. It was 1979, and South Africa simmered with rage over the apartheid, segregating white and non-white people through forced removals, loss of citizenship, repression, and state-sponsored violence. James was a young Jewish politician who keenly grasped the opportunities and imperfections of his South African homeland.

Still, Ron was taken back when James suddenly blurted out, "God told me that if I come to this conference he will tell me things about his Son." Ron was a speaker at this Christian leadership conference and felt more than prepared to address James' yearning. Ron was known not only for his sharp intellect, but also for his ability to explain difficult biblical concepts in a clear manner. After all, Ron was a Yale trained academic who participated in InterVarsity Christian Fellowship, a college ministry with a tradition of campus witness and thoughtful dialogue.

Ron and James struck up a conversation that lasted several days. For Ron, James' political insights provided a glimpse into the potential of one of the African continent's most populated countries. And for James, Ron was able to rationally explain

> Today the sinfulness of the social order offends thoughtful Christians everywhere . . . The great inequalities of wealth and poverty among the haves and have-nots, and the revolting treatment meted out to oppressed minorities, are clearly contrary to the will of the God and Father of our Lord Jesus Christ.
>
> —Donald McGavran[1]

Christ's resurrection, the fundamentals of Christian faith, and God's purposes for humankind. After a three-hour conversation, Ron sensed James was ready to act. But James responded with an unexpected retort that almost derailed the journey.

He said, "But what I've seen is that Christians just like to sing happy songs and talk about Jesus. They are not committed to abolishing apartheid or helping oppressed minorities." For James, the God Ron described seemed so different from how Christians acted.

This view was not new to Ron. Since his college years he had been passionate about sharing his faith in Christ. But he had also seen the church's lack of holistic ministry create misperceptions, skepticism, and often rejection of the good news. He observed that in most people's minds the good news was divorced from good works. This misperception had led Ron Sider to write a book.[2] In it Ron recounted how concern for the whole person, both physical and spiritual, was a hallmark of Jesus' ministry. As a result, Ron slowly helped James negotiate Waypoint 14, assisting him in understanding that his initial awareness of the good news had been skewed.

While James was right that oftentimes Christians focus on the joy and celebration in knowing Christ, the good news is much greater than just conversionary festivities. The good news includes the fact that Jesus stands in solidarity with the poor, the disenfranchised, and the oppressed. The Lausanne Movement, whose goal is "to reframe the Christian mission of evangelization in a world rife with social, political, economic, and religious upheaval" states in its covenant that "the message of salvation implies also a message of judgment upon every form of alienation, oppression and discrimination, and we should not be afraid to denounce evil and injustice wherever they exist."[3]

Ron and James met a number of times over the next three days. Slowly, James' initial awareness of the good news came into perspective, and at one meeting James asked to personally meet the Son of God. James accepted Jesus as Messiah. Ron recalls, "All I could do was walk around my room praising God . . . I wish this would happen to me once a week!"

WAYPOINT CHARACTERISTICS

SIGNS OF TRAVELERS AT WAYPOINT 14

Skeptical Travelers. These are wayfarers who are skeptical that the church really deep down cares for the needs of others or the world. This may occur because churches sometimes feign care for the poor because of their own need of survival or for numerical increase. We shall see shortly that churches that care for the needy because of selfish goals have poor theology, especially when it comes to a theology of God's creation. And the lack of a clear theology of social ministry only confirms in skeptical minds that the church is self-serving rather than serving humanity. One participant in the Lausanne Conference summed up, "If we turn a blind eye to the suffering, the social oppression, the alienation and loneliness of people, let us not be surprised if they turn a deaf ear to our message of eternal salvation."[4]

Travelers Who Ignore the Problem. Research into how people handle new ideas has led some researchers to conclude that people react in one of four ways called the EVLN paradigm.[5] Some people, when confronted with a conflicting idea, such as the good news, *exit* the situation. These people run away from the thought of discussing spiritual matters. They may best be reached by the principles outlined in Waypoints 16 and 15 respectively. Other people *voice* their objections. These people are often the skeptical travelers noted above. Still others remain *loyal*, not wanting to rock the boat, and thus they quietly agree. The most difficult segment to engage, however, is those who react to news by *neglecting* or ignoring the problem. They nod politely in affirmation but do not yet recognize the seriousness of the situation. They hope to avoid new ideas because they reject things that cause a change in their lives. Travelers who ignore the problem of their eternal destiny must be gently and logically led to understand the momentousness and seriousness of their journey. Let us look at how ministry to both of the above kinds of travelers can take place.

ACTIONS THAT HELP WAYPOINT 14 TRAVELERS

ACTION 14.1: NEWS YOU CAN'T IGNORE

Let us look at the last category of travelers first—the traveler whose initial awareness of the good news results in a neglect of it. There are two steps for helping someone deal with such a difficult issue. The first is to help the person grasp the seriousness of the subject, and the second is to visualize the future.

Point 1: The Seriousness of the Topic. C. S. Lewis, an organic intellectual, skillfully illuminated grand biblical themes. Regarding the seriousness of the good news he said, "Christianity is a statement which, if false, is of *no* importance, and, if true, of infinite importance. The one thing it cannot be is moderately important."[6] What Lewis meant by this is that if the claims of eternal life (John 14:1–3) are true and if the parallel claim that only through Christ can eternal life be reached (John 14:6) are also true, then Christianity holds the all-important key to infinity.

Describing a bright future of enjoying children and grandchildren was almost 80 percent effective in helping patients change their lifestyle. When sharing the good news, a depiction of a happy future may be more powerful than depicting a fiery doom.

Point 2: Picture the Future. But how does a congregation emphasize the importance of the topic? For most travelers, it will not be enough to just logically explain (as Lewis did) that eternal life is possible and attainable. Instead, most people will need a mental picture. Alister McGrath analyzed how the Bible and Christians looked at heaven and said, "The Christian concept of heaven is iconic, rather than intellectual . . . [Heaven is] something that makes its appeal to the imagination, rather than the intellect, which calls out to be visualized rather than merely understood . . . It is much easier to reflect upon an image than an idea."[7]

This fact was driven home to the American medical community when a study on heart patients found scaring patients into changing their behavior did not work. When future illness was graphically described, only 10 percent of the patients changed their behaviors. On the other hand, 77 percent changed their behavior when they were given a mental picture of a healthy future life (for example, enjoying life with their family, friends, and grandchildren).[8] In other words, describing the poor health associated with heart disease only motivated one in ten people to change. But describing a bright future enjoying children and grandchildren was almost 80 percent effective in helping patients change their lifestyle. When sharing the good news, a depiction of a happy future may be more powerful that depicting a fiery doom. The church should focus on the penalty and punishment of hell, but in today's world only about 10 percent of the people will change their outlook because of scare tactics. If Christians focus on the bliss of heaven and the wholeness of a Christian life, then perhaps up to 80 percent may change their outlook.

The Bible is replete with verses that visualize eternal joy. Jesus underscore the communal and residential nature of heaven when he stated:

> Do not let your hearts be troubled. Trust in God; trust also in me. In my Father's house are many rooms; if it were not so, I would have told you. I am going there to prepare a place for you. And if I go and prepare a place for you, I will come back and take you to be with me that you also may be where I am. (John 14:1–3)

Peter knew the Jewish people pictured their "promised inheritance" as Canaan (Num. 32:19), but he suggested they visualize this everlasting inheritance as eternal life stating, "In his great mercy he has given us new birth into a living hope through the resurrection of Jesus Christ from the dead, and into an inheritance that can never perish, spoil or fade—kept in heaven for you" (1 Pet. 1:3–4). Throughout Scripture, it is emphasized that Jesus is the only way to this bliss. When Thomas asked Jesus to clarify the above statement about "going to prepare a place" (John 14:2), Jesus decisively and authoritatively responded, "I am the way and the truth and the life. No one comes to the Father except through me" (John 14:6).

How then can points 1 and 2 be fostered in our churches? A good place is in what we read and discuss. Many popular books today are inspirational guides aimed at Christians. There is nothing wrong with this. But when a church wants to engage travelers at Waypoint 14, the church may need to recast its reading lists. There are many books that give descriptive and positive images of heaven or Christian life that could become book studies in our churches and communities. C. S. Lewis's *Chronicles of Narnia* (especially *The Last Battle*), *The Great Divorce* (especially the sections on heaven), and the Space Trilogy (especially the last book), are but of few of his books that paint inspiring pictures of the future. Lewis's friend and Christian mentor, J. R. R. Tolkien, painted pictures of an idyllic world where good triumphs over evil, sacrifice leads to nobility, and ultimately humankind and nature conspire to overthrow evil (The Lord of the Rings trilogy). John Milton's classic *Paradise Regained* illustrates in luminous words the worlds that lie ahead (and in *Paradise Lost* those luminous realms that lie behind). Even modern stories such as Trudy Harris's *Glimpses of Heaven: True Stories of Hope and Peace at the End of Life's Journey* and Don Piper and Cecil Murphey's *90 Minutes in Heaven: A True Story of Death and Life* can help travelers at Waypoint 14 focus on the promise of the good news.

ACTION 14.2: THE GOOD NEWS THAT GOD CARES

A church also must understand and articulate a theology regarding God's concern for his creation if its congregants are going to help people move beyond Waypoint 14. A theology of creation must be a holistic theology and include not just God's creative activity but also humankind's woeful response. For in response to God's gracious creation of a paradise on earth, humans chose a selfish route, disobeying God's directives and forfeiting paradise.[9] Though there are many elements to a theology of creation, let us look at five points that bear upon our current conversation.

Point 1: Injustice and Poverty Are the Result of Human Activity. God does not desire it for his creation. When Adam and Eve forfeited the paradise of Eden, they embarked upon a journey of selfish arrogance. Scripture tells us their journey led to self-centeredness, injustice, and greed (Gen. 3–5). Ron Sider reminds us that this disappoints God: "The Bible clearly and repeatedly teaches that God is at work in history casting down the rich and exalting the poor, because frequently the rich are wealthy precisely because they have oppressed the poor or have neglected to aid the needy."[10]

Point 2: This Injustice Was not Always So. God provided Adam and Eve an Eden of goodness and wholeness in every aspect of their lives. Old Testament scholar Walter Brueggemann pointed out that the Hebrew word *shalom*[11] comes closest to describing this "wholeness in every area of life, where God, creature, and creation enjoy harmonious relationships."[12] God had warned that disobeying him would result in a loss of this life of shalom (Gen. 2:15–17). But Adam and Eve made selfish choices, putting to an end this world of balance and blessing (Gen. 3).

Point 3: Humankind Was Put in Charge of Caring for God's Creation. Early on in the Genesis story, before the fall of humankind from the era of shalom, God gave humankind the task caring for the garden and being stewards of it (Gen. 1:26–30). This requires Christians to be good stewards of God's earth and life upon it.

Point 4: Humankind Was Put in Charge of Caring for the Needy, Oppressed, and Disenfranchised. Proverbs 19:17 says, "He who is kind to the poor lends to the LORD, and he will reward him for what he has done." Judah was punished in part because of her mistreatment of the poor: "Woe to those who make unjust laws, to those who issue oppressive decrees, to deprive the poor of their rights and withhold justice from the oppressed of my people, making widows their prey and robbing the fatherless. What will you do on the day of reckoning, when disaster comes from afar?" (Isa. 10:1–3). King David said, "I know that the LORD secures justice for the poor and upholds the cause of the needy" (Ps.140:12). Howard Snyder reminds us that "God especially has compassion on the poor, and his acts in history confirm this."[13]

Point 5: God Requires His People to Sacrifice for This Task. Adam and Eve were put in charge of caring for and cultivating the garden (Gen. 1:26–30). This required sacrificing their own desire to taste the forbidden fruit. From this beginning, serving a loving, creative God required self-sacrifice. At this sacrifice, Adam and Eve failed. In doing so, they condemned their children and their children's children to laborious toil, hostility, repression, and ultimately death (Gen. 3:16–24). Still, God's desire is that his children serve and sacrifice for others. Jesus stated, "When you give a luncheon or dinner, do not invite your friends, your brothers or relatives, or your rich neighbors . . .

But when you give a banquet, invite the poor, the crippled, the lame, the blind, and you will be blessed. Although they cannot repay you, you will be repaid at the resurrection of the righteous" (Luke 14:12–14). This sacrifice for others is exemplified in the sacrificial actions of godly men and women in the Bible, ultimately culminating in the sacrifice of Jesus for humankind's disobedience.

When a congregation grasps the five points above, wayfarers will understand that evil, oppression, and the like are not God's doing but human doing. And wayfarers such as James from the beginning of this chapter can see that God wants Christians to help the oppressed, disenfranchised, and neglected. The church must help travelers at Waypoint 14 see the good news that "the sinfulness of the social order offends thoughtful Christians everywhere."[14]

INTERVIEW WITH RON SIDER

President of the Evangelicals for Social Action and professor of theology, holistic ministry, and public policy at Palmer Theological Seminary

Whitesel: How did your experience with James renew or challenge your view of the good news?

Sider: While at Yale in the 1960s, I felt a call to be a social activist. I resolved very early on that I would not make the same mistake of the old social gospel movement that developed a poor theology and lost its compassion for evangelism. Both passions, good news and good works, are needed to change the person for the better—and the world for the better too. My conversations with James reaffirmed my thinking.

"Thirty years ago it seemed the primary mission of most evangelical churches was saving souls. If you had a little money and a little time left over, you could do a few good works."

Whitesel: How are churches doing on this issue of balance today?

Sider: Thirty years ago it seemed the primary mission of most evangelical churches was saving souls. If you had a little money and a little time left over, you could do a few good works. I don't think that's biblical. I'm committed to loving the whole person as Jesus did. Now, evangelism is central. We don't want to lessen that. But a theology of creation means we want to care for and meet the needs of the people created in God's image. And we've made some progress. Many evangelical leaders today understand that we should do both. It's growing everywhere today. Churches are doing both social ministry and evangelistic action—holistic mission.

Whitesel: What do you say about the criticism that social action can be manipulative—that you are just leading them to Christ for your own need for scale?

Sider: You're right, this is a danger. The way to avoid it is to first of all be clear that a theology of creation tells us that it is important to assist people in attaining a good, wholesome life. It is a good thing to take care of people's physical needs. Jesus showed us that dramatic conversion restores families, overcomes despair, heals relationships, and changes lives for the better. But if you care about them, you will also want to do more than just meet their physical needs; you will want to help them with their eternal destiny. Walking with Jesus is a good deal now and an even better deal later!

Whitesel: Who can we learn from?

Sider: The Salvation Army has continued to do an excellent job. The Booths (William and Catherine) knew that social structures were unfair and needed to be changed, and the Salvation Army passionately carries on that care today. The result is that they are respected because they do it. Vineyard Fellowships are increasing in holistic ministry, and the Church of the Nazarene is working on this, creating Good Samaritan Congregations who balance their ministry by reaching out to help the poor.[15]

Whitesel: Any final thoughts?

Sider: The Pentecostals may be the ones to watch. Donald Miller and Tetsunao Yamamori wrote a book on the emerging movement for social concern in global Pentecostalism.[16] If the global Pentecostal movement embraces this, then the next twenty to thirty years will be a remarkable time for the spread of the gospel and social ministry. I'm pretty excited about the journey!

QUESTIONS FOR GROUP OR PERSONAL STUDY

1. Have you read or watched a story, movie, or narrative that impressed you with the momentousness of the biblical good news? Do you know of others who have read or watched the same narrative? If so, what elements of that story made it so memorable? Was their experience similar to yours?

2. What books, poems, movies, short stories, passages of Scriptures, or other resources have helped you visualize heaven? Have you shared this experience with someone who had only a limited awareness of the good news? If so, what was the outcome? If not, what will you do?

3. What changes have you made as a result of a mental picture of the future? Did you change some habit, go in some different direction, or change your outlook on some topic? How helpful was visualizing the future? Could telling a story help you explain your faith to a person who is new to the good news? If so, create an explanation of some facet of the good news and share it with your Christian friends. Ask them to help you fine-tune it to increase clarity.

4. Which of the following books explains your most memorial image? Why does it linger with you? If you have not read one of the books below, decide to read the one that most appeals to you in the next three weeks, and then complete the above task.

   - C. S. Lewis, the Chronicles of Narnia (any volume)
   - C. S. Lewis, *The Great Divorce*
   - C. S. Lewis, *The Screwtape Letters*
   - C. S. Lewis, the Space Trilogy (any volume)
   - J. R. R. Tolkien, the Lord of the Rings trilogy (any volume)
   - Charles Williams, *War in Heaven, a Novel*

- Charles Williams, *The Place of the Lion*
- John Milton, *Paradise Lost*
- John Milton, *Paradise Regained*
- John Bunyan, *Pilgrim's Progress*
- Trudy Harris, *Glimpses of Heaven: True Stories of Hope and Peace at the End of Life's Journey*
- Don Piper and Cecil Murphey, *90 Minutes in Heaven: A True Story of Death and Life*

5. How does your church care for God's creation? How energetically and enthusiastically do you care for the oppressed, the poor, the estranged, the outsider, the lonely, and those suffering from health issues? What percentage of your effort is directed toward meeting the needs of these disenfranchised individuals? How does this percentage compare with the time, effort, and money your church directs toward the Christian community? Is there a balance? Should there be?

AWARENESS OF THE
FUNDAMENTALS
OF THE GOOD NEWS

I t was a question Dan had not heard before, but it intrigued him. For several months, a young Hindu girl had been attending the church Dan pastored. A gifted poet, she approached one of the church staff with an offer to host a poetry slam at the church. An informal event where attendees share poetry in front of a crowd, this poetry slam would be an official event of the church. "It seemed like it would be a fun night for people, so the poetry slam was held, and it turned out to be a successful event," recalls Dan.

Dan's reaction to have the poetry slam emerged from years of listening to the faith stories of church attendees. Having people who aren't yet Christians involved in the life of the church community is a

> A journey is best measured in friends, rather than miles.
> —TIM CAHILL[1]

significant form of outreach for this church in Santa Cruz, California. "They aren't in teaching roles or in roles of spiritual leadership, but there are many ways for people to get involved in the church community—even as a non-Christian," declares Dan. "I remember one guy. He was really skeptical of Christians for a long time. In fact, the only reason he came to church was because he liked a girl who attended here. The relationship was totally the motive. But through being a part of the church community, he grew in his awareness of the gospel and Jesus. It took time, but eventually he put his trust in Christ. You come to know Christ through his Word and through seeing the gospel lived out among his people."

Another church attendee recently pulled Dan aside in the church hallway. "It was the same story," he says. "Friendship without pressure, building trust.

Eventually the person came to the larger worship gathering because the friend was a part of it. The person related to the vibe of the community and eventually put saving faith in Jesus. It doesn't happen with everyone, of course. There are many who don't put faith in Jesus. But with the ones who do, it seems the pattern overall is the same."

Dan's desire to not rush, manipulate, or incentivize the process has allowed attendees to become aware of the good news through the faith community and God's working in their hearts. "I came to understand this by listening to their stories. Before anyone is baptized, I meet with them to hear their story. And I repeatedly hear about how they became participants in our community before they knew Jesus. One person who is not a Christian recently helped with a project doing some gardening around our church. After the work was done, she stayed and got to know other Christians who are part of our church. This past Sunday, she introduced me to two friends she brought to the worship gatherings. They aren't Christians either. She isn't a Christian yet, but I have hope.

"It almost feels like popcorn," Dan continues. "You put something in the pot, it starts simmering as misconceptions are broken down, and then in God's timing, a new life breaks out. Some may not pop so to speak, but over time others do. God can do anything, but it seems that today he is using a more communal way to help people navigate their spiritual journey."

Dan Kimball's approach has led to amazing growth at Vintage Faith Church amid the often skeptical culture of Santa Cruz, California. "Don't get me wrong, the basics of what it means to be a Christian must be taught, grasped, and wrestled with, and a person must have a transformation experience. But oftentimes, the church doesn't realize that this takes time and it presses for a decision too soon. Providing ways for those interested in Jesus to join in our community and serve together gives them an opportunity to grow without pressure. It gives them a chance to experience people who love them and who live out their lives authentically as those who follow Jesus."

WAYPOINT CHARACTERISTICS

SIGNS OF TRAVELERS AT WAYPOINT 13

Spiritual Curiosity. Wayfarers at this point are usually inquisitive, curious, perplexed, and frustrated by all things spiritual. They have been drawn to investigate further their initial experience with the good news at Waypoint 14. But they may bring with them the skepticism about religion that is rising in North America.[2]

At Waypoint 13, some travelers have not yet grasped the differences between varying religious viewpoints. They may be drawn to investigate the occult, mysticism, and other religions. Once spiritual curiosity has been stirred, they often launch full bore into multiple religious directions. Though natural, their openness to varying viewpoints challenges Christians.

The church sometimes overreacts, humiliates, or banishes such inquisitiveness. Instead, we must see these individuals as normal explorers on a spiritual journey and expect their curiosity. Churches can best help travelers by encouraging discussion, inquisitiveness, disagreement, and even prying. The church must not be defensive, closed, or inauthentic. Doing so can belie that it has the truth the traveler seeks.

Frustrated By Language. Another sign that travelers are at Waypoint 13 is that they can be confounded by the language of Christian culture. Christians frequently employ terminology that is not broadly understood. Terms such as *sanctification, the kingdom of God,* and *the blood of Christ* can express grand concepts in concise terms. But to those newly introduced to the journey, these terms may be too much too soon. The result is that travelers may feel that the ardor of the journey coupled with learning a new language is too much to bear. In addition, not knowing the terminology may make the traveler feel ignorant, naïve, and possibly excluded.

Churches must undertake the task of adapting their terminology to the metaphors of the hearer without sacrificing content. Action 13.2 below will describe how to create metaphors that are equivalent to images in the traveler's world. Finding and utilizing such equivalent metaphors is a challenging task. But it is part of every missionary's work, and in North America's cultural mosaic, it must be the work of every church.

Travelers Are Accepted but not Accepted Enough. Travelers at Waypoint 13 often feel they are being courted by Christians, but then when they try to volunteer, the church often tells them they are not yet ready. This is the frustration that Kimball observed at the beginning of this chapter and sought to address. Some churches feel that God's intention is to utilize only Christians to serve the community. While this should be true in distribution of the sacraments and certain religious ministries (see Acts 6:1–3; 14:23; 1 Tim. 5:17), the Scriptures are replete with examples of those who traveled with a faith community and even assisted it prior to partaking in that community's faith (see Josh. 2; Ruth 1; Matt. 2; 9).[3]

A popular Christian musician once told me he only employed Christians in every aspect of his musical recordings. This might be an appropriate strategy if Christians were being excluded because of their beliefs and his action was designed to bring parity. But to me it seemed that many non-Christian musicians missed an opportunity to work alongside and learn from this gifted Christian artist. Kimball is focused on ensuring this does not happen at the church he pastors.

ACTIONS THAT HELP WAYPOINT 13 TRAVELERS

ACTION 13.1: WE JOURNEY WITH THEM AND THEY WITH US

At Vintage Faith Church, wayfarers are encouraged to participate in administrative tasks. Most churches reserve administrative involvement for those who have experienced new birth. Yet such involvement can be an important learning opportunity for three reasons. First, it helps people at Waypoint 13 recognize they have God-given gifts. Second, it helps people at Waypoint 13 understand that the community of faith is there to support them in their service to others. Third, it helps people at Waypoint 13 see that participation in the community is not reserved for only a privileged group. This keeps a church from developing elitism.

It is also best if the church's volunteer opportunities are directed toward serving those outside the church, rather than serving the church. This is because a person at Waypoint 13 may have only recently departed a realm of inequalities, injustices, deprivations, and oppression. Therefore, to them, the organizational needs of the church will pale in comparison. They can easily, and rightly, be offended when we ask them to clean up the church, arrange chairs in the sanctuary, or paint a nursery. Though these organizational tasks are necessary to support outreach, to the wayfarer these connections can be too obscure. Instead, it is important to let the wayfarer become involved in volunteer actions that help people at waypoints the volunteer has recently experienced. The needs of others are fresh in their mind, as is the difference they've experienced by moving forward on their journey.

Still, two caveats must be considered. First, as Kimball noted, some activities require a level of spiritual maturity, sensitivity, or organizational history that the volunteer at Waypoint 13 may lack. Therefore, it becomes important for leaders to tactfully guide the person into appropriate volunteer opportunities.

Second, many wayfarers do not want to volunteer. Many may be reeling from disappointments, resentments, oppression, or other setbacks and thus only desire our assistance, not our recruitment.

At Waypoint 13, it therefore becomes essential for the Christian to move slowly with fellow travelers, never manipulating or forcing them. The Holy Spirit is the one who draws a person on this journey (John 16:8–9), and the faith community must ensure that we assist and not replace the Holy Spirit.

ACTION 13.2: TRANSLATE THE GOOD NEWS

At the same time that the traveler is growing in knowledge of the good news, the Christian is often bombarding the traveler with a specialized language. Earlier in this chapter we saw how travelers can become frustrated with a Christian's cryptic language.

To underscore such a communication breakdown, a Christian troubadour named Larry Norman created an imaginary dialogue between a Christian and a person at Waypoint 13. "Have you been saved?" began the Christian. The traveler replied, "I fell out of a canoe at camp once, and the lifeguard rescued me." "No, I mean have you been born again?" continued the Christian. "I don't believe in reincarnation," came the traveler's answer. "Have you been washed in the blood?" replied the Christian in growing exacerbation. "Ugh! I don't think I would want to," came the wayfarer's astonished response. After which the flustered Christian blurted out, "I'm trying to tell you the good news!" "What's that?" came the traveler's hopeful reply. "You're going to hell," retorted the Christian, and the conversation ended.[4]

This narrative illustrates how Christian musicians have grappled with translating their message to a non-churched culture. Though we do not want to change our message or its content, Christians helping those at Waypoint 13 must translate the good news. Missionaries and Bible translators spend years honing their skills in translating truth without sacrificing content. But regrettably, most Christian leaders in North America rarely try. With the growing mosaic of cultures and subcultures in North America, coupled with a large unchurched population that is unfamiliar with Christian terminology, churches must begin to learn the important skills of translating the good news from missionaries and translators.[5] The following are four basic steps for translation.[6]

Step 1: Decide What Are the Essential Principles That Must Be Translated. For a person at Waypoint 13 headed toward Waypoint 12 (grasp of the implications of the good news), this means explaining that the good news holds promises as well as requirements. Jesus reminded his hearers of these requirements but also reminded them that they are not odious or overwhelming, saying, "Come to me, all you who are weary and burdened, and I will give you rest. Take my yoke upon you and learn from me, for I am gentle and humble in heart, and you will find rest for your souls. For my yoke is easy and my burden is light" (Matt. 11:28–30). Initial principles that should be broached at Waypoint 13 include but are not limited to God's unconditional love (John 3:16), that wrongdoings destroy lives and separate us from God (Rom. 3:23), how Jesus bore the penalty for our wrongdoings (Rom. 5:8; John 14:6), in order that we might have a better life here and ultimately eternal life (John 17:3; 1 John 5:13).

Step 2: Put the Basics of the Good News into the Language of the Hearer. This step is best accomplished by a team. And it is good to have non-churchgoers involved, so that through dialogue, questioning, and discussion, an up-to-date translation is created. While non-churchgoers should not have veto power, their involvement helps ensure that the translation is relevant and accurate. In addition, the Christian must be careful not to be offended or affronted by another culture's terminology. Anthropologist Eugene Nida recalls how the tribal people of Papua New Guinea, had never seen a lamb and the phrase "Look, the lamb of God" (John 1:29) was confusing.

> The Christian must gather regularly with others to discuss and improve the translation of the basics of the good news. Too often, churches ignore the need for updating their terminology and become mired in language from earlier and outdated renditions.

Yet in their tribal culture, they raised and valued pigs in similar fashion to the way ancient Israelites prized sheep. The missionaries therefore translated John the Baptist's declaration "Look, the Lamb of God" as "Look, the Pig of God." To many Christians this is distasteful for most Christians are sensitive to the Jewish repulsion to unclean animals such as pigs. However, the tribal people of Papua New Guinea have no knowledge of such aversion, and because they value their swine so greatly, Jesus was to them the cherished, sacrificial "Pig of God."[7]

Step 3: Keep Modifying and Improving Your Terms. Translation is an ongoing process because the meaning of words can change, as well as our understanding of them. Thus, translated terms must be updated and modified in an ongoing fashion, from Waypoint 13 forward. The Christian must gather regularly with others to discuss and improve the translation of the basics of the good news. Too often, churches ignore the need for updating their terminology becoming mired in language from earlier and outdated renditions. A result is that wayfarers often view the church's terminology as outdated, obsolete, and incoherent.

Step 4: Sift Out the Bad and Keep the Good. Each culture has elements that run counter to the good news of Christ. Yet at the same time, each culture has elements that are consistent with Christ's good news. For example, postmodernism emphasizes that people should not just talk about changing the world but actually be engaged in changing it. Karl Marx famously intoned, "philosophers have only interpreted the world in various ways; the point is to change it."[8] The result has been that postmodern-influenced young people exhibit a growing concern for changing the plight of the poor. This is also a major element in Jesus' good news; for example, when he proclaimed in the Nazareth synagogue, "The Spirit of the Lord is on me, because he has anointed me, to preach good news to the poor. He has sent me to proclaim freedom for the prisoners and recovery of sight for the blind, to release the oppressed, to proclaim the year of the Lord's favor" (Luke 4:18–19). Thus, this postmodern passion for helping the needy should be lauded.

The task of explaining the good news to wayfarers at Waypoint 13 also carries the requirement that we sift between elements of a culture that go against Christ's news and those that do not. To not fully explain God's expectations is to misinform and ill prepare the traveler.

But there are also elements of a culture that can run counter to the good news. For example, premarital or extramarital affairs can be viewed by postmodern culture as a natural and recurrent part of life. But this runs counter to the biblical injunction against pre- and extramarital sex. *The Message* paraphrase crafts a good translation of this biblical injunction: "Honor marriage, and guard the sacredness of sexual intimacy between wife and husband. God draws a firm line against casual and illicit sex" (Heb. 13:4). Thus, when translating the good news, a translator must be careful to not deemphasize or obscure God's commands and expectations.

When elements of a culture run counter to the good news and others are in agreement with it, what should be done? Eddie Gibbs has provided a helpful metaphor in the image of cultural "sifting."[9] Sifting separates unwanted elements from wanted elements, most notably in cooking, where a mesh strainer such as a colander will sift out impurities. The task of explaining the good news to wayfarers at Waypoint 13 also carries the requirement that we sift between elements of a culture that go against Christ's news and those that do not. To not fully explain God's expectations is to misinform and ill prepare the traveler. Some Christians avoid the task of doing this because championing God's requirements is awkward in comparison to lauding his rewards. But both must be undertaken. A leader who is not ready to sift elements of a culture and tactfully explain what can be retained and what must be abandoned is not ready to travel forward with the wayfarer.

INTERVIEW WITH DAN KIMBALL

Pastor of Vintage Faith Church, Santa Cruz, California

Whitesel: You told the story of a talented Hindu poet who volunteered to host and organize a poetry slam. And you let her do this before she experienced new birth. Aren't you afraid that a person could unintentionally do something egregious or morally wrong while representing the church?

Kimball: If it was a teaching role or an event that placed her in a position of spiritual authority, then we wouldn't have let her lead that. But because it was a fun event and there were also Christians in our church helping out, it was fine. It got her involved and it allowed her to meet other people in our church.

Whitesel: Did you always see evangelism as a journey where non-Christians often travel along with the church before they are ready to go deeper?

Kimball: I didn't understand this at first. As a high school pastor fifteen years ago, I did regular altar calls. It was more like as soon as people get in our building, present the gospel so they can respond right away. God moved in a lot of people's hearts, so I don't think this was ineffective. But I think today we have a shift in culture and people that has occurred. The church has lost its voice in most places and isn't trusted. So we have to build a lot of trust before people will listen to our message. That's why when people are part of a church community, trust is built and then they are more open to really hearing what Christians believe and why.

Whitesel: Let's make sure our readers understand. You do believe in a point of decision—where a person becomes a new person in Christ.

Kimball: Certainly. For most people there still is a decision point where they pray to put faith in Jesus. But I see the journey leading up to that decision as slower, often unfolding in community, and guided by the Holy Spirit. Churches need to be places where such non-Christians are expected and welcomed into community before they are even Christians. Again, they should not take on a role of spiritual leadership if they aren't Christians yet. But they can become a regular part of the church community in various ways. As they do, their hearts soften and are more open to the gospel. We never hold back on teaching the hard and difficult things. This is not a water-things-down approach or seeker approach. It is almost the opposite, as we can directly talk and teach about difficult doctrines and things people may not like to hear, such as the reality of hell or that Jesus is the only way of salvation. But as they are in community, people become more receptive. It is the Spirit who changes someone's heart, but we still have our part in setting up the missional environment and culture in our churches.

QUESTIONS FOR GROUP OR PERSONAL STUDY

1. What volunteer opportunities do you have at your church that could be undertaken by a gifted and willing person who is not yet a Christian?

   - List three such jobs that primarily serve non-churchgoers.
   - Create a job description for one.
   - List two people who have the knowledge and skills to undertake this job.
   - Select people you know personally.
   - Select people who have attended the church at least once in the past year.
   - Begin to pray that God will open an opportunity for you to reach out and invite one of these two people to join the church in its efforts to meet the needs of others.

2. What translation of the Bible do you use when communicating with an unchurched person?

- Does it use language that is more familiar to you than it is to them? If so, what will you do about this?
- List six ways that you can employ understandable terminology in your communication.

3. Look up three of the passages below in the Bible translation you customarily use. Then look them up in four other translations. Be sure to use at least one paraphrased translation. What did you learn from this exercise? How will this exercise help you better explain biblical passages to non-churchgoers?

- Matthew 22:37–40
- Matthew 28:18–20
- John 4:21–24
- Acts 2:40–47
- 1 Corinthians 4:20
- Ephesians 4:11–16
- 1 Timothy 1:5

4. What terms do you use that may not be familiar to non-churchgoers? List four terms in each of the following categories. Then translate a total of six words (two from each category) into terminology that is more newcomer-friendly.

- *Places*. What are some names for places in your church that may not be readily understood by those who are not regular attendees? Do you have a narthex, baptismal, parlor, or nave?
- *Liturgical Structure*. Do you use words in your order of worship that may be confusing to non-churchgoers? Do you have benedictions, invocations, sacraments, the Eucharist, vespers, consecrations? While some

visitors may be intrigued by the mystery of uncommon terminology, if not carefully explained such terminology may confuse the traveler.[10]

- *Verbal Communication.* Do you use terms in your explanation of the good news that are uncommon in non-churchgoers' vocabulary? Do you talk about regeneration, justification, sanctification, atonement, deacons?

PERSONAL RELEVANCE OF
THE GOOD NEWS

L auren, a self-described nerd, had an insatiable appetite for all things
spiritual. A religion major, she had grown up in a Jewish home that
provided a foundation for her spiritual sensitivity and quest. Yet along her
route, there had been three events—waypoints—that now were culminating
in Lauren's most momentous decision. "It all happened while I was going to
school in New York. I was caught in a process of moving from the intellectual
to the personal in my view of Christianity.
I had several experiences that kept turning my
attention to Jesus. I gradually crossed over
from an intellectual understanding of the good
news to a grasp of the implications of the good
news for me."

Lauren says, "The first thing that really hit
me was that God would come down to earth in human form. That got me
thinking that if this Christian God was real, then this was pretty great: a God
who cared enough about his creation that he would come down and join them.
That really hit me.

"A second event happened in my sophomore year. I had a dream in which I
was kidnapped by mermaids and lived underwater with them.[2] I have wacky
dreams all the time, but most of the time they don't mean anything. But this one
seemed to have a message. I was rescued by a figure I eventually realized was
Jesus. When I awoke I was sure that this dream was from God. Some people

> Existence is no more than
> the precarious attainment of
> relevance in an intensely
> mobile flux of past, present,
> and future.
>
> —SUSAN SONTAG[1]

have a definitive conversion date, but for me this dream was a second event en route to a gradual change.

"Finally, the summer before my senior year of college, I was going on a vacation and writing retreat. While waiting for my friends in a bookstore, I picked up a couple books in the Mitford series.[3] The novels are set in a fictional town, and the main character is a fictional priest named Father Tim, who hangs out with his neighbors. I was totally hooked; I read them six times. Though these were not set in New York City (where I lived), they had spiritual resonance for me. These fictional people seemed to be living lives that were pervaded by faith. The stories helped me become aware that although I was religiously observant and in many ways organized my whole life around Judaism, my life wasn't really infused with a life of faith or God.

"That was the third element. At first I realized God was personal and cared about everyone, including me. Then I saw that this personal relationship resulted in God wanting to rescue me from my captivity to myself. And finally, I saw that God has a wonderful life for you if you infuse that life with faith and God.

"To sum it all up," concludes Lauren, "I do not have a story about a specific conversion date. My change was dramatic because I was Jewish. And there was quite a dramatic process in that. I can't say there is a moment when it clicked and a conversion took place, but I can tell you when I was baptized. That I have a date for, but the good news broke upon me over time."

Lauren eventually enrolled at Duke University to pursue her master of divinity degree. Today she is an author and professor at the Duke University School of Divinity. "But," says Lauren, "I am here today because through a series of experiences, God broke into my life and became more relevant."

WAYPOINT CHARACTERISTICS

SIGNS OF TRAVELERS AT WAYPOINT 12

The Personal Trekker. At this point, the journey becomes terribly personal for the traveler. Trekkers begin to realize that the good news has ramifications for them personally. For Lauren, it was the recognition that God is a personal God and had sent his own offspring into Lauren's world to rescue her from herself. The implications of this for Lauren's personal journey fostered a huge impact.

The Traveler Caught between Two Opposites. At this waypoint, travelers will often experience diametrically opposed forces between Christianity and their former worldview. While the Christian may wonder why this bothers them so, travelers feel as if they are crossing over an all-encompassing threshold. Travelers are comparing and contrasting their former worldview with an emerging Christian perspective. They will need time to make comparisons, assessments, and conclusions.

ACTIONS THAT HELP WAYPOINT 12 TRAVELERS

ACTION 12.1: UNDERSTAND A POST-CHRISTIAN WORLDVIEW

The very term *post-Christian* requires some definition. This term indicates in part that we live in an age where Christianity is not the dominant belief system or the religious culture. The American Religious Identification Survey (ARIS) indicates that the majority of North Americans consider themselves religious, but do not necessarily embrace a Christian belief.[4] Researchers of American church history note that at one time, much of North America embraced a Christian worldview, though there were various permutations and factions.[5] Yet the dominance of the Christian worldview has dissipated, and it can now be said that North America is in a post-Christian era. Darrell Guder says, "rather than occupying a central and influential place, North American Christian churches are increasingly marginalized, so much so that in our urban areas they represent a minority movement. It is by now a truism to speak of North America as a mission field."[6]

> The term *post-Christian* in part indicates that we live in an age where Christianity is not the dominant belief system or the religious culture.

There have been numerous attempts to describe this post-Christian milieu. However, for succinctness, let me tender six basic (but not exhaustive) characteristics of a post-Christian environment.[7]

1. God, if he exists at all, is just an impersonal moral force.

2. The Bible is nothing other than a book written by humans.

3. Humankind basically has the capacity within itself to improve morally and make the right choices.

4. Happiness consists of unlimited acquisition of possessions, knowledge, experience and so forth.

5. There is no objective basis for right and wrong.

6. If a person lives a good life, then eternal bliss is probable.

Each of these distinctives must be understood and addressed by the Christian who travels with others through Waypoint 12. Therefore, Action 12.2 will address the importance of dialogue and companionship, and Action 12.3 will discuss how each of the above distinctives can be addressed.

ACTION 12.2: DISCUSS THE POST-CHRISTIAN AND BIBLICAL WORLDVIEW

The metaphor of a journey reminds us that a trekker will encounter fellow travelers, guides, and hosts along the way. Yet the church has lost her way in creating dialogue with travelers who embrace a post-Christian worldview. Richard Peace regrets the church has lost this art of companionship, and thus he suggests the church must renew her efforts to assist, engage, and travel with wayfarers with divergent points of view.[8] Here are three guidelines for reviving the lost art of journey companionship.

If Christians join travelers on the journey and only laud their own journey and the primacy of that route, then travelers will feel that Christians have no respect or understanding for the wayfarer's personal passage.

Don't Have a Goal in Mind. For many Christians, the goal of companionship is to lead the traveler to a new birth. But as we have seen in the forgoing chapters, it is the Holy Spirit's role to draw wayfarers to this waypoint (John 16:8–9). Thus the church's role is conversation not conversion, assistance not damnation. The church must resist the temptation to be goal oriented, for we do not know the length or the route of the traveler's journey. When Peter asked Jesus about the apostle John's destiny, Jesus reminded Peter that his role was to be faithful and to feed Jesus' sheep (John 21:15–25). Destiny is in God's hands, but accompaniment is in ours.

FIGURE 12.1

RESOURCES TO ANSWER A POSTMODERN WORLDVIEW

God, if he exists at all, is just an impersonal moral force.
- The good news: Genesis 2; Exodus 15:11; 20:2–6; John 3:16; Galatians 2:20; Ephesians 5:1
- Books: "Why I Believe God Exists" in *Why I Am a Christian*[9] and *How Does Anyone Know God Exists?* (Tough Questions series)[10]

The Bible is nothing other than a book written by humans.
- The good news: 1 John 5:13; 2 Timothy 3:15–17; Mark 13:31; Luke 24:44–45
- Books: "Why I Believe the New Testament is Historically Reliable" and "Why I Believe the Bible is Scientifically Reliable" in *Why I Am a Christian*, "Examining the Record" in *The Case for Christ*,[11] and *The Ring of Truth: A Translator's Testimony*.[12]
- Research: Biblical scholar F. F. Bruce has stated that critics of the Bible's text have uncovered no variants that affect any historical fact or belief on which Christianity is founded.[13]

Humankind basically has the capacity within itself to improve morally and make the right choices.
- The good news: Psalm 51:1–4; 143:2; Ecclesiastes 7:20; Ezekiel 18:4; Romans 2:14–16; 3:10–18; 3:23; Ephesians 2:8–9; 1 John 5:1–10
- Books: "Postmodernism: A Declaration of Bankruptcy"[14] and "Evangelism in a Post-modern World" in *The Challenge of Postmodernism*.[15]

Happiness consists of unlimited acquisition of material, knowledge, experience, etc.
- The good news: Romans 1:18–32; 2 Peter 2:18–22; Titus 2:11–14
- Books: *Your God is Too Small: A Guide for Believer and Skeptics Alike*,[16] *The Hole in Our Gospel: The Answer That Changed My Life and Might Just Change the World*,[17] *Money, Possessions, and Eternity*,[18] and *The Irresistible Revolution: Living as an Ordinary Radical*.[19]

There really is no objective basis for right and wrong.
- The good news: Jeremiah 6:16–19; John 8:34–44; Romans 2:1–16; Galatians 2:15–16
- Books: *God in the Dock; Essays on Theology and Ethics*,[20] *Christian Apologetics*,[21] and *Simply Christian: Why Christianity Makes Sense*.[22]

If a person lives a "good life," then eternal bliss is probable.
- The good news: Matthew 7:13–14; Luke 13:23–25; John 14:6; Romans 5:12–21
- Books: *Why I Am a Christian*,[23] *Faith on Trial*,[24] *The Case for Christ*,[25] and *The Prodigal God*.[26]

Respect post-Christian and Even Anti-Christian Worldviews. For honest and candid discussion to emerge, respect must be the foundation. If a Christian joins a traveler on the journey and the Christian only lauds his or her own journey and the primacy of that route, then the traveler will feel the Christian has no respect or understanding for the wayfarer's personal passage.

Understand that Modern Culture Is Fascinated with Spirituality. Though there is a growing agnosticism and atheism in North America, still almost three out of four people say they are interested in spiritual things.[27] Yet many may have divergent belief systems to Christianity.[28] To foster authentic dialogue, the Christian must show respect and reverence for different religious beliefs.

ACTION 12.3: EXPLAIN THE RELEVANCE OF THE BIBLICAL WORLDVIEW

Figure 12.1 deserves an extended discussion beyond this book. However, to begin addressing each, I have listed suggestions, ideas, and books in Figure 2.2. These can be the starting place for the leader that wishes to increase his or her knowledge of the relevance of the good news.

FIGURE 12.2

RESOURCES TO SUPPORT A BIBLICAL WORLDVIEW

To aid in this dialogue, the five elements below of a Christian worldview are accompanied by applicable Scriptures, suggestions, ideas, and books.

1. There is one God, Creator, who actually exists in space and time.
   - The good news: Genesis 1–2; Exodus 15:11; 20:2–6; Deuteronomy 6:4; Isaiah 45:5–6, 21–22; Malachi 3:6
   - Books: "Why I Believe the God of the Bible is the One True God" in *Why I Am a Christian*,[29] *Faith on Trial*, and *The Case for Christ* (these books are also useful with the following four elements).

2. Because of a willful act of disobedience, people (humankind) became severed from a personal relationship with the God who made him and her. The consequence is that humankind has become imprisoned and most live a self-seeking life with no possibility on their own of restoring this lost communion.
   - The good news: Genesis 2:16–17; 3:7–8; Romans 3:9–18; 3:23; 6:23; Ephesians 2:13–16
   - Books: *Tears of God*,[30] *Know Why You Believe*,[31] and *Epic: The Story God is Telling*.[32]

3. Jesus Christ, a human being who actually lived on earth, is God's Son who has provided, through his death and resurrection, the only way for humankind to be restored to fellowship with God.
   - The good news: Isaiah 53:5; Matthew 1:21; John 1:29; 6:47; 14:6; Romans 5:8; 6:23; 2 Corinthians 5:21; Ephesians 2:8–9; Colossians 1:4; 1 Timothy 2:5; Hebrews 9:22; 11:6; 1 John 1:7–9
   - Books: "Why I Believe Jesus Is The Promised Messiah" and "Why I Believe Jesus Is the Son of God" in *Why I Am a Christian*,[33] "Analyzing Jesus" in *The Case for Christ*,[34] *How to Give Away Your Faith*,[35] and *The Jesus I Never Knew*.[36]

4. The Bible is a valid witness to eternal spiritual truth.
   - The good news: Psalm 119; 2 Timothy 3:16–17; Jude 3
   - Books: "Why I Believe the Bible Alone Is the Word of God" in *Why I Am a Christian*[37] and *The New Testament Documents: Are They Reliable?*[38]

5. Restoration of fellowship between God and humankind requires an acceptance by humans of the free gift God offers but only on the terms that God has provided.
   - The good news: Zechariah 13:9; Matthew 6:33; 7:7–8; Romans 5:1; 8:1, 38–39; 10:9–13; 2 Peter 3:9
   - Books: "Why I Have Made Jesus Christ Lord of My Life" in *Why I Am a Christian*,[39] *Live to Tell*,[40] *The Sacred Romance*,[41] and *Peace with God*[42]
   - This point will be discussed further in the remainder of this book, especially along the journey between Waypoints 11 and 4.

INTERVIEW WITH LAUREN WINNER

Author and Duke Divinity School professor on Christian practice, the history of Christianity in America, and Jewish-Christian relations

Whitesel: How did the good news become relevant to you?

Winner: What seemed relevant at first was the doctrine of incarnation. I was Jewish, and I was grasped by the notion of incarnation, meaning Jesus came in the flesh to relate to us. Even before I was personally attracted to Christianity, I thought on an intellectual level that it was totally great that God might become a person so he can fully understand everything we are experiencing. I was in college studying religion, and I envied this way of understanding God. The idea of the incarnation really grabbed my imagination.

Whitesel: How did this unfold in your life?

Winner: I really experienced this change through an extended process. There was the idea of the incarnation, the dream of a rescue, and the community depicted in the Mitford novels. But that doesn't mean there are not "the" moments for other people. But in my life, my encounter with God was a developing thing. And it continues. If one's life is long, then there will continue to be these moments, almost mini epiphanies, where God breaks into his or her personal life. I would be scared if I didn't think that God wanted to barge into our lives now and then.

Whitesel: Have these mini epiphanies happened again?

Winner: There was a moment five years after my conversion. My mother was ill and she was in the hospital. And I thought, "This world is really not like it is supposed to be!" Illness and suffering are not supposed to be in this world. And then I experienced a personal awareness of the brokenness of the world, summarized by the intense environment of that hospital wing. The whole peace of the Christian story became relevant to me, more than it had before. This was another example of a mini epiphany, where God broke into my life to remind me who he is. Every year or so there will be another such experience where I will encounter a real doctrine in real life. And the good news becomes relevant to me again and again.

Whitesel: How do you explain this to others?

Winner: I simply try to tell people about my friendship with God. I don't dwell too much on my conversion. What I dwell on is the many ways in which God continues to make me his friend. Jesus does not call his disciples servants, but friends. What do we need to be God's friend? Following my colleague Sam Wells, I say that God gives us everything we need to be his friend. So when I try to explain this to others, I am just as likely to talk about the Lord's Supper—the place we come to eat with one another and to eat with God, a place where God draws near to us. Or I will talk about the moments when Scripture has seemed so alive to me it practically glows. Or I will talk about the ways some of my Christian friends have at times stunned me with their self-sacrificial generosity, their ability to love well. To me, all of this is part of the ongoing-ness of conversion—of the ways we continue to be made into Christians and into friends of God.

QUESTIONS FOR GROUP OR PERSONAL STUDY

1. When was the last time your church leadership discussed the tenets of Christianity? Do your leaders have a good grasp of these basics? Ask four leaders to give you five of the basics of Christian belief, and then compare them with the list in this chapter. Are some missing? What will you do about this?

2. Pick one of the following elements of a post-Christian milieu and develop a Bible study that explains the biblical perspective on this element.

   - God, if he exists at all, is just an impersonal moral force.
   - The Bible is nothing other than a book written by humans.
   - Humankind basically has the capacity within itself to improve morally and make the right choices.
   - Happiness consists of unlimited acquisition of possissions, knowledge, experience, and so forth.

- There is no objective basis for right and wrong.
- If a person lives a good life, then eternal bliss is probable.

3. Pick one of the following elements of a post-Christian milieu and develop a fictional dialogue that tactfully and biblically engages a person holding these perspectives. Write this dialogue down, limiting yourself to two pages.

- God, if he exists at all, is just an impersonal moral force.
- The Bible is nothing other than a book written by humans.
- Humankind basically has the capacity within itself to improve morally and make the right choices.
- Happiness consists of unlimited acquisition of possessions, knowledge, experience, and so forth.
- There is no objective basis for right and wrong.
- If a person lives a good life, then eternal bliss is probable.

POSITIVE ATTITUDE TOWARD
LIVING THE GOOD NEWS

H"ow did it come to this?" Mike wondered. One day, NBC news anchor Tom Brokaw was calling Mike the "the prince of the Mafia," and the next day Mike was beginning a sentence in the prison's notorious hole. "You can't get much lower than spending three years in the hole," remembers Mike. "But it was there I began to see that God had a plan for me. I read my Bible forward and backward looking for answers. And I began to write in prison. Nothing earth shattering, but I began to write. And I found I had a talent for it. Before I went into prison, people said I was a brilliant businessman. But it was in prison that I realized God had made me a people person. I'm not a businessman but a person who likes and wants to encourage people."

Not long before Mike went to prison he began to grasp the implications of the good news. "I met this beautiful woman, and I fell in love. But then I realized she was in love with someone else! She was in love with Jesus!

> God enters by a private door into every individual.
>
> —RALPH WALDO EMERSON[1]

She talked to him daily and asked for his guidance through prayer. That was something I had never seen! I grew up in a Catholic home but I always saw Jesus as a person in the Bible, not someone you could talk to and make the navigator for your life! But in Cammy, I saw how Jesus wants a personal friendship with us. It began to change my attitude about Jesus and his good news. In that hole, I realized I wanted and needed that personal friendship with Jesus."

Soon Mike, committed his life to Jesus Christ. "Boy, did that take some guts," recalls Mike. "I was raised on the streets. And on the streets surrendering to Jesus was a sign of weakness. You wouldn't broadcast it; you would hide it! But Cammy is for real, her family is real, and Jesus is real to them. It came to a head, and I had to publicly make a choice. I labored for months and months on my journey to that decision. I'd go to sleep thinking one way and then wake up thinking the other way. My wife, her mom, and their pastor were patient, but also very firm in their faith. Jesus became my hero and when I made a decision to follow him, all the other terrible things that I feared started to work out."

Today, Michael Franzese is the author of a few autobiographical books.[2] Once dubbed "the Prince of the Mafia," the Mafia's youngest and most financially powerful superstar is now a spokesperson for Jesus. "I'm a Barnabas-type person: an encourager. I can relate to people from all walks of life. I don't know what it is, but God seems to be able to reach people through how I communicate. I've known that I could connect with people since I was in the family business. It was an asset that I used in the mob, but God meant me to use it for him. And you can't ignore his orders."

WAYPOINT CHARACTERISTICS

At Waypoint 11, the traveler is growing with an increasingly positive attitude toward the act of accepting Christ and joining his community. Yet this is a very fragile and complicated waypoint. As noted earlier, media and popular culture may have painted a pessimistic picture of the Christian lifestyle. Therefore, the Christian community must be prepared to patiently, unwaveringly, and lovingly help the traveler gain an authentic picture of a faith community, as well as the person God intended the traveler to be.

SIGNS OF TRAVELERS AT WAYPOINT 11

The Lost Traveler. This is a traveler who has exhausted all other road maps. Like Mike Franzese, the trekker may be at the end of their options. It is here that the faith community must begin to help travelers understand the direction and basics of this new route. But often at this waypoint the church will feel compelled to remind hikers of the errant paths they have taken. However, one of the lessons of the parable of the prodigal son (Luke 15:11–32) is that the unwavering older brother should celebrate the return not reprimand it.

The Returning Traveler. Other travelers may be returning to the road map of their youth. Again, it becomes tempting for the faith community to disparage the years trekkers have squandered. Still, the parable of the prodigal son reminds us that the faithful older brother should not only celebrate his own faithfulness, but also celebrate his brother's recovery. Jesus concluded this parable by putting the spotlight on the trekker's return, saying, "His father said, 'Son, you don't understand. You're with me all the time, and everything that is mine is yours—but this is a wonderful time, and we had to celebrate. This brother of yours was dead, and he's alive! He was lost, and he's found!'" (Luke 15:31–32 MSG).

ACTIONS THAT HELP WAYPOINT 11 TRAVELERS

SWOT is an acronym for a helpful analysis tool. Though often employed to analyze businesses, its holistic nature makes it a good tool for understanding a person's aspirations, fears, hopes, and dreams.[3] Each of the letters of SWOT stands for an area that must be studied. When a community of faith is helping a traveler at Waypoint 11 gain a positive attitude toward living the good news, it is critical to look at these four areas.

ACTION 11.1: EMPOWER STRENGTHS

The "S" in SWOT stands for *strengths*. These are strengths that each person possesses. Leadership researcher Peter Northouse believes such strengths can be traits, abilities, skills, or behaviors.[4] Traits are inherent and natural qualities with which a leader is endowed. Abilities are aptitudes developed by experience. Skills are means and methods for carrying out leadership responsibilities. And behaviors are what people do with the traits, abilities, and skills they have been given. Though we will discuss their differences more in the next chapter, for

Every person has redeeming strengths, and it is the Christian community's task to nurture what God has planted.

this chapter, the reader should keep in mind that people's giftings include things they are born with (traits), things they learn through experience (abilities and skills), and the behaviors that result.

There is little doubt that everyone possesses strength in some traits, abilities, skills, and behaviors. Yet the Scriptures indicate that a full unleashing of such gifts awaits a new birth experience that originates in God's Spirit. Such strengths and gifts testify to the goodness of the divine giver. Speaking to the Corinthian church, Paul states:

God's various gifts are handed out everywhere; but they all originate in God's Spirit. God's various ministries are carried out everywhere; but they all originate in God's Spirit. God's various expressions of power are in action everywhere; but God himself is behind it all. Each person is given something to do that shows who God is: Everyone gets in on it, everyone benefits. All kinds of things are handed out by the Spirit, and to all kinds of people! The variety is wonderful:

- wise counsel
- clear understanding
- simple trust
- healing the sick
- miraculous acts
- proclamation
- distinguishing between spirits
- tongues
- interpretation of tongues.

All these gifts have a common origin, but are handed out one by one by the one Spirit of God. He decides who gets what, and when. (1 Cor. 12:4–7 MSG)

When encountering a wayfarer who has arduously traveled a spiritual journey, churches can easily be put off by the demeanor, appearance, habits, and opinions of the traveler at Waypoint 11. Yet every person has redeeming strengths, and it is the Christian community's task to nurture what God has planted. Helping travelers at Waypoint 11 means helping them uncover their fledgling strengths and to see these gifts were given by God as they await his full empowerment. The following two actions will assist in that process.

ACTION 11.1A: RECOGNIZE THE DIVERSITY OF GOD'S GIFTS

The Scriptures describe a variety of God-given gifts. Romans 12; 1 Corinthians 12; and Ephesians 4; along with secondary lists in 1 Corinthians 7; 13–14; Ephesians 3; and 1 Peter 4, describe many of the gifts of the Spirit that God uses to empower people for service and ministry. Here is a brief yet annotated list:[5]

1. *Administration*. Effective planning and organization (1 Cor. 2:28; Acts 6:1–7).

2. *Discernment*. Distinguishing between error and truth (1 Cor. 12:10; Acts 5:1–11).

3. *Encouragement*. Ability to comfort, console, encourage, and counsel (Rom. 12:8; Heb. 10:25; 1 Tim. 4:13).

4. *Evangelism*. Building relationships that help travelers move toward a personal relationship with Christ (Luke 19:1–10; 2 Tim. 4:5).

5. *Faith*. Discerning with extraordinary confidence the will and purposes of God (1 Cor. 12:9; Acts 11:22–24; Heb. 11; Rom. 4:18–21).

6. *Giving*. Cheerfully giving of resources without remorse (Rom. 12:8; 2 Cor. 8:1–7; 9:2–8; Mark 12:41–44).

7. *Hospitality*. Creating comfort and assistance for those in need (1 Pet. 4:9; Rom. 12:9–13; 16:23; Acts 16:14–15; Heb. 13:1–2).

8. *Intercession*. Passionate, extended, and effective prayer (James 5:14–16; 1 Tim. 2:1–2; Col. 1:9–12; 4:12–13).

9. *Knowledge*. To discover, accumulate, analyze, and clarify information and ideas that are pertinent to the well-being of a Christian community (1 Cor. 2:14; 12:8; Acts 5:1–11; Col. 2:2–3).[6]

10. *Leadership*. To cast vision, set goals, and motivate in order to coopera-tively accomplish God' purposes (Luke 9:51; Rom. 12:8; Heb. 13:17).

11. *Mercy*. To feel authentic empathy and compassion accompanied by action that reflects Christ's love and alleviates suffering (Rom. 12:8; Matt. 25:34–36; Luke 10:30–37).

12. *Prophecy*. Providing guidance to others by explaining and proclaiming God's truth (1 Cor. 12:10, 28; Eph. 4:11–14; Rom. 12:6; Acts 21:9–11).[7]

13. *Helps*. Investing time and talents in others to increase their effectiveness (1 Cor. 12:28; Rom. 16:1–2; Acts 9:36).

14. *Service*. A tactical gift that identifies steps and processes in tasks that results in ministry to others (2 Tim. 1:16–18; Rom. 12:7; Acts 6:1–7).

15. *Pastor*. Long-term personal responsibility for the welfare of spiritual travelers (Eph. 4:1–14; 1 Tim. 3:1–7; John 10:1–18; 1 Pet. 5:1–3).

16. *Teaching*. Communicating relevant information that results in learning (1 Cor. 12:28; Eph. 4:11–14; Rom. 12:7; Acts 18:24–28; 20:20–21).

17. *Wisdom*. To have insight into how to apply knowledge (1 Cor. 2:1–13; 12:8; Acts 6:3, 10; James 1:5–6; 2 Pet. 3:15–16).[8]

18. *Missionary*. Using spiritual gifts effectively in a nonindigenous culture (1 Cor. 9:19–21; Acts 8:4; 13:2–3; 22:21; Rom. 10:15).

19. *Miracles*. To perform compelling acts that are perceived by observers to have altered the ordinary course of nature (1 Cor. 12:10, 28; Acts 9:36–42; 19:11–20; 20:7–12; Rom. 15:18–19; 2 Cor. 12:12).

20. *Healing*. To serve as a human intermediary through whom it pleases God to restore health (1 Cor. 12:9, 28; Acts 3:1–10; 5:12–16; 9:32–35; 28:7–10).

21. *Tongues*. There are various explanations of this gift. For instance it can be (a) to speak to God in a language the speaker has never learned or (b) to receive and communicate an immediate message of God to his people.[9] Another option is that this can mean an ability to speak a foreign language and convey concepts across cultures (1 Cor. 12:10, 28; 14:13–19; Acts 2:1–13; 10:44–46; 19:1–7).[10]

22. *Interpretation*. To make known a message of one who speaks in tongues.[11] Or it can mean, "Those who help build bridges across cultural, generational and language divides"[12] (1 Cor. 12:10, 30; 14:13, 26–28).

23. *Voluntary Poverty*. To renounce material comfort and luxury to assist others (1 Cor. 13:1–3; Acts 2:44–45; 4:34–37; 2 Cor. 6:10; 8:9).

24. *Celibacy*. To remain single with joy and not suffer undue sexual temptation (1 Cor. 7:7–8; Matt. 19:10–12).

25. *Martyrdom*. Ability to undergo suffering for the faith even to death, while displaying a victorious attitude that brings glory to God (1 Cor. 13:3).

There is no biblical reason why some of these gifts are not given in some measure before conversion, awaiting the regenerative experience to unleash them with divine empowerment. Therefore, the Christian community should look for signs of such pre-empowered giftings in travelers at Waypoint 11, then move to the next step.

ACTION 11.1B: NEW BIRTH WILL UNLEASH AND EMPOWER THESE STRENGTHS

A Christian community can help a traveler grasp that along with new birth will come divine empowerment for good deeds. And these good deeds will rise from the traveler's traits, abilities, skills, and behaviors. People today often suffer from poor self-esteem, yet God's intention is that each person has gifts to contribute to the common good (1 Cor. 12:7; 1 Pet. 4:10). Christian communities should be a place where travelers with such emerging giftings discover:

1. Gifts, as listed in Scripture, are from God (Rom. 12:5–6; 1 Cor. 12:18; 1 Pet. 4:10).

2. These gifts were given so that travelers can serve others (Rom. 12:6; 1 Cor. 12:7, 18).

3. The full empowerment and release of these gifts occurs following new birth (1 Pet. 4:10).

ACTION 11.2: OFFSET WEAKNESSES

The "W" in SWOT stands for personal *weaknesses*. A Christlike community can help travelers grasp that new birth (Waypoint 7) and growth in God's new community (Waypoints 5–0) can result in the traveler overcoming personal weaknesses. The Scriptures promise the following:

95

- "Don't you realize that this is not the way to live? Unjust people who don't care about God will not be joining in his kingdom. Those who use and abuse each other, use and abuse sex, use and abuse the earth and everything in it, don't qualify as citizens in God's kingdom. A number of you know from experience what I'm talking about, for not so long ago you were on that list. Since then, you've been cleaned up and given a fresh start by Jesus, our Master, our Messiah, and by our God present in us, the Spirit" (1 Cor. 6:9–11 MSG).

- "Don't panic. I'm with you. There's no need to fear for I'm your God. I'll give you strength. I'll help you. I'll hold you steady, keep a firm grip on you" (Isa. 41:10 MSG).

- "Is anyone crying for help? GOD is listening, ready to rescue you" (Ps. 34:17 MSG).

- "And do not set your heart on what you will eat or drink; do not worry about it. For the pagan world runs after all such things, and your Father knows that you need them. But seek his kingdom, and these things will be given to you as well" (Luke 12:29–31).

- "I can do everything through him who gives me strength" (Phil. 4:13).

ACTION 11.3: CAPITALIZE ON OPPORTUNITIES

The "O" in SWOT stands for *opportunities*. God's good news is that his intentions are to help his offspring make the most of opportunities. The Scriptures state:

- "Be ready with a meal or a bed when it's needed. Why, some have extended hospitality to angels without ever knowing it! Regard prisoners as if you were in prison with them. Look on victims of abuse as if what happened to them had happened to you" (Heb. 13:1–4 MSG).

- "Sitting down, Jesus called the Twelve and said, 'If anyone wants to be first, he must be the very last, and the servant of all'" (Mark 9:35).

- "Anyone who sets himself up as 'religious' by talking a good game is self-deceived. This kind of religion is hot air and only hot air. Real religion, the kind that passes muster before God the Father, is this: Reach out to the homeless and loveless in their plight, and guard against corruption from the godless world" (James 1:26–27 MSG).

- "'For I know the plans I have for you,' declares the LORD, 'plans to prosper you and not to harm you, plans to give you hope and a future'" (Jer. 29:11).
- "Come, you who are blessed by my Father; take your inheritance, the kingdom prepared for you since the creation of the world" (Matt. 25:34).
- "Don't hoard treasure down here where it gets eaten by moths and corroded by rust or—worse!—stolen by burglars. Stockpile treasure in heaven, where it's safe from moth and rust and burglars. It's obvious, isn't it? The place where your treasure is, is the place you will most want to be, and end up being" (Matt. 6:20 MSG).
- "What a God we have! And how fortunate we are to have him, this Father of our Master Jesus! Because Jesus was raised from the dead, we've been given a brand-new life and have everything to live for, including a future in heaven—and the future starts now! God is keeping careful watch over us and the future. The Day is coming when you'll have it all—life healed and whole" (1 Pet. 1:3–4 MSG).

ACTION 11.4: OVERCOME THREATS

The "T" in SWOT stands for *threats*. These are things beyond people's control and which they fear. Death, illness, and estrangement are but a few of the threats that humans can be anxious about. Again, here are just a few Scriptures that paint an image of triumph over anxiety and adversity:

- Fear of persecution: "Fear nothing in the things you're about to suffer—but stay on guard! Fear nothing! The Devil is about to throw you in jail for a time of testing—ten days. It won't last forever. Don't quit, even if it costs you your life. Stay there believing. I have a Life-Crown sized and ready for you" (Rev. 2:10 MSG).
- Fear of death: "'Where, O death, is your victory? Where, O death, is your sting?' The sting of death is sin, and the power of sin is the law.

But thanks be to God! He gives us the victory through our Lord Jesus Christ. Therefore, my dear brothers, stand firm. Let nothing move you. Always give yourselves fully to the work of the Lord, because you know that your labor in the Lord is not in vain" (1 Cor. 15:55–58).

- Fear of hardship: "That's why I don't think there's any comparison between the present hard times and the coming good times. The created world itself can hardly wait for what's coming next. Everything in creation is being more or less held back. God reins it in until both creation and all the creatures are ready and can be released at the same moment into the glorious times ahead. Meanwhile, the joyful anticipation deepens" (Rom. 8:18 MSG).

- Fear of not being successful: "Don't be obsessed with getting more material things. Be relaxed with what you have. Since God assured us, "I'll never let you down, never walk off and leave you," we can boldly quote, God is there, ready to help; I'm fearless no matter what. Who or what can get to me?" (Heb. 13:5–6 MSG).

At Waypoint 11 the church must be careful to not overly romanticize nor paint a rosy picture of the future, even with Christ. The Bible states that challenges lie ahead on our route, but advises: "Friends, when life gets really difficult, don't jump to the conclusion that God isn't on the job. Instead, be glad that you are in the very thick of what Christ experienced. This is a spiritual refining process, with glory just around the corner" (1 Pet. 4:12–13 MSG). The Christian community must realistically and authentically let the traveler know that there will be barriers, detours, and challenges on the road ahead, but Christ and his community provide aid and strength to continue the journey.

INTERVIEW WITH MICHAEL FRANZESE

Author, speaker, Colombo family member, and formerly number 18 on Fortune *magazine's "Fifty Most Wealthy and Powerful Mafia Bosses" list*

Whitesel: You grew up attending a parochial school, but it wasn't until later that you gained a positive attitude toward the good news. Is that correct?

Franzese: Yes, that's right. Maybe it was because I was young, but I never understood Jesus could be the friend and the navigator of your life. To me, Jesus was a figure in the Bible. I believed he lived, but I wasn't interested in him calling the shots.

Whitesel: And that changed when you met Cammy, her family, and went to prison?

Franzese: That's right. All of those things helped me understand Jesus, and that changed my attitude toward his good news. I began to see that the good news was that God loved you, he had given you talents you were supposed to use for him, he could make you a better person, he would take care of you, and he had a purpose for you.

Whitesel: You started writing while in the prison hole. And you discovered God had made you a people person, not a businessman. Did you sense that God was preparing to one day use these abilities for him?

Franzese: That's correct. My testimony is not about me. It's about God having a purpose for you and preparing you for his work throughout your upbringing. I see God as nurturing our strengths and trying to get rid of our weaknesses. I later realized that there were so many things God had put in my life, and he placed them there because one day he was going to use them. When people ask me what my greatest asset is, I used to say it was that I was a skillful businessman. In hindsight, I don't really think I was good at that. Instead, I am a people person. I encourage people around me to succeed, and that is my most important asset: I encourage others. I thought these abilities were given to me to use for the mob, but now I see God gave them for me to use for him. You don't mess with that giver.

QUESTIONS FOR GROUP OR PERSONAL STUDY

1. When a person possesses a gift of the Holy Spirit, others usually notice it.[13] Which gifts of the Spirit do others notice in you? Were these gifts evident in some form before your conversion? If so, how?

2. What is a weakness you have overcome? (Be careful not to share something that may be improper for the setting of your discussion.) How did others view you when you were ensnared by that weakness? And how has Christ helped you overcome the weakness? Are you viewed differently now? Take a piece of paper and make two columns. In the left column, list former unattractive characteristics, and in the right column, list the positive characteristics God has fostered in you. Ask God to help you look beyond characteristics from the left column that you see in other wayfarers. Do not condone sin, but learn to reach out to and love those who live primarily in the left column.

3. Translate this passage in order to make it clear to a traveler at Waypoint 11: "Keep on loving each other as brothers. Do not forget to entertain strangers, for by so doing some people have entertained angels without knowing it. Remember those in prison as if you were their fellow prisoners, and those who are mistreated as if you yourselves were suffering" (Heb. 13:1–3).

4. What worries you most about the future? List three such things and write a paragraph about each. Then read Revelation 2:10; 1 Corinthians 15:55–58; and Romans 8:18. Take each of the three paragraphs and put one in your Bible at each of these three verses. Next time you come across these passages, read the Scripture, then the paragraph, then the Scripture again. Finish by reading Isaiah 41:10, from a modern translation such as *The Message*: "There's no need to fear for I'm your God. I'll give you strength. I'll help you. I'll hold you steady, keep a firm grip on you."

PERSONAL PROBLEM
RECOGNITION

I f you're going to do some good today, you'll have to do it yourself.

Al was an athlete, an A-student, and popular. Perhaps because so many students looked up to him, Al felt that he could only rely on himself to get things done. Thus, his friend Jane was surprised when Al responded to her invitation to join her at a church meeting.

Al had shown little interest in church; in fact, he viewed the church with disdain. A Filipino-American growing up as a nominal Roman Catholic, he rarely attended church. "Easter and Christmas, and even that was spotty," remembers Al. When his parents eventually divorced and

> The day you take complete responsibility for yourself, the day you stop making excuses, that's the day you start your move to the top.
>
> —O. J. SIMPSON[1]

both remarried within a year, when he was fourteen, Al began a journey of reckless and dangerous behavior. "I decided that there was no god," recalls Al. "I believed that we're basically on our own, and circumstances in my life were bearing that out."

Al immersed himself in the drug culture of his school. To everyone who knew him, Al was an enigma. He remained a good student, participated in athletics, and even supported worthy causes. As a quasi-member of Greenpeace, he helped in various environmental consciousness-raising activities such as "Walk for the Whales" and "Skate for the Seals." Still, Al says "there was still a restlessness, a hopelessness . . . in the midst of all of this I knew there had to be something more to make sense of life. Not a rational God thing, but something. Drugs were the first option to still that restlessness."

It was during a drug-induced conversation that Al and a friend created an alternative to fill this restlessness—their own religion. "A friend and I decided we should create a personal religion. The center of our religion was us. Basically, our religion was that it was up to us to make life meaningful. I would pray to a mirror every morning and say, 'You're it. If you're going to do something good today, you'll have to do it yourself.'"

These episodes highlighted Al's dilemma. In a world of chaos and disorder, Al had come to depend only on himself. And though he was outwardly brimming with self-reliance, inside Al knew his problem was bigger than one young man could tackle.

To Jane, Al's eccentric behavior made his openness to her invitation all the more surprising. Al went with her that night to a community of faith gathering where he began to see that he no longer needed to chafe under the weight of self-reliance, for there was another who could help.

"I still remember the message," recalls Al. "There were three points. Point one: God is real. The pastor didn't justify it or try to support it. He just said it. Deep down inside I knew that God or something was out there, that this God was here to help me. I didn't need to be totally self-reliant. Then the pastor said, 'Point two: God can be known through the person of Jesus.' It didn't make intellectual sense, but it made sense that God would try to help humans by being relatable. I realized that God can be talked to, learned from, and he could help me make a difference. Then the pastor said, 'God loves you; he laid down his life for his friends.' I could relate to that because I really cared for others. And Jesus cared the same way, even to the point of dying."

Al's personal problem came into view because since childhood, he had been overly self-reliant. Now he realized he was not alone in his struggle to be a better student, a better athlete, or to make the world a better place. God was there to help and empower him. "In Christ, I began to see myself as part of the solution to life's problems. Today's problems are too big for humans. God's participation is needed. Though this insight started that day, God had to reconfirm this a few years later."

Al's passion for the needy intensified as God opened his eyes to the enormity of the need. "I was in Central America working with street kids and slum dwellers," he remembers. "And again, the need overwhelmed me. But then I remembered that God did not want me to be overly self-reliant. He reminded me that if I partner with him, anything is possible. I decided right then and there to partner with God to impact people who are in great need. My wife and I eventually became missionary development workers in the Philippines, first in Metro-Manila and then in Zambales province.

"I think many of us can relate to a chronic problem with self-reliance. God has to remind me constantly that I am not the savior of the world—he is. The job is much bigger than me. But by God's grace, I can be part of making a difference in Christ's name."

WAYPOINT CHARACTERISTICS

SIGNS OF TRAVELERS AT WAYPOINT 10

Feelings of rejection or despondency can result in depression or excessive self-reliance. At this juncture the personal failings of a wayfarer can become so overwhelming that the traveler suffers from one or a combination of four maladies: rejection, despondency, depression, or excessive self-reliance. Let us look at each of these characteristics that often accompany travelers at Waypoint 10.

Rejection. This arises from lack of acceptance. People may feel that they are not accepted due to background, personal habits, status, lifestyle, and so on.[2] Though people usually yearn to be accepted, they may view themselves as not living up to community standards, and thus see themselves as unacceptable and an outsider.[3] Subsequently, they often feel they must rely only upon themselves for survival.

Despondency. This malady signifies hopelessness about the future. Psychologist William McDougall coined the classic definition that "despondency drives out hope."[4] A person suffering from despondency will view the future as uncontrollable, bleak, and unwelcoming.[5]

From rejection and despondency result two debilitating reactions: depression or self-reliance.

Depression.[6] This malady is sadness, helplessness, and hopelessness.[7] Depressed people see little chance for change in their failings or in their outsider status. Thus, they give in to despondency, gloominess, or mood swings. Because the magnitude of these outward behaviors makes the person socially unacceptable, depression is often easier to spot than the underlying forces of rejection and despondency.[8]

Excessive Self-Reliance.[9] This is another reaction that can arise from feelings of rejection or despondency. While moderate self-reliance is laudable, excessive self-reliance can be dangerous. Excessively self-reliant people may feel they can tackle unreasonable tasks and will set about to do so with frenzied energy. Excessive self-reliance eventually leads to grand failures which can devastate the exceedingly optimistic traveler. O. J. Simpson's quote that began this chapter may be an example of excessive self-reliance.

ACTIONS THAT HELP WAYPOINT 10 TRAVELERS

ACTION 10.1: GOOD NEWS FROM FELLOW TRAVELERS

Biblical stories of optimism and divine accompaniment can provide a starting place for helping travelers experiencing rejection, despondency, depression, or excessive self-reliance. Let us look at just a few illustrations that can provide an introductory understanding.

Excessive Self-Reliance. Others have felt like you. The story of Samson (Judg. 13–16) yields a powerful story of a failed leader who once was brimming with leadership potential. Peter Northouse says that leadership is made of five elements. Let us look how each is manifest in the life of Samson.

1. Leadership *traits* are inherent and natural qualities with which a leader is endowed, according to Northhouse. Samson was given enormous strength to deliver Israel from its enemies (Judg. 13:5; 14:5–6).

2. Leadership *abilities* are aptitudes developed by experience. Samson's political savvy was developed by his keen understanding of ancient customs and politics (Judg. 14:12–20).

3. Leadership *skills* are the means and methods of carrying out leadership responsibilities. For example, "a skilled leader in a fund-raising campaign

knows every step and procedure in the fund-raising process."[10] Samson knew every step in the process of leading Israel (Judg. 15–16), even though he subverted the process for his own gain and sensuality.

4. Leadership *behavior* is what leaders do with the traits, abilities, and skills they have been given. Here we see Samson's shortcomings as his great skills, abilities, and traits were squandered by a behavior of excessive self-reliance. His self-centered and self-reliant behaviors were exhibited in his peevish demands to marry a forbidden Philistine woman (Judg. 14:1–7), to frequent prostitutes (Judg. 16:1–3), and to marry an alluring yet avaricious Delilah (Judg. 16:4–22). Samson's end came while captive by his enemies where, in a final act of protection of Israel, he brought down the Philistine temple upon his captors (Judg. 16:23–31). Samson's story is a biblical tale of self-reliance that evolved into selfishness and self-serving and ultimate shame.

You are not alone; God promises help. The story of Samson's failings is dwarfed by biblical examples of women and men who overcame their temptation to be self-reliant. Paul was a great example of this, noting that his elite religious status was compost in comparison to the benefits of knowing Christ:

> You know my pedigree: a legitimate birth, circumcised on the eighth day; an Israelite from the elite tribe of Benjamin; a strict and devout adherent to God's law; a fiery defender of the purity of my religion, even to the point of persecuting the church; a meticulous observer of everything set down in God's law Book.
>
> The very credentials these people are waving around as something special, I'm tearing up and throwing out with the trash—along with everything else I used to take credit for. And why? Because of Christ. Yes, all the things I once thought were so important are gone from my life. Compared to the high privilege of knowing Christ Jesus as my Master, firsthand, everything I once thought I had going for me is insignificant—dog dung. I've dumped it all in the trash so that I could embrace Christ and be embraced by him. (Phil. 3:4–9 MSG)

Depression. Others have felt like you. Even in small doses, depression is a part of the journey of life. F. F. Bruce describes the bitterness and difficulty of biblical life even beyond what most modern readers can comprehend.[11] The biblical times were not an idyllic time of tranquility but times of oppression, starvation, abuse, and depravity.

You are not alone, God promises help. The Scriptures promise: "The righteous cry out, and the LORD hears them; he delivers them from all their troubles. The LORD is close to the brokenhearted and saves those who are crushed in spirit. A righteous man may have many troubles, but the LORD delivers him from them all" (Ps. 34:17–19). "For everything that was written in the past was written to teach us, so that through endurance and the encouragement of the Scriptures we might have hope" (Rom. 15:4). "We also rejoice in our sufferings, because we know that suffering produces perseverance; perseverance, character; and character, hope. And hope does not disappoint us, because God has poured out his love into our hearts by the Holy Spirit, whom he has given us" (Rom. 5:3–5). "We have this hope as an anchor for the soul, firm and secure" (Heb. 6:19).

Despondency. Others have felt like you. Jonah was a prophet called by God. He wallowed in racial prejudice to the point that he wanted the Assyrians in Nineveh to die. So disappointed was Jonah with God's love, mercy, and forgiveness toward Nineveh that Jonah protested, "I knew that you are a gracious and compassionate God, slow to anger and abounding in love, a God who relents from sending calamity. Now, O LORD, take away my life, for it is better for me to die than to live" (Jon. 4:2–3).

In despondency over a loss of racial pride, Jonah sat down to die. Here he exhibited the first of two characteristics that often accompany despondency: thoughts of death. Yet God would not let him die, reminding Jonah of God's love, mercy, and forgiveness (Jon. 4:5–11). A second sign of despondency is to withdraw and even run from responsibility. Jonah's exemplified this as he set sail to Tarshish to avoid going to Nineveh, only to find God chasing him first through a storm and then through the belly of a whale (Jon. 1:4—2:10). English poet Francis Thompson has called God, the "hound of heaven," for God sees our potential and chases his offspring with love and call.[12]

You are not alone, God promises help. Scriptures that explain God's assistance in battling despondency include (but are not limited to): "When I said, 'My foot is slipping,' your love, O LORD, supported me. When anxiety was great within me, your consolation brought joy to my soul . . . But the LORD has become my fortress, and my God the rock in whom I take refuge" (Ps. 94:18–19, 22). "He reached down from on high and took hold of me; he drew me out of deep waters. He rescued me from my powerful enemy, from my foes, who were too strong for me. They confronted me in the day of my disaster, but the LORD was my support" (2 Sam. 22:17–19).

Especially helpful for envisioning how God helps when things look bleak is the story of Abraham. The writer of Romans retells the story:

> He didn't tiptoe around God's promise asking cautiously skeptical questions. He plunged into the promise and came up strong, ready for God, sure that God would make good on what he had said.
>
> —Rom. 4:19–22 (MSG)

We call Abraham "father" not because he got God's attention by living like a saint, but because God made something out of Abraham when he was a nobody . . . When everything was hopeless, Abraham believed anyway, deciding to live not on the basis of what he saw he couldn't do but on what God said he would do. And so he was made father of a multitude of peoples. God himself said to him, "You're going to have a big family, Abraham!" Abraham didn't focus on his own impotence and say, "It's hopeless. This hundred-year-old body could never father a child." Nor did he survey Sarah's decades of infertility and give up. He didn't tiptoe around God's promise asking cautiously skeptical questions. He plunged into the promise and came up strong, ready for God, sure that God would make good on what he had said. (Rom. 4:17–22 MSG)

Rejection. Others have felt like you. Jesus experienced rejection as the throngs that shouted, "Hosanna . . . blessed is he who comes in the name of the Lord!" (Matt. 21:9), and who would soon shout all the louder, "Crucify him!" (Matt. 27:23).

You are not alone, God promises help. Rejection is best addressed by a community of love and acceptance. The Scriptures describe the faith community as a new kind of extended family (Eph. 2:19) where inter-reliance, cooperation, and clemency are hallmarks (Acts 2:42–47). The community of Christ is the abode of imperfect humans where affronts and failings still occur. But it is also a community that reflects God's love, mercy, and forgiveness. To understand this, Luke chronicled the expansion of the good news in the book of Acts. This is another good starting place to help those feeling rejected recognize that God can reform and transform ordinary and fallible fishermen, tax collectors, Pharisees, and contentious siblings into tenacious leaders who will adventurously spread the good news across the world.

ACTION 10.2: THREE LANTERNS TO ILLUMINATE THE ROUTE

Al's view about self-reliance changed the night a church leader explained three simple yet weighty lines of reasoning. Al had felt all along that there must be something more to make sense of his life. But he felt outside forces were unable to navigate for him in his plight. He sought to become self-reliant even though he had a feeling that help was available.

At Waypoint 10, where a personal problem is recognized, three foundational principles will illuminate the traveler's path. These are the three philosophical lanterns that illuminated Al's life that night.

Lantern 1: God Is Real. The leader Al heard did not seek to rationalize or confirm this statement; he simply stated it. Too often Christians spend inordinate amounts of time validating God's existence, but, in my experience, most people sense God's presence deep inside. Most people, by the time they have reached Waypoint 10, are not questioning God's existence but, like Al, are wondering what that existence means for them. By stating the certainty of God's existence, the church leader affirmed what Al had already been feeling inside. And then the leader began to take Al to the next step: What does this mean for Al?

Lantern 2: God Can Be Known in the Person of Jesus Christ. God sent his Son, Jesus Christ, to be the supernatural, personal guide and rescuer for humankind. The relational nature of Christ, who experienced every temptation that we have experienced (Heb. 4:15), creates a unique and compelling bond between God and humans. And with the empowerment and inner accompaniment of his Holy Spirit in each believer (Acts 1:8), God has created the ultimate relationship. This relationship is so dynamic, celestial, and supernatural that it can only be described as birthing a new "being."

Lantern 3: God Loves You, and Jesus Christ Laid Down His Life for All Humankind. Sacrificing oneself for others may not be a popular action. But travelers like Al sense that assistance is needed. The church must help wayfarers understand that though humans can't solve life's problems, God can. The magnitude of God's sacrificial action must be carefully explained to the wayfarer. The community of faith must recapture in word and deed the enormity of Jesus' death and resurrection where graves opened, departed saints reappeared (Matt. 27:51–53), and Sheol spewed forth her wrath and eventually her captives (Eph. 4:8–10).

Christ's regeneration of Al did not supplant his passion to help the needy, but empowered it. Al's sensitivity to the oppressed had been a preconversion characteristic. Though Northouse would call this a trait, it can also be thought of as a God-given gift.[13] The New Testament lists approximately twenty-six gifts that are given by God to bring a focus to ministry.[14] One of these is the gift of mercy, which has been described as follows:

> The gift of mercy is . . . to feel genuine empathy and compassion for individuals (both Christian and non-Christian) who suffer distressing physical, mental, or emotional problems, and to translate that compassion into cheerfully done deeds which reflect Christ's love and alleviate the suffering.[15]

There is no biblical reason why these gifts could not be given in some measure before conversion, awaiting the regenerative experience for them to then be supernaturally empowered and expanded. God did not supplant Al's gift of compassion for the poor, but after regeneration, he empowered it. In the following interview, we will look at Al's current ministry and see how God is using him to infect thousands of people with a passion to share the good news in word and deed.

INTERVIEW WITH AL TIZON

Director of the Word and Deed Network of the Evangelicals for Social Action and assistant professor of evangelism and holistic ministry at Palmer Theological Seminary

Whitesel: As the director of the Word and Deed Network, which integrates the good news with good deeds, you seem to have combined your heart for the needy that you exhibited in school with a heart to share the good news of salvation. What happened?

Tizon: I came to realize that personal and social transformations are inseparable. True change needs to happen from the heart to sociopolitical structures. So if I was going to be a true agent of change, I had to be about good works and good news.

Whitesel: You talk about a refocus that occurred in Central America as being a second conversion. Was it the same as your salvation experience?

Tizon: No, it wasn't another spiritual salvation, but I do half-jokingly call it my born again, again experience. I describe it as a conversion because it was an eye-opening experience that radically changed or converted, both my understanding of God and my ministry direction. It reminded me that the task of helping the needy is a huge part of what God is doing in the world, and that I must participate in that as a bearer of good news. I came home from that trip feeling like I had encountered God amid the poor and the oppressed. The good news was no good at all unless it dealt with the needs of the oppressed and needy. Within this new understanding, God completely destroyed my feelings of self-reliance. We won't be able to change the world without God.

Whitesel: So, it wasn't selfishness that your mirror-facing religion exemplified; it was self-reliance. God had to remind you that you couldn't change the world alone. Is that the problem you recognized?

Tizon: Exactly. Yes, that was much of the problem with my former view of things. As my worldview slowly but surely conforms to Christ's, I see the world and its needs differently. I see great possibilities that we can accomplish—with Christ's help.

QUESTIONS FOR GROUP OR PERSONAL STUDY

1. What does your church do when you encounter people suffering from dejection, despondency, depression, or excessive self-reliance? Do you have trained professionals you can recommend to help them? Are these trained professionals part of your local faith community? If not, how will you train and prepare local congregants to be part of this task so that you can make local connections with people suffering from rejection, despondency, depression or excessive self-reliance.

2. Describe two biblical stories that would illustrate each of the following principles:

   • God is real.
   • God can be known in the person of Jesus Christ.
   • God loves you, and in Jesus Christ he laid down his life for all humankind.

3. Recall examples of people who had preconversion passions, and after conversion found themselves supernaturally empowered. Give two examples. What does this tell you about people you know today who are non-Christians? What does this tell you about God's love, concern, and potential for them? Do you see them in a new light?

4. Look for a person who exhibited excessive self-reliance. What was his or her life like in the early years? What was his or her life like in later years? What does this tell you about travelers with excessive self-confidence? Do you know one? Share an encounter.

DECISION TO ACT

Jim[1] joined the army for financial reasons, so he may not have been prepared for the spiritual clash he was about to experience. The rigors and pressures of boot camp fostered a deepening connection to Christ. "One day while marching in formation, Jim began to feel an extraordinary weight to the rifle he was carrying," recalls Shane from a letter he received from Jim. "He knew right then that he was not supposed to be there. But when he told his leader, the reaction was not what Jim expected." According to the letter, the officer embarrassed and derided Jim before his squad. This humiliation had followed closely on the heels of Jim's deepening relationship with Christ.

But in the midst of the humiliation, Jim grew stronger in his decision to act and follow Christ, not weaker. "In that moment, Jim felt that he could understand what Christ had felt by being rejected by his friends, by Peter, and the others."

> "I am the Road, also the Truth, also the Life."
> —JOHN 14:6 (MSG)

Right then Jim made a decision to act and fully follow Christ because he at last knew what Christ had undergone for him.

"This is the story he wrote in that letter," remembers Shane. "And it accentuates what happens when a person is ready to act. They often identify with the suffering Christ. They see in Christ someone who understands their pain and humiliation. We all need to understand that."

The purpose of this story is not to debate the moral rectitude of the soldier's action, but to emphasize the identification with Christ's redemptive action that often occurs among travelers at Waypoint 9. At this juncture, the traveler often realizes that Christ has undertaken an amazing feat of identification and rectification. This fuels the traveler's decision to act.

The recipient of this letter, Shane Claiborne, is an author, speaker, and advocate for the poor. A member of The Simple Way, a faith community in inner-city Philadelphia that helps birth and connect faith communities around the world, Shane states one of his goals is "to follow Jesus to the margins of the empire in which we love and to become friends of the poor."[2]

WAYPOINT CHARACTERISTICS

SIGNS OF TRAVELERS AT WAYPOINT 9

Caught in a Gap. One of the most common sensations at Waypoint 9 is a feeling of hopelessness and suspension between two lives, two worlds, two monarchies, and two calls. Interestingly, church altars in the Middle Ages were often painted with scenes of heaven and hell with many people perched precariously between both.[3] This may have been an attempt to portray sensations of being caught in the middle. But once those who are tussling in this gap grasp a glimpse of their rescuer in Christ, they have an uncommonly strong urge to identify and escape. And this leads to the second sign that can accompany travelers at Waypoint 9: an urge to act without delay.

If travelers are accustomed to having others make decisions for them, they may reel from moving forward, being brought to a standstill by the magnitude of the gulf.

An Urge to Act Immediately. At this waypoint, the traveler often has a strong desire to do something, though what that something is can be vague and foggy. Still, the traveler feels an overwhelming impulse to act. Engel describes this as "a firm intention to act one way or another."[4] This compulsive urge has been brought on by the many waypoints that have led up to this juncture. Travelers now feel they are on the cusp of a new awakening, a new life, a new destiny—and they are. But if travelers rush too quickly into this decision, they can do so without fully understanding of what they are embracing.

Vacillation Due to the Magnitude of the Gap. At the same time, travelers can also be intimidated by the magnitude of the gap that separates them from an all-powerful God. And if travelers are accustomed to having others make decisions for them, they may reel from moving forward, being brought to a standstill by the magnitude of the gulf. The community of faith must help the traveler see that God understands this gap, and that God himself has erected a bridge to span it.

Therefore, it is important for the faith community to gradually, yet steadily, help the traveler perceive the gap, the one bridge, and the necessity of a decision to cross it. The following actions will examine this assistance in detail.

ACTIONS THAT HELP WAYPOINT 9 TRAVELERS

ACTION 9.1: UNDERSTAND THE TREKKER'S FEELINGS

The Feeling of Being Caught in the Middle. As the soldier in Shane's story came to grasp, Christ understands the travels and travails his offspring have experienced. Jesus experienced both the wayfarer's frailty and defenselessness: "We don't have a priest who is out of touch with our reality. He's been through weakness and testing, experienced it all—all but the sin. So let's walk right up to him and get what he is so ready to give. Take the mercy, accept the help" (Heb. 4:14–16 MSG).

The soldiers assigned to the governor took Jesus into the governor's palace and got the entire brigade together for some fun. They stripped him and dressed him in a red toga. They plaited a crown from branches of a thornbush and set it on his head. They put a stick in his right hand for a scepter. Then they knelt before him in mocking reverence: "Bravo, King of the Jews!" they said. "Bravo!" Then they spit on him and hit him on the head with the stick. When they had had their fun, they took off the toga and put his own clothes back on him. Then they proceeded out to the crucifixion. (Matt. 27:27–31 MSG)

Yet in many Protestant churches, the image of Christ portrayed is that of a victorious or everyday Christ. There is nothing wrong with such imagery, but the images within Catholicism of a Christ on the cross may be more helpful for the traveler at Waypoint 9. Often before arriving at this waypoint, travelers have undertaken an arduous journey, and before they make a decision to act, they need to know that Christ understands their predicament and journey. Thom Rainer's research revealed that most people visit a community of faith because a crisis in their life has driven them there.[5] When they visit our churches because of a crisis, they may be looking for a Christ (as well as his followers) who can identify with their calamities and afflictions. The community of faith must understand that although for many mature Christians the image of a victorious Christ overcoming all enemies is exhilarating, for travelers at Waypoint 9 who are pleading for help to overcome their own inadequacies, the images of a Christ who suffered as they are suffering is obligatory.

The Feeling that They Must Act Immediately. Travelers at this juncture will have a resolute determination that they must act. But the seemingly impulsive and rash nature of this act is really due to this being the culmination of a long process. This does not mean, however, that a person should be rushed through this stage. On the contrary, the faith community must let travelers know they appreciate and understand their impetuous feelings, and they are normal. It is important that the community of faith not chide them for this impulsiveness, but acknowledge it as a natural part of the process. Then they can slowly lead them to the next area of assistance.

The Feeling of Vacillation Due to the Magnitude of the Gap. Because many travelers will find this decision intimidating, the community of faith must help them move forward neither in haste nor delay. This is a decision of eternal destiny, and thus a choice cannot be put off indefinitely even if it needs to be slowed down. The community of faith will want to take into account each traveler's predicament and then help them navigate Waypoint 9 at the pace that is right for them.

ACTION 9.2: THE GAP, THE ONLY BRIDGE, AND THE DECISION

Subsequently, the community of faith will want to let trekkers know that there are three important works of God that must be grasped in order to fully understand the importance of the act they are about to undertake. These three understandings will be discussed in the following two chapters. But here it will be important for the traveler to be introduced to an overview of three critical scriptural truths: the gap, the only bridge, and the decision.

The Gap. There is a gap that separates humankind from God. The community of faith must slowly help the wayfarer grasp that every person who travels this journey makes mistakes and falls short of God's ideal. In theological terms, every trekker is a sinner.[6] Scriptures that emphasize this gap include, but are not limited to:

- "There's nothing wrong with God; the wrong is in you. Your wrong-headed lives caused the split between you and God. Your sins got between you so that he doesn't hear" (Isa. 59:2 MSG).
- "If we claim that we're free of sin, we're only fooling ourselves. A claim like that is errant nonsense. On the other hand, if we admit our sins—make a clean breast of them—he won't let us down; he'll be true to himself. He'll forgive our sins and purge us of all wrongdoing" (1 John 1:8–9 MSG).
- "For all have sinned and fall short of the glory of God" (Rom. 3:23).

The Bridge. Travelers must also understand that a sympathetic and compassionate God has erected a bridge to span their gap. And travelers must grasp that this is the only bridge that can cross this chasm. The following are some representative Scriptures of the bridge that was built by One who understands and has experienced the traveler's anguish and suffering:

- "This is how much God loved the world: He gave his Son, his one and only Son. And this is why: so that no one need be destroyed; by believing in him, anyone can have a whole and lasting life. God didn't go to all the trouble of sending his Son merely to point an accusing finger, telling the world how bad it was. He came to help, to put the world right again. Anyone who trusts in him is acquitted" (John 3:16–17 MSG).
- "Since we've compiled this long and sorry record as sinners (both us and them) and proved that we are utterly incapable of living the glorious lives God wills for us, God did it for us. Out of sheer generosity he put us in

right standing with himself. A pure gift. He got us out of the mess we're in and restored us to where he always wanted us to be. And he did it by means of Jesus Christ" (Rom. 3:23–24 MSG).

- "But God demonstrates his own love for us in this: While we were still sinners, Christ died for us" (Rom. 5:8).
- "But God's gift is real life, eternal life, delivered by Jesus, our Master" (Rom. 6:23 MSG).
- "But we see Jesus, who was made a little lower than the angels, now crowned with glory and honor because he suffered death, so that by the grace of God he might taste death for everyone. In bringing many sons to glory, it was fitting that God, for whom and through whom everything exists, should make the author of their salvation perfect through suffering. Both the one who makes men holy and those who are made holy are of the same family. So Jesus is not ashamed to call them brothers" (Heb. 2:9–11).

Yet, with all of the usefulness and convenience of the bridge, some find such a decision intimidating. For some it seems easier to stand on the cusp of the gap and gaze at the future from afar than to actually cross the bridge and reach it.

There is only one bridge. Sometimes travelers wonder if there is another bridge spanning the same chasm. They wonder if perhaps Buddha, Mohammed, or Shiva has built a bridge. While other religious personages may claim to have spanned the chasm, Jesus clearly states that though others may claim else wise, no other bridge exists. "Jesus answered, 'I am the way and the truth and the life. No one comes to the Father except through me'" (John 14:6). Another translation adds traveler imagery: "Jesus said, 'I am the Road, also the Truth, also the Life. No one gets to the Father apart from me. If you really knew me, you would know my Father as well. From now on, you do know him. You've even seen him!'" (John 14:6–7 MSG).

The Decision. Yet with all of the usefulness and convenience of the bridge, some find such a decision daunting. For some, it seems easier to stand on the cusp of the gap and gaze at the future from afar than to actually cross the bridge and reach it. Thus, the community of faith must help the traveler cross this span not in haste, but not in delay either. Remaining perched on one side of the gap is not crossing it, nor getting travelers any closer to their destination. The Scriptures accentuate the importance of decision:

- "But if serving the LORD seems undesirable to you, then choose for yourselves this day whom you will serve . . . But as for me and my household, we will serve the LORD" (Josh. 24:15).
- "Here I am! I stand at the door and knock. If anyone hears my voice and opens the door, I will come in and eat with him, and he with me" (Rev. 3:20).
- "Everyone who calls on the name of the Lord will be saved" (Rom. 10:13).
- "Yet to all who received him, to those who believed in his name, he gave the right to become children of God" (John 1:12).
- To the young businessman, Jesus replied, "First things first. Your business is life, not death. Follow me. Pursue life" (Matt. 8:22 MSG).

It is important that the community of faith introduce, discuss, and receive questions about these three truths in an unhurried manner. These are world-changing truths that take time to digest and absorb.

INTERVIEW WITH SHANE CLAIBORNE

*Author, advocate, circus performer, and founding member of the
Potter Street Community, a new monastic community*

Whitesel: How did the story of Jim turn out?

Claiborne: Jim left the military base. But because a relationship with Christ had been deepened by this experience, Jim eventually realized that he must own up to his departure, and return. He did and was discharged.

Whitesel: What does this say to you about the waypoint where people decide to act upon their understanding of Christ?

Claiborne: Jim was really in a place of uncertainty about Jesus. That is the place where many find themselves. When God was calling the Israelites out of Egypt, there was uncertainty regarding where they were going and what it would mean. That place of decision and identification with Christ is the very place where faith is born. Jim didn't even know the path that was before him. But he sensed that Jesus had been down that road, and Jesus would guide him.

Whitesel: Is there a political or spiritual message in this?

Claiborne: Both. But the message for Waypoint 9 is that Jim had a life-changing identification with Jesus. God used it to hit Jim with the magnitude of the decision he was making to follow Christ. It was a confirmation that God could make a way for Jim.

QUESTIONS FOR GROUP OR PERSONAL STUDY

1. How do you feel when comparing yourself to an all-powerful God? Do you feel deficient, imperfect, inadequate, or embarrassed? How does this affect your relationship with God? Do you feel more in need of his assistance and love? Or do you feel more estranged and unable to live up to his expectations because of your misdeeds? Look up biblical Scriptures that address each of these feelings:

   - Do you feel deficient, imperfect, or inadequate? Look up three Scriptures that tell how God feels about our inadequacies. Here are two to start your list:

     - "Don't panic. I'm with you. There's no need to fear for I'm your God. I'll give you strength. I'll help you. I'll hold you steady, keep a firm grip on you" (Isa. 41:10 MSG).
     - "But he said to me, 'My grace is sufficient for you, for my power is made perfect in weakness.' Therefore I will boast all the more gladly about my weaknesses, so that Christ's power may rest on me. That is why, for Christ's sake, I delight in weaknesses, in insults, in hardships, in persecutions, in difficulties. For when I am weak, then I am strong" (2 Cor. 12:9–10).

- Do you feel estranged and unable to live up to God's expectations because of your misdeeds? Look up three Scriptures that tell how God feels about his imperfect creation. Here are two to start your list:

  - "Christ arrives right on time to make this happen. He didn't, and doesn't, wait for us to get ready. He presented himself for this sacrificial death when we were far too weak and rebellious to do anything to get ourselves ready. And even if we hadn't been so weak, we wouldn't have known what to do anyway. We can understand someone dying for a person worth dying for, and we can understand how someone good and noble could inspire us to selfless sacrifice. But God put his love on the line for us by offering his Son in sacrificial death while we were of no use whatever to him" (Rom. 5:6–8 MSG).

  - "So, what do you think? With God on our side like this, how can we lose? If God didn't hesitate to put everything on the line for us, embracing our condition and exposing himself to the worst by sending his own Son, is there anything else he wouldn't gladly and freely do for us? . . . Do you think anyone is going to be able to drive a wedge between us and Christ's love for us? There is no way! Not trouble, not hard times, not hatred, not hunger, not homelessness, not bullying threats, not backstabbing, not even the worst sins listed in Scripture . . . None of this fazes us because Jesus loves us. I'm absolutely convinced that nothing—nothing living or dead, angelic or demonic, today or tomorrow, high or low, thinkable or unthinkable—absolutely nothing can get between us and God's love because of the way that Jesus our Master has embraced us" (Rom. 8:38–39 MSG).

2. How did you navigate the gap, the bridge, and the decision? Write a paragraph about:

- How you experienced the gap.
- How you experienced the bridge.
- How you experienced the decision.

Share your three paragraphs with two friends. Gain their input then rewrite each paragraph. Place these rewritten paragraphs in your Bible at John 3:16.

3. How do you picture Christ—as a victorious leader or a suffering servant? How did you picture him when you first came to know him? Has the picture changed and in what way? What will you do to help others understand the picture of a suffering Christ who is also triumphant?

REPENTANCE AND
FAITH IN CHRIST

I was baptized at age twelve because of peer pressure, not passion. I was in the church youth choir, and my teacher asked me if I had been saved. I knew I wanted to go to heaven, but beyond that, I was spiritually naïve. So I didn't reply. When it came time for the next baptism service, I signed up. At a meeting with the pastor, I was asked when I was saved. So I gave him the date I signed up for baptism. I guess I was saved from peer pressure, not my sins.

Needless to say, my life changed little. I grew interested in music, joined a rock-and-roll band, and played music throughout high school and college. I joined the largest and most prestigious fraternity at my college, and on the outside it looked like I was living the successful college lifestyle. I studied psychology and became a political activist so I could make the world a better place. But deep down inside I felt powerless to really, and permanently, change the world. I agreed with Engel when he said, "A sense of intolerable discomfort that compels the individual to make a choice."[2]

> There are only two kinds of people in the end, those who say to God "Thy will be done," and those to whom God says in the end, "Thy will be done."
>
> —C. S. Lewis[1]

While I lived my college dreams, my mother, Fern, prayed fervently for her child. Slowly Mom's prayers were answered through Barb. Though we had never been romantically involved, we shared a passion for rock and roll and marijuana. You can imagine my surprise when Barb declared she was no longer going to do drugs with me. She said, "I've become a Christian and I'm not doing drugs anymore. Jesus changed me, and he wants to change you too!" That was something I had never heard from someone in my rock-and-roll culture. Not wanting to lose a friend, I protested, "I'm a Christian too because I believe in God." To which Barb responded with a Scripture stating, "Agreeing with your mind is not enough. You have to follow too. James 2:19 says 'you believe that there is one God. Good! Even the demons believe that—and shudder.'" Suddenly it dawned on me, that believing was not enough. I had to live a life consistent with that belief. Christ is who he claims to be and is the only way to God, for "no one comes to the Father except through me" (John 14:6).

Barb's words haunted me that entire week. On Thursday night, before a big psychology test, I was studying late. I'd found an old Bible my mom had sent with me to college. And I had been carrying it around all week. When I got bored studying that night, I flipped it open and in the back was something called the "Romans Road." It led me through Romans 3:23; 6:23; and 10:9. Suddenly, it was clear to be! I was miserable because I was not who God wanted me to be. And I had made myself that way! I saw that Jesus died for my sins to gave me a new lease on life. I made a decision right there in the library to accept Jesus' salvation and to turn my life over to him. I had no idea the hardest part, a declaration, was still coming!

I'd been a political activist, but now I was ready to be an activist for Christ. On the way back to my fraternity, I told God I would go wherever he sent me. "I'll go to India, to Africa, to wherever you want me to go," I declared. And God replied, "Go to your fraternity and minister to your brothers there." This was the worst possible scenario! I had no problem telling strangers about Jesus, but my fraternity brothers were another matter entirely. I had worked hard to be accepted into this large and prestigious fraternity. My brothers looked up to others based on their social standing. Religion was not looked upon favorably—partying and drinking were. I pleaded with God to send me overseas. But he kept telling me, "Go to your fraternity brothers. That is your mission field."

As I drove back to the fraternity house, God made his expectations even clearer: "Declare your love for me when you arrive," he said. I sensed what that meant. There was a large four-by-eight-foot blackboard next to the main entrance where people could post messages. God told me, "Write 'Jesus is my Lord' on that blackboard and sign it." Again, I pleaded with God to send me to some nondescript alien culture where my declaration for Christ would only be witnessed by those I did not know. But he persisted, and I relinquished as I pulled into the parking lot. After all, the blackboard was usually filled with notices and there would probably only be a small gap near the bottom were I could scrawl "Jesus is my Lord" in tiny lettering. Imagine my surprise upon entering the fraternity and seeing the blackboard had been wiped clean with a wet towel! Not a chalk mark was on it! It lay there empty, ready for me to proclaim my allegiance. And I did, writing in large letters "Jesus is my Lord—Bob Whitesel." I've never looked back.

Later I became an author and a professor of Christian leadership and evangelism. But I've never lost my passion for my fraternity brothers. I realized that to have an impact upon the people I lived with, I had to live a godly lifestyle. I led Bible studies in my fraternity and always tried to be authentic and loving. I was respected by my brothers because I daily lived out my Christian faith. Eventually I was elected president of my fraternity alumni association, serving the second longest tenure as chapter alumni president in Phi Kappa Theta history. But it was not just repentance I experienced that night in the library, though I am grateful for that. I also experienced a new understanding of Jesus Christ, that he would use me to tell others about his good news, and that it starts with right living, and it starts right where you live.

WAYPOINT CHARACTERISTICS

SIGNS OF TRAVELERS AT WAYPOINT 8

A Traveler Mistakes Belief for Following. As a youth, I thought mental assent was all I needed to get into heaven. Living a changed life seemed optional. But as a fuller understanding of God's words emerged, I began to understand that God requires holy living as well.[3] Scriptures that underscore this include, but are not limited to, the following:

- "As obedient children, let yourselves be pulled into a way of life shaped by God's life, a life energetic and blazing with holiness. God said, 'I am holy; you be holy'" (1 Pet. 1:15–16 MSG).

- "For physical training is of some value, but godliness has value for all things, holding promise for both the present life and the life to come" (1 Tim. 4:8).
- "Submit yourselves, then, to God. Resist the devil, and he will flee from you. Come near to God and he will come near to you. Wash your hands, you sinners, and purify your hearts, you double-minded. Grieve, mourn and wail. Change your laughter to mourning and your joy to gloom. Humble yourselves before the Lord, and he will lift you up" (James 4:7–10).

A Traveler Is Struggling with Surrendering His or Her Will to God. C. S. Lewis once wrote, "There are only two kinds of people in the end, those who say to God 'Thy will be done,' and those to whom God says in the end, '*Thy will be done.*'"[4] Travelers at this waypoint may be struggling with the thought of relinquishing control of their lives. They may have grown up in an environment that required them to be self-sufficient. Regardless of the genesis, they now find the thought of relinquishing control to an unseen deity very unnerving. Yet Jesus reminds us:

> What is required is serious obedience—doing what my Father wills. I can see it now—at the Final Judgment thousands strutting up to me and saying, "Master, we preached the Message, we bashed the demons, our God-sponsored projects had everyone talking." And do you know what I am going to say? "You missed the boat. All you did was use me to make yourselves important. You don't impress me one bit. You're out of here." (Matt. 7:21–23 MSG)

A Self-Centered Aspiration for Impersonal Ministry. The good news travels best over what Donald McGavran called the "bridges of God" or the natural relationships that God has brought into our lives.[5] While it seemed to me somewhat romantic and impersonal to be called to a mission field far away, God knows that we are the ones who can best reach out to those around us. For example, it must have been embarrassing for Peter to preach his first sermon on the day of Pentecost. Many in the crowd would have known the hot-headed

126

fisherman, and some would have heard about his swearing and denials only fifty days before. Yet preaching in Jerusalem, the social center of his world, was where Peter would have the greatest impact.

A key to understanding the life-changing magnitude of the good news is to understand the role of the heart, the seat of the emotions, and the mouth through which we proclaim our emotions. As Paul says, "For it is with your heart that you believe and are justified, and it is with your mouth that you confess and are saved" (Rom. 10:9–10). Thus the journey into the good news is a public excursion because God wants more people to join the journey.

ACTIONS THAT HELP WAYPOINT 8 TRAVELERS

This waypoint and Waypoint 7 address conversion, which is a topic of great interest to both religious and secular scholars.[6] Among such scholars, psychologist and philosopher William James' definition remains one of the most accepted:

[Conversion is] the process, gradual or sudden, by which the self hitherto divided and consciously wrong, inferior and unhappy, becomes united and consciously right, superior and happy, in consequence to its firmer hold upon religions realities.[7]

Let us briefly recap the three most recent waypoints that have led up to this definition:

Waypoint 10: Problem recognition with "a sense of intolerable discomfort that compels the individual to make a choice."[8]

Waypoint 9: Christ is who he claims to be and is the only way to God. As Jesus said in John 14:6, "No one comes to the Father except through me."

Waypoint 8: The Holy Spirit now works to "intensify the perceived gap between what is and what might be, thus leading to a firm intention to act one way or another with respect to Christ. No human persuasion enters into this process."[9]

To understand how this process unfolds at Waypoint 8, let us look at four actions that communities of faith can undertake to help travelers at this juncture.

ACTION 8.1: EMBRACE THE SUPERNATURAL

Much of the research on conversion by psychologists and philosophers has ignored or downplayed a supernatural connection.[10] Yet Scripture makes it clear that a supernatural intersection is at the heart of this experience: "For it is by grace you have been saved, through faith—and this not from yourselves, it is the gift of God—not by works, so that no one can boast. For we are God's workmanship" (Eph. 2:8–10). One translation paraphrases this passage to make God's participation even more blunt:

> Saving is all his idea, and all his work. All we do is trust him enough to let him do it. It's God's gift from start to finish! We don't play the major role. If we did, we'd probably go around bragging that we'd done the whole thing! No, we neither make nor save ourselves. God does both the making and saving. He creates each of us by Christ Jesus to join him in the work he does, the good work he has gotten ready for us to do, work we had better be doing. (Eph. 2:8–10 MSG)

Therefore, a faith community helps wayfarers by allowing the supernatural to participate and to guide the process. This does not mean sanctioning spiritual anarchy. When Paul wrote to the Corinthians, a church struggling with spiritual disorder and chaos, he emphasized that God works in a logical and reasonable manner, stating, "But everything should be done in a fitting and orderly way" (1 Cor. 14:40).

ACTION 8.2: AUTHENTICITY AND RELEVANCE

Human Manipulation Should not Enter into This Process. As seen above, human manipulation is inauthentic and ultimately fruitless. God's Holy Spirit is working, and only an all-loving God could ensure that this process is free of manipulation and coercion. The process is organic, with dialogue and intersection with a loving heavenly Father guiding the process. Christians must pray, support, and aid but let the Holy Spirit guide.

Relevance and Free Will Are Involved. Though there are different theological options regarding the degree to which choice is involved in human decisions, free will does exist at the point of decision.[11] The Scriptures make it clear that a human must make an individual decision regarding the relevance of God's declarations to them (Rom. 3:23), their personal estrangement from God (Rom. 6:23), and a willingness to accept God's rescue plan through Jesus Christ (John 3:16).

ACTION 8.3: FALLEN, IMPRISONED, AND THE ULTIMATE SOLUTION

The Holy Spirit now works to "intensify the perceived gap between what is and what might be, thus leading to a firm intention to act one way or another with respect to Christ. No human persuasion enters into this process."[12] This takes place as the traveler grasps three "realities."[13]

Reality 1: Fallen. The wayfarer has fallen short of God's expectations. The traveler at this point is coming to the conclusion that he or she has fallen short of God's expectations and is a sinner. Below are foundational verses for understanding this:

- "For all have sinned and fall short of the glory of God" (Rom. 3:23).
- "But your iniquities have separated you from your God; your sins have hidden his face from you, so that he will not hear" (Isa. 59:2).

Reality 2: Imprisoned. The wayfarer, imprisoned by self-seeking, can thus never please God and will ultimately experience spiritual death. Below are a few foundational verses:

- "For the wages of sin is death, but the gift of God is eternal life in Christ Jesus our Lord" (Rom. 6:23).
- "As for you, you were dead in your transgressions and sins" (Eph. 2:1).

Reality 3: The Ultimate Solution. The wayfarer becomes willing to go in a new direction, seeking the ultimate solution through an act of will to accept Christ's salvation. Foundational verses include:

- "For God so loved the world that he gave his one and only Son, that whoever believes in him shall not perish but have eternal life" (John 3:16).

- "This is the real and eternal life: that they know you, the one and only true God, and Jesus Christ, whom you sent" (John 17:3 MSG).

ACTION 8.4: CULTIVATE DECLARATION

Paul wrote, "That if you confess with your mouth, 'Jesus is Lord,' and believe in your heart that God raised him from the dead, you will be saved. For it is with your heart that you believe and are justified, and it is with your mouth that you confess and are saved" (Rom. 10:9–10). Paul is emphasizing that faith and repentance result in a conversion, "a turn around . . . a change of mind . . . [to turn] from something to something [else]."[14] In addition, Paul emphasizes that such a turnaround should be conspicuous.[15]

Reality 1: Fallen—the wayfarer has fallen short of God's expectations.

Reality 2: Imprisoned—the wayfarer, imprisoned by self-seeking, can thus never please God and will ultimately experience spiritual death.

Reality 3: The Ultimate Solution—the wayfarer becomes willing to go in a new direction, seeking the ultimate solution through an act of will to accept Christ's salvation.

Thus, this declaration should be in public behavior, and not just words. Engel notes that when Paul says, "For it is with your heart that you believe and are justified" (Rom. 10:9), he is emphasizing that this is more than mental agreement.[16] The reference to the heart means a decision "that penetrates to the very core of one's being." Engel notes that this is "betting your life" on the route you are taking.[17] A public statement or action verifies this bet.

Faith communities must provide relevant, authentic, and appropriate circumstances for such declaration and community accountability. Such proclamations in word and deed are not biblically optional (Rom. 10:9–10), but they must be culturally relevant. For example, for me an appropriate venue for declaration was the more than a hundred men who lived in the same fraternity with me. The common bonds, experiences, and inter-reliance we shared had created bridges of God, which I crossed for the next thirty-five years.

INTERVIEW WITH BOB WHITESEL

Author, speaker, and professor

(The following was conducted by Rebecca Whitesel, my wife of thirty-three years and a professional journalist.)

Rebecca Whitesel: Your life changed that night on the way back to your fraternity. Why was this different from the baptism you experienced at age twelve?

Bob: When I was baptized at twelve, I bowed to peer pressure. When I wrote my declaration on that fraternity blackboard, I stood up to peer pressure. In a secular college, you are under a lot of pressure to live the excesses of a college lifestyle. But Christ made it clear right from the start that I must be a testimony to my fraternity brothers in not just word, but also deed.

Rebecca: How did you change?

Bob: On the outside, I quit smoking, drinking, cursing, and partying. I still played music, but I became a leader at a Christian music café. But on the inside even more profound changes took place as I became more compassionate, sympathetic, thoughtful, loving, and honest.

Rebecca: Didn't this ostracize you from your fraternity brothers?

Bob: There is a lot of pressure in a fraternity to be like everyone else. But I let my brothers know that I had a calling to serve Jesus. They respected that, and they saw changes in me for the better. I think deep down, many of them needed a change too. Seeing that I could do it with God's help gave them hope.

Rebecca: How would you sum this up?

Bob: My desire was to let my brothers see that God had made me a better person in words and actions. In response, they honored me by electing me to the second-longest term ever as alumni president.

QUESTIONS FOR GROUP OR PERSONAL STUDY

1. "Let every detail in your lives—words, actions, whatever—be done in the name of the Master, Jesus" (Col. 3:17 MSG). What does this mean to you? Is there a warning here? And if so, why is this warning given?

2. In this chapter, we saw the three realities that wayfarers must grasp to move onward in their journey. Read each of the realities below and write a paragraph about how you encountered each. Some readers may have experienced some of the realities at a datable time, while for others it will be an unfolding process. To note the different ways God works, share your three paragraphs with two friends and compare and contrast how God has been working.

   - *Reality 1: Fallen*—the wayfarer has fallen short of God's expectations (Rom. 3:23; Isa. 59:2).
   - *Reality 2: Imprisoned*—the wayfarer, imprisoned by self-seeking, can thus never please God and will ultimately experience spiritual death (Rom. 6:23; Eph. 2:1).
   - *Reality 3: The Ultimate Solution*—the wayfarer becomes willing to go in a new direction, seeking the ultimate solution through an act of will to accept Christ's salvation (John 3:16; 17:3).

3. Think of a friend, coworker, or relative who has not made a commitment to Christ. With one of these persons in mind, take the following Scripture and translate it to make it understandable to them. Before you begin your translation, write a short descriptive paragraph about this person. Without giving the name, explain who it is and why you will translate Ephesians 2:8–10 the way that you will:

   Saving is all his idea, and all his work. All we do is trust him enough to let him do it. It's God's gift from start to finish! We don't play the major role. If we did, we'd probably go around bragging that we'd done the whole thing! No, we neither make nor save ourselves. God does both the making and saving. He creates each of us by Christ Jesus to join him in the work he does, the good work he has gotten ready for us to do, work we had better be doing. (Eph. 2:8–10 MSG)

4. Recount the first time you declared your faith in Jesus Christ. What were the circumstances? What were the outcomes? Was it important for you? Was it important for others?

5. How do you regularly declare your faith? Are you more or less effective today? And what will you do about this?

NEW BIRTH

et's wait until your father gets home," was the loving reply to Scot's request. "But I can't wait. What if I die before Dad gets home?" came the five-year-old's retort. Scot had returned from an evening service at his church, and the hellfire-and-brimstone message had made an impression. Yet Scot's decision that night was more the result of his wish to avoid damnation, than it was to embark upon a new life. "That's probably why it didn't have much effect on me," remembers Scot. "I got baptized perfunctorily at age twelve because we were supposed to get baptized. It wasn't until I was seventeen that the avoidance of the penalty of my sins caught up to my desire to serve God sacrificially."

Repentance: "The idea of turning, but focuses on the inner, cognitive decision to make a break with the past."[1]

Scot was an avid athlete, and in the summer of his seventeenth year he was impressed by the spiritual depth and athletic prowess of his camp counselor, Duane. "I wasn't impressed by him so much as I was impressed about how he could be a good athlete and also live out his faith in Christ. I saw a new direction I wanted to go. I was tired of being thought of as a Christian

> "So don't be so surprised when I tell you that you have to be 'born from above'— out of this world, so to speak. You know well enough how the wind blows this way and that. You hear it rustling through the trees, but you have no idea where it comes from or where it's headed next. That's the way it is with everyone 'born from above' by the wind of God, the Spirit of God."
>
> —JOHN 3:7–8 (MSG)

when, really, I was putting myself first, and God was way down the list. I saw an example of how a Christian can live out his life and be an athlete too. I had a change of mind and wanted to turn from the way I have been living, to something else . . . the way I saw Duane living."

Faith: "To trust, to [have] confidence in God."[2]

"We began talking about the Bible all night in our cabin," remembers Scot. "And out of that grew a new understanding of the Holy Spirit and a new confidence in God. I sensed he had a plan for my future. I had wanted to be an athlete, and I was being courted by Division 1 colleges. But all of that changed. All of my passions changed. I wasn't as interested in sports, for now, I had confidence in God's handling of my future. Before, I was full of pride and doing what I wanted to. All of a sudden, I wanted to do what Christ wanted me to do."

Conversion: To "turn around . . . a change of mind . . . [to turn] from something to something [else]."[3]

"I didn't know if I wanted to be a pastor, a professor, or a missionary," continues Scot. "I just knew I wanted to serve God and not me. It happened the next day while I sat under an oak tree. No longer did I care about getting into a Division 1 school. Now I just wanted to serve God. I was ready to go where he called me."

WAYPOINT CHARACTERISTICS

Waypoint 7 may be the most important and misunderstood juncture in the journey. Subsequently, the reader will notice some overlap with the previous chapter, and this is intentional. The intersection of the Holy Spirit with the human soul is so critical that this is best observed from several perspectives. Thus, to understand this event, it will be necessary to look at several aspects.

KINDS OF CONVERSION

Conversion to Christianity. I will limit this present discussion about conversion to Christianity. There is an abundance of literature dealing with different types of conversion, and I am indebted to Richard Peace for classifying these varieties.[4] There are secular conversions where a drug addict might be transformed from drug dependence to a drug-free lifestyle. There are manipulative conversions where coercion is used by a cult[5] or a government.[6] There is conversion between religious worldviews such as the change from Sikhism to Hinduism that is taking place in India. And there is conversion from one Christian denomination to another, like when popular Catholic priest Rev. Alberto Cutie (nicknamed "Father Oprah") converted to the U.S. Episcopal denomination. Though all of these areas are of interest to scholars and researchers, we will limit this discussion to conversion about Christianity.

What Is Conversion? A look at Church history reveals that a wide range of experiences, tempos, and progressions is associated with conversion.[7] However, there are common characteristics and elements that run through all of these conversations. Philosopher William James best summed up these common aspects when he defined conversion as follows:

> To be converted, to be regenerated, to receive grace, to experience religion, to gain an assurance, are so many phrases which denote the process, gradual or sudden, by which a self hitherto divided, and consciously wrong, inferior and unhappy, becomes unified and consciously right, superior and happy, in consequence of its firmer hold upon religious realities.
>
> —WILLIAM JAMES

To be converted, to be regenerated, to receive grace, to experience religion, to gain an assurance, are so many phrases which denote the process, gradual or sudden, by which a self hitherto divided, and consciously wrong, inferior and unhappy, becomes unified and consciously right, superior and happy, in consequence of its firmer hold upon religious realities.[8]

The Bible uses several Greek words to describe this conversion process. Each of these terms will help us more accurately understand conversion.

- *Epistrophe* is the most basic term, and means to "turn around . . . a change of mind . . . (to turn) from something to something (else)."[9] Peace notes this is a "reversing direction and going the opposite way."[10]

- *Metanoia* often appears with *epistrophe*, and is the Greek word for repentance that "conveys the idea of turning, but focuses on the inner, cognitive decision to make a break with the past."[11]
- *Pistis* is the Greek for "faith, trust, confidence in God," and conveys a reliance and assurance in God that can lead to conversion.[12]

Combining these three terms is important to understanding the matrix of conversion. Peace sums this up, stating, "*Metanoia* [repentance] must be combined with *pistis* [faith] in order to bring about *epistophe* [conversion]."[13]

HOW AND WHEN CONVERSION OCCURS

Does conversion occur in a flash, with miraculous transformations and heavenly encounters? Does conversion take place over time? Or perhaps conversion is a stumbling process, where the conversionary experience takes place in what has been called "fits and starts." Richard Peace, Scot McKnight, and others have looked at the New Testament record and concluded that the answer is "all of the above."[14] Let us look at three basic categories.

Sudden Conversion. Sometimes conversion takes place "in a flash . . . a sudden point-in-time transformation based on an encounter with Jesus."[15] This is the experience of Saul/Paul in Acts 9, and has became the standard way the evangelical church looks at conversion.[16] At the altar, sudden and dramatic responses are often expected, door-to-door visits lead to a "prayer of commitment," and mass rallies end with an appeal to come forward for conversion.[17] While this may be required to facilitate a person on the verge of a sudden conversionary experience, not all conversions happen in this manner. Psychologist Lewis Rambo, in an exhaustive look at religious conversion, concluded that "for the most part it [religious conversion] takes place over a period of time."[18] Thus, the evangelical church may be limiting the number of wayfarers she can help by focusing too exclusively on sudden conversion.

Progressive Conversion.[19] A closer look at the gospel of Mark reveals that Mark was describing a different, more gradual paradigm of conversion. As Peace notes,

What Mark sought to communicate in his Gospel was the process by which these twelve men gradually turned, over time, from their culturally derived understanding of Jesus as a great teacher to the amazing discovery that he was actually the Messiah who was the Son of God. In showing how the Twelve turned to Jesus, step-by-step, Mark was inviting his readers to undergo the same journey of conversion.[20]

Peace concludes that "what happened to Paul and what happened to the Twelve was identical in terms of theological understanding, though quite different experientially."[21]

Scot McKnight describes how progressive conversion can take place in churches that practice infant baptism. "For many Christians conversion is a process of socialization," meaning that nurture is confirmed later by personal affirmation.[22] For example, an infant baptism or dedication can be seen as a public affirmation that the church community and parents will nurture that child (via spiritual socialization). After living in this environment of spiritual socialization and religious community, the young adult will be expected to ratify this effort through further instruction (that is, catechism) and confirmation.

Travelers at Waypoint 7 experience an inner, mental decision to make a break with their past. Mental gyrations are occurring where memories of the positive attributes of the past are being superseded by visions of what an ideal future can contain.

Liturgical Acts and Conversion. McKnight also notes that in some liturgical traditions, such as the Roman Catholic Church and the Orthodox Church, while conversion is experienced, the sacraments are more involved. Thus, baptism, the Eucharist, and official rites of passage are where conversionary experiences often take place for "liturgical converts."[23] There is nothing to preclude that God can use such spiritual rites as touchstone experiences where *metanoia* (repentance) is combined with *pistis* (faith) in order to bring about *epistophe* (conversion).

SIGNS OF TRAVELERS AT WAYPOINT 7

Travelers at Waypoint 7, the new birth, are usually experiencing three growing yet competing feelings: repentance, faith, and conversion. Let us look at signs the traveler is wrestling with each.

Wrestling with Repentance. Travelers at Waypoint 7 experience an inner, mental decision to make a break with their past. Mental gyrations are going on where memories of the positive attributes of the past are being superseded by visions of what an ideal future can contain. The traveler will often be vacillating between anticipation of the future and guilt over the past. The church must be prepared to gracefully and gradually help travelers make sense of these polar forces and to focus on God's design for their future.

Wrestling with Faith. At this juncture, travelers often feel a new inner certainty and confidence in God and his good news. Sometimes Christians are taken aback by such passionate belief. This may be especially hard to understand if the observer has experienced a liturgical or progressive conversion, and the traveler is experiencing a sudden conversion. And the converse is true: if a person experiences a progressive conversion, this can often mystify and confuse the sudden convert because it has not been her or his experience. We will talk more about overcoming this confusion under Action 7.4.

Wrestling with Conversion. Travelers at Waypoint 7 are on the cusp of reversing course and setting about in a new direction. Phrases such as *new outlook*, *new beginning*, or *new lease on life* occur in their vocabulary. The traveler is encountering a powerful sensation that a new direction is warranted. But as noted above, this feeling can be lived out in a slow, sudden, or even sacramental encounter. Regardless of the venue or pace, the key to repentance is in William James' words: "by which a self hitherto divided, and consciously wrong, inferior and unhappy, becomes unified and consciously right, superior and happy."[24]

ACTIONS THAT HELP WAYPOINT 7 TRAVELERS

Actions 7.1, 7.2, and 7.3 will deal with helping the traveler wrestle with repentance, faith, and conversion.

ACTION 7.1: HELPING THOSE WRESTLING WITH REPENTANCE

Repentance is the process of focusing on the inner, cognitive decision to make a break with the past. Here, the church assists the traveler through prayer, support, and by getting out of the way and allowing the Holy Spirit to work. The church's job is not to convict of sin, for that is the Holy Spirit's role (John 16:8–9). Usually at this stage, the traveler is so riddled with shame and guilt due to the Holy Spirit's working that any additional derision lumped on by the unaware Christian can thwart the process.

Also, the church must help the traveler see that others have experienced similar remorse for the past. And the church must help the traveler see that Christ can create a new creature, "and what we see is that anyone united with the Messiah gets a fresh start, is created new. The old life is gone; a new life burgeons! Look at it!" (2 Cor. 5:17 MSG).

At this waypoint, travelers are summing up all they have known of the past and are now comparing that to an emerging understanding of God's future for their lives. The reality of the past is now being compared to the hope of the future, and overcoming the concreteness of the past will take some support.

ACTION 7.2: HELPING THOSE WRESTLING WITH FAITH

At this waypoint, travelers are often in the final gestation of faith develop-ment that leads to conversion. They will be inquisitive, confused, and befuddled because they are growing in faith, trust, and confidence in God.

The church can help travelers at this waypoint see God's promises as reflected in Scripture. The Scriptures are filled with examples of stories, poems, and songs given to people who are struggling with trusting God in the midst of calamity. I have often found that, at this juncture, Psalm 23, and its emphasis upon trust in times of trial is appropriate for it emphasizes the positive future of God's assistance even over the calamity of the present.

ACTION 7.3: HELPING THOSE WRESTLING WITH CONVERSION

Travelers at Waypoint 7 will be ready to experience a "turn around . . . a change of mind . . . [to turn] from something to something [else]."[25] The traveler will seek help in reversing direction and going the opposite way. This may require significant effort by the church.

For example, the church may need to help an abused spouse find a new place to live if that spouse is to reverse his or her direction and move away from an abusive relationship. Or a church may need to provide housing, counseling, a job, and a host of other assistance. While this type of ministry was described as a congregational action at Waypoints 14, 15, and 16, it must be offered again here. At the conversion stage, travelers are making a lifestyle change along with their spiritual decision. They are deciding to turn in a new direction that will be of such radical nature that they will need significant help to reverse course.

ACTION 7.4: CONVERSION IS A MYSTICAL MATRIX OF FORCES

Many churches today focus on one of the three variations of conversion. McKnight says that "each is aligned with a major component of the church and each appears to be allergic to the others."[26] Let us look briefly at each in Figure 7.1.

FIGURE 7.1

	Types of Conversion		
	Sudden Conversion	Socialization	Liturgical Acts
Customary Denominational Context	Evangelicals,[c][e] Pentecostals[c][e]	Mainline Protestants[c][e]	Roman Catholics,[c][e] Orthodox Church[c][e]
Strengths	Radical departure from the past.	Point of conversion does not require a sordid past.	Mystery and encounter with the supernatural.
Weaknesses	In some studies, only 10 percent of these decisions "resulted in long-term changes in personal behavior."[d] Mechanical tools can replace community.[e]	The work of conversion can "drift from the center of one's ecclesiastical vision."[e] Faith can become a matter of duty and obligation.[e]	Liturgy has to be learned, as well as how to participate in it before conversion.[e]
Adage	"Conversion is an individual experience that can be dated exactly."[e]	"Belonging before believing."[e]	"To arouse the sleeping faith in the nominal Christian."[e]
Customary Participants	Raised in a secular environment.[e] First-generation Christians[a]	Raised in a Christian home.[b] Second-generation Christians[a]	Second-generation Christians[a]

a. Charles Kraft, "Christian Conversion As a Dynamic Process," in *International Christian Broadcasters Bulletin* (Colorado Springs, Colo.: International Christian Broadcasters, 1974), Second Quarter.
b. Scot McKnight, Personal Interview, June 2, 2009.
c. Scot McKnight, *Turning to Jesus: The Sociology of Conversion in the Gospels* (Louisville, Ky.: Westminster John Knox Press, 2002).
d. Donald Miller, *Reinventing American Protestantism: Christianity in the New Millennium* (Berkley, Calif.: University of California Press, 1997), 171–172.
e. Richard Peace, "Conflicting Understandings of Christian Conversion: A Missiological Challenge," in *International Bulletin of Missionary Research*, Vol. 28, No. 1, 8.

As noted in this chapter, the New Testament and experience tells us that conversion takes place in several ways and with different cadences. Scot's story that began this chapter mirrors that of many of the people I have met over the years as well as my personal experience. Scot's experience was a combination of personal decision and socialization. For Scot, this was a culmination of three personal encounters (ages five, twelve, and seventeen). God had been connecting with Scot for some time via the influence of friends, family, and the Holy Spirit.

INTERVIEW WITH SCOT McKNIGHT

Author, speaker, and professor in Religious Studies
at North Park University

Whitesel: Tell me about your story as it relates to a "turn around . . . a change of mind . . . [to turn] from something to something [else]."[27]

McKnight: What awakened in me under that oak tree at age seventeen was a devout and sincere passion to give my life to Christ. That was a radical change of mind for me. I was an athlete. Suddenly, I had no interest in that anymore. I wanted to go to a Christian college and study theology. And I didn't know what I wanted to do, but it was something like a pastor, professor, and missionary rolled into one.

Whitesel: Were there three parts to your conversion, one at age five, another at age twelve at baptism, and another at age seventeen at camp?

McKnight: It was not so much three parts, but three segments of a journey. I look at my conversion at age five and twelve as a very typical decision as a child. But when I was seventeen, I experienced an individuation of faith. For me, it was an awakening of my faith as a result of an encounter with the Holy Spirit. I think conversion is an ongoing experience, and very much so for kids that grow up in Christian homes. I became an adult Christian that day underneath that oak tree. I accepted the implications of the good news as an emerging adult. I became an adult at that moment. My life had meaning, purpose, and new direction from then on.

Whitesel: Would you sum up your experience as conversion through socialization or conversion through personal decision?

McKnight: Both. You cannot get away from conversion as a process of socialization if you grow up in a Christian home. It is the combination of the personal decision and a socialization process. I didn't see what happened to me as a seventeen-year-old who decided to receive Christ. In my mind, I had already done that. This was a decision to let Christ have his way in my life.

Whitesel: What resulted?

McKnight: My experience was a conversion, a turning around, a change of mind from one way to a new way. It was regenerating, purifying, and a complete change from the inside out. People who knew me saw dramatic changes in my life. I received new life at that point. It was the convergence of the decisions I made as a child. There were influences coming from my parents that were at work in me, which I've called conversion through socialization. But that was only part of it. There was also a personal decision at seventeen too. It was all part of a unique, personalized, and God-ward process.

QUESTIONS FOR GROUP OR PERSONAL STUDY

1. Was there a time when you had a significant, nonreligious change of mind accompanied by a mental decision to make a break with the past? When was this? What happened? Did it last?

2. Was there a time when you had a reversing of some nonreligious actions? Was there a significant turning from something to something else? When was this? What happened? Did it last?

3. Do you recall a time when you increased in faith, trust, and confidence in someone? How did your reliance and assurance in them change? When was this? What happened? Did it last?

4. Now answer, from a religious point of view, the following variations of the questions above:

- Was there a time when you had a significant, religious change of mind accompanied by an inner, cognitive decision to make a break with the past? When was this? What happened? Did it last?
- Was there a time when you had a reversing of some spiritual actions? Was there a significant turning from one thing to something else? When was this? What happened? Did it last?
- Do you recall a time when you increased in faith, trust, and confidence in God? How did your reliance and assurance in God change? When was this? What happened? Did it last?

5. Sharing your personal story can be helpful to travelers at Waypoint 7.[28] Write out (in three paragraphs) your personal story of conversion. Use the following structure:

- Paragraph 1: Tell about how you mentally turned from your past and decided to make a break with it (repentance).
- Paragraph 2: Tell about how you increased in faith, trust, confidence, reliance, or assurance in God (faith).
- Paragraph 3: Tell about how you reversed direction and went the opposite way (conversion).

POST-DECISION EVALUATION

Len grew up in an austere but loving home with a mother who led holiness revivals and a father who worked at a local bank. "I was one of three boys," says Len, "and Mom didn't isolate us from the world, but she did insulate us. We went to the public schools, but we were home-schooled in Christianity with twice-daily devotionals and Bible memorization assignments. Our Pilgrim Holiness Church looked like people from another era with old-fashioned dresses—hair in a bun, hankies unfurled when people got 'happy.' My mother conducted revivals and camp meetings in the hills of Appalachia, and some of my earliest memories were of my brothers and me being dragged kicking and singing as part of Mother's presentations." Len played the piano and organ for worship, and it was during one final "great preaching" service at a Free Methodist camp meeting that Len had a powerful spiritual experience he later described as his "de-conversion."

> My one regret in life is that I am not someone else.
>
> —WOODY ALLEN[1]

"In my first seventeen years, I totally lived the faith through my parents," Len recalls. "But when I was seventeen I de-converted. I can date my de-conversion to the song and verse. I was playing the organ for Pine Grove Camp meeting. In the front row sat the girl I was dating. She was Linda, the district superintendent's daughter. I thought I was pretty hot stuff and couldn't wait until the end of the invitation song to get what I thought would be my good-bye kiss. On the third of six verses of 'Softly and Tenderly,' I saw my mother's best friend, Ruth, get out of her seat and 'hit the sawdust trail,' as they used to call it.

"I couldn't believe my eyes. Ruth was the closest thing I knew to a saint next to my mother. I was brought up pretribulationist and expected a rapture of the saints before the seven-year great tribulation. When I came home from school and mother wasn't there, I got nervous. And after twenty minutes, I started to sweat. Had the rapture occurred? I knew my mother would be taken up to meet Jesus in the air, but I knew Jesus wouldn't want anything to do with my brothers. I wasn't sure about myself. In addition, I was afraid I would be left with my brothers, and since I was the oldest, I would have to take care of them during the horrors of the tribulation. To relieve my anxiety, I would call Ruth's number on a rotary phone (and her number had two zeros in it). If she answered, I would quickly hang up and breathe a big sigh of relief. To this day, I am tender toward hang-ups—you never know who and why someone is calling and hanging up.

"So Ruth is this person on whom I banked all my eschatological hopes," Len says. "She finally made her way up to the front. But instead of going to the altar, she came right up to me, threw herself on me, and started crying out, 'Now is your appointed time, Lenny! Now is your time!' As she wailed these words, she tried to pull me from the organ bench to the altar.

"This is the worst thing that can happen to a seventeen-year-old. Especially one who is dating the superintendent's daughter! At first I tried ignoring her, hoping she'd go away. Then I tried reasoning with her. Then I tried shooing her away. But the more I tried to push Ruth away, the more determined she was to haul me to the altar.

"We were now at the end of the altar call. The preacher said, 'Obviously the Lord is at work here this morning. We must give the Spirit plenty of time to work. Let's sing this song one more time. All the verses, please.' That's when I realized that I was playing for my own altar call! Ruth kept crying and pulling at me. I kept playing. The harder she pulled, the louder I played. When we get to the third verse, she suddenly stopped. She removed herself from being my drape, shook herself off, turned around, and retraced her steps back to her seat. About a third of the way down the center aisle, she stopped, hung her head, and shook it a couple of times. And when I saw her shake her head, I knew what that meant, and that was the moment I de-converted from Christianity.

"When Ruth shook her head, she was releasing me to the Devil. In her mind, I had quenched the Spirit, the one unpardonable sin, and from now on I was on my own, with no protection from God. And when I saw her do that, I said to myself, 'I'm out of here. God, I hate you. I no longer believe there is a God, but if you do exist, God, I hate you. I want nothing to do with you.' When Mother came up to me afterward, it was as if I had contracted Tourette's syndrome. I spewed out every swear word I had ever heard but never uttered until that moment. Needless to say, I never saw or heard from the superintendent's daughter again."

WAYPOINT CHARACTERISTICS

SIGNS OF TRAVELERS AT WAYPOINT 6

Some might wonder if Len had been a Christian before this experience and thus the applicability of this story to this chapter. But this illustration yields a poignant illustration of a post-decision evaluation where a person must decide if the new restrictions, culture, and costs of following Christ are worth the effort.

Len had been immersed in a Christian culture, doing the right thing on the outside. He played the organ for camp meetings and dated the superintendent's daughter. But it was evident to others, especially Ruth, that Len's outward appearance was not a personal choice. Len's sham of a life was now subject to a post-decision evaluation, and Len decided that his lifestyle was not worth the effort or the scorn.

The Interrogator: Bursting with Questions. Many people experience a post-decision evaluation when a barrage of questions surface in their minds. Will they enjoy this new life? What are the restrictions? Will they be accepted? Will they be ridiculed? Will they lose their former friends? Will they make new ones? Due to such questions, the church must be prepared to spend hours in conversation with new converts, explaining the benefits and detriments to following Christ. While the benefits are often willingly described by churches, the challenges and detriments are usually glossed over. We shall see shortly that the Church must not shirk her duty to clearly explain both the benefit and cost of discipleship.

The Runner: Bristling with Annoyance. Here, Len serves as a classic example. His journey through Waypoints 11, 10, 9, 8, and 7 had been to please and appease his parents. This was not his chosen lifestyle, and once he was confronted with this spirituality by proxy and ridiculed for it, he stormed away from Christian culture. Not until years later would he regain an appreciation for it, as well as be able to pull from it the toxins that contaminated his relationship with God.

When Christians undergo a post-decision evaluation, they often bolt the situation. They may, like Len, spew forth profanity and vulgarity which will grieve loved ones. But the church must see in this the working of God's navigation and not grieve, but pray. This action will be emphasized later in this chapter as well.

To understand what churches can do to help people at this stage, it will be necessary to depart our custom of addressing church actions next. Instead, we will go directly to an interview with Len Sweet and allow him to explain how he negotiated Waypoint 6.

INTERVIEW WITH LEN SWEET
Theologian, author, futurist, and professor at
Drew Theological School and George Fox University

Whitesel: Len, the story ended with you immersed in a verbal flood of filth. What happened next?

Sweet: Some people plant wild oats; I planted a prairie. For the next six years, I totally went the other way. I became an atheist who told people I didn't believe in God and told God I didn't believe in him. The irony was that it was only after my de-conversion that God started working on me big time. You see, even though I was now telling God how bad a divine being he was and that I didn't really believe he existed anyway, I was no longer talking to God through my parents. I was talking to God directly. I was now engaged in a conversation, and that conversation was the beginning of a relationship that has brought me to where I am today. What does God want more than anything from us? A relationship. And even an argumentative and negative relationship is better than rote and ritual obedience.

Whitesel: Explain the conversation.

Sweet: The minute I de-converted, I began a very passionate conversation with God and a personal quest to determine what was truth with a capital "T." I earned an undergraduate degree in psychology and history, then enrolled simultaneously in a Ph.D. program in history and an M.Div. in church history. I was trying to figure out the historical background of my upbringing, and why it was the way it was from an intellectual standpoint. It felt like I had been mugged, and I needed to learn everything I could about the mugger and the mugging. The seminary I chose was one with faculty who embraced a "death of God" theology and was known for its social justice emphasis, so I felt right at home studying church history there.

Whitesel: But you stayed connected with Christians.

Sweet: The key component of every liminality, as anthropologist Victor Turner noted, is that the water that has left the river and has become wetlands or streams keeps tracking with the river. In liminal stages of life, you need to leave the main stream so that the toxins can be removed and the water cleansed. But while that purifying process is taking place, you must keep tracking alongside the river so that you can return to it. And when you return to the river, you enter it with a higher degree of passion and purity than when you left it. That's what happened to me. I said, "I'm no longer in that river," but I kept tracking with it, I kept talking to it, I kept engaging it. And that's how God kept me in relationship, a relationship that was being cleansed and purified even when I didn't know it. Our head wants to know God, but our heart wants to be known by God. And the more my head was buzzing, the more my heart was growing in its desires.

During my seminary education, I had a requirement of field education, meaning that I had to work in a church. My faculty mentor invited me to be his teaching assistant so I wouldn't have to do church work. But the dean vetoed it. My mentor got the whole faculty to pass a resolution against forcing me to work in a church. But the dean vetoed it again! So there I was, headed to a Presbyterian church for supervised ministry. I was not happy, but wanted my A, so I had to do what I was assigned. This pastor, whose name was Fred Yoos, helped me fall in love with Jesus and the Church again. He sent me on a blind pastoral call to someone in need. I had no idea what I would find. He just told me I was going to have to handle it pastorally. I was sent to the home of Marge Wilke, and I found her crying when she answered the door. It was the anniversary of her husband's death in Vietnam. I had a number of friends who had been killed or maimed in the war, and it suddenly hit me that Marge's husband could have been me. But for the grace of God I could have been killed in Vietnam. Why was I still alive when so many I knew weren't? As I started to minister to her, she ministered to me. And I ended my first pastoral call on my knees in her living room, asking God to forgive me and for Christ to come into my life.

Whitesel: Did you tell anyone?

Sweet: Yes, and it started right away with my graduate school friends and seminary colleagues. After our pastoral calls, we were supposed to write up our experience. But mine was so personal, I just couldn't. So I've made verbal confessions about that day through today.

Whitesel: How does this relate to your experience at the camp meeting?

Sweet: When I was seventeen, I evaluated where I was with God. And it wasn't where I wanted to be. I was living my Christianity through my parents. I had a hand faith with no head and no heart. It is now clear to me that I had to go away in order to come back. That's the definition of *liminality*. Though it looked like I was moving away from God, I was still tracking with God, talking to God, studying God, and I found myself moving closer to God, not farther.

Whitesel: Is there a message in this for others?

Sweet: I hope there is a comforting word here, especially for parents of adolescents. Sometimes people appear to be on a fight-or-flight pattern in their faith. But when people seem hostile and resistant, that's when God is most at work in their life, and we just have to be patient. There is an old saying, "Methinks thou dost protest too much . . ." I love people who are arguing with God the loudest.

Whitesel: Do you regret your upbringing?

Sweet: I really appreciate my religious heritage and celebrate the Holiness tradition today. In fact, I don't live in my heritage but out of it. I appreciate how I was brought up. I even talk to Ruth at least once a month. I have an unresentful, respectful relationship with her. But I had to clear out the toxins.

Whitesel: How would you describe this?

Sweet: It is not so much a process, but something more organic. My faith was planted as a seed by my family. They really wanted to grow a whole plant, but I ripped that out with my de-conversion. What remained planted was a seed. And that seed was watered by the prayers of my parents and the ministries of many preachers and laypeople. I am grateful for the nurturings and waterings of my upbringing. That's why I think of it as organic evangelism—faith is a seed that is planted, nurtured, and fertilized, but it takes time to grow. "God's clock keeps perfect time" was another of my mother's favorite sayings.

ACTIONS THAT HELP WAYPOINT 6 TRAVELERS

ACTION 6.1: THE COST OF DISCIPLESHIP

Oftentimes, Christians are coy, if not deceptive, about the price tag of following Christ. Such practices must end, for to do so is a bait and switch. While the cost of following Christ pales in comparison to the benefits, the cost of discipleship must always be examined.

The Scriptures are filled with examples of those who answered the call and found it rewarding. Hebrews 11, often labeled the "Hall of Faith," lists the faith adventures of Abel, Enoch, Noah, Abraham, Sarah, Isaac, Jacob, Joseph, Moses, and others. The church must carefully explain, examine, and discuss these stories with those new to discipleship. In today's world, there is an increasing interest in biblical stories among unchurched people.[2] And these stories can provide multifaceted illustrations of the costs and rewards of following Christ.

Modern stories can also put the cost of discipleship into perspective. Billy Graham tells that after his conversion at Dr. Ham's revival meeting, he was ridiculed at school. "'I understand we have Preacher Graham with us today,' one of my teachers said to the class some days later," Graham recalled. "Everybody laughed. She was making fun of me, and I felt some resentment. Then I remembered what Dr. Ham had said: When we come to Christ, we're going to suffer persecution."[3] That early encounter with persecution led Graham to make a post-decision evaluation to follow Christ regardless of the cost.

Similar illustrations can be drawn from the lives of others, including German pastor Dietrich Bonhoeffer, who famously penned *The Cost of Discipleship* and *Letters and Papers from Prison* while imprisoned in a Nazi death camp.[4] Bonhoeffer first learned about the cost of discipleship years earlier as he observed how African-American churches reacted with Christ's love, yet dissonance, to North American prejudice. Adam Clayton Powell Sr. was the pastor of Abyssinian Baptist Church in New York City where Bonhoeffer once attended. He was the founder of the National Urban League, an early leader of the NAACP (National Association for the Advancement of Colored People) and an organizer of the Silent Protest Parade of 1928.[5] Bonhoeffer witnessed grace, power, promise, and the cost of discipleship in the African-American church's reaction to prejudice.[6]

> We have stories of those who were . . . homeless, friendless, powerless— the world didn't deserve them!—making their way as best they could on the cruel edges of the world.
>
> —Heb. 11:32–38 (MSG)

Churches today have elaborate assimilation programs that seem more concerned about assimilating persons into the life of the organization than into the cost and rewards of discipleship. Churches must include in these ministries an honest look at the cost of discipleship. Churches can utilize stories such as those of Adam Clayton Powell Sr., Dietrich Bonhoeffer, and biblical champions, to introduce new believers to the rewards and sacrifice of following Christ.

ACTION 6.2: THE REWARD OF DISCIPLESHIP

Though there are costs, there are rewards that outshine the hardship. To foster a balance, these should be addressed as well. The "Hall of Faith" from Hebrews 11 (noted above) concludes with this heartening refrain:

I could go on and on, but I've run out of time. There are so many more— Gideon, Barak, Samson, Jephthah, David, Samuel, the prophets . . . Through acts of faith, they toppled kingdoms, made justice work, took the promises for themselves. They were protected from lions, fires, and sword thrusts, turned disadvantage to advantage, won battles, routed alien armies. Women received their loved ones back from the dead. There were those who, under torture, refused to give in and go free, preferring something better: resurrection. Others braved abuse and whips, and, yes, chains and dungeons. We have stories of those who were stoned, sawed in two, murdered in cold blood; stories of vagrants wandering the earth in animal skins, homeless, friendless, powerless—the world didn't deserve them!—making their way as best they could on the cruel edges of the world.

Not one of these people, even though their lives of faith were exemplary, got their hands on what was promised. God had a better plan for us: that their faith and our faith would come together to make one completed whole, their lives of faith not complete apart from ours. (Heb. 11:32–40 MSG)

Paul reminded the Corinthian church that despite challenges, the benefits ahead can keep travelers moving forward:

So we're not giving up. How could we! Even though on the outside it often looks like things are falling apart on us, on the inside, where God is making new life, not a day goes by without his unfolding grace. These hard times are small potatoes compared to the coming good times, the lavish celebration prepared for us. There's far more here than meets the eye. The things we see now are here today, gone tomorrow. But the things we can't see now will last forever. (2 Cor. 4:16–18 MSG)

Churches are usually adept at extolling the benefits of discipleship, and this should continue. Yet, to help travelers negotiate a post-decision evaluation is to balance both the costs and the rewards of following Christ.

ACTION 6.3: THE ROUTE IS DIFFICULT, BUT THERE IS HELP

When wayfarers have second thoughts about continuing their journey, the church must help them grasp the assistance that God and his people provide. God is an omnipresent help, as the following Scriptures remind us:

- "God is our refuge and strength, an ever-present help in trouble" (Ps. 46:1).
- "Stalwart walks in step with GOD; his path blazed by GOD, he's happy. If he stumbles, he's not down for long; GOD has a grip on his hand" (Ps. 37:23 MSG).
- "He who dwells in the shelter of the Most High will rest in the shadow of the Almighty. I will say of the LORD, 'He is my refuge and my fortress, my God, in whom I trust'" (Ps. 91:1–2).
- "The LORD is near to all who call on him, to all who call on him in truth. He fulfills the desires of those who fear him; he hears their cry and saves them" (Ps. 145:18–19).
- "I have told you these things, so that in me you may have peace. In this world you will have trouble. But take heart! I have overcome the world" (John 16:33).
- "Cast all your anxiety on him because he cares for you" (1 Pet. 5:7).
- "For the eyes of the Lord are on the righteous and his ears are attentive to their prayer" (1 Pet. 3:12).

A community of believers also provides a support network for fellow travelers. In fact, there is a global village of fellow travelers. Some will be at different points on their journey, but all will be on the same trek. Again, the Scriptures extol the power of this companionship:

- "When two of you get together on anything at all on earth and make a prayer of it, my Father in heaven goes into action. And when two or three of you are together because of me, you can be sure that I'll be there" (Matt. 18:19–20 MSG).
- "The body is a unit, though it is made up of many parts; and though all its parts are many, they form one body. So it is with Christ" (1 Cor. 12:12).
- "In this way we are like the various parts of a human body. Each part gets its meaning from the body as a whole, not the other way around. The body we're talking about is Christ's body of chosen people. Each of us finds our meaning and function as a part of his body. But as a chopped-off finger or cut-off toe we wouldn't amount to much, would we? So

since we find ourselves fashioned into all these excellently formed and marvelously functioning parts in Christ's body, let's just go ahead and be what we were made to be, without enviously or pridefully comparing ourselves with each other, or trying to be something we aren't" (Rom. 12:4–6 MSG).

- "They devoted themselves to the apostles' teaching and to the fellowship, to the breaking of bread and to prayer. Everyone was filled with awe, and many wonders and miraculous signs were done by the apostles. All the believers were together and had everything in common. Selling their possessions and goods, they gave to anyone as he had need. Every day they continued to meet together in the temple courts. They broke bread in their homes and ate together with glad and sincere hearts, praising God and enjoying the favor of all the people. And the Lord added to their number daily those who were being saved" (Acts 2:42–47).

ACTION 6.4: THE TRAVELER MUST SIFT TOO

Travelers seem to intuitively know that some things must be left behind. But what exactly? Should friends, places, opinions, and attitudes be forfeited? Or are some of these to be retained?

This task is similar to what missionaries do when they encounter a new culture. Charles Kraft says Christianity is "supra-cultural," meaning it is not a culture, but rather principles and powers that are higher than culture—and thus can permeate all cultures.[7] This means that when new believers look back upon their pre-new-birth travels (Waypoints 16 to 7), they will see things that agree with Christ's good news, and things that run counter to it. To address this predicament, Eddie Gibbs suggests that Christians focus on "sifting a culture," in order to separate out elements that go against the good news from those that support it.[8] We saw back at Waypoint 13 that sifting out the impurities of a culture was a step in translating our good news.

But now the traveler must learn to sift too. At the post-decision evaluation, the traveler must be introduced to cultural sifting, separating out elements of a culture that go against Christ's news from those that do not. For example, some friends and habits may be harmful for the new Christian's growth and might need to be sifted out. However, many other friends and habits will not be detrimental, and they should not be excluded.

People often choose the easy route when it comes to the delicate task of sifting, and just sift out large segments. Christians will say, "You have to leave your friends behind." And yet, this would be an error of simplicity. In fact, some of the new believer's most powerful communication channels will be with friends. God may be opening up opportunities for them to share this fresh experience of new birth. Donald McGavran called these the "bridges of God" and wrote, "again and again I observed that though [new] Christians were surrounded by thousands of fellow citizens, the Christian faith flows best from . . . close friend to close friend."[9] When churches uncritically demand that new converts leave all their friends behind, the Church may be burning bridges that God intends his good news to travel.

"Again and again I observed that though [new] Christians were surrounded by thousands of fellow citizens, the Christian faith flows best from . . . close friend to close friend," states McGavran. When churches uncritically demand that new converts leave all of their friends behind, the Church may be burning bridges that God intends his good news to travel.

We must not be naïve. God gives travelers a set of parameters. The Ten Commandments form the most basic map (Ex. 20:1–21), but so do Ephesians 4 and 1 Thessalonians 5.

ACTION 6.5: PRAYER, PRAYER, AND MORE PRAYER

When assisting travelers, we can be frustrated because we may not understand or relate to their journey. As we saw in the introduction, this is because each wayfarer takes a different route (though the waypoints may be similar). At such times, it is helpful to remember that God is the only true guide for such journeys. But too often his assistance is overlooked or disregarded. Since only God knows the plans he has for us (Jer. 29:11), prayer for the traveler becomes a powerful navigational aid. When travelers are floundering and guides are perplexed, the assistance of the Mapmaker becomes essential.

The Scriptures remind us that God is the Mapmaker. This is important to recognize when encountering the post-decision evaluation. One can only imagine how Ruth must have felt as she shook her head at the thought of losing Len. There is little doubt that Ruth prayed for Len. The following are but a few of the Scriptures addressing God's important part in this journey:

- "'For I know the plans I have for you,' declares the LORD, 'plans to prosper you and not to harm you, plans to give you hope and a future'" (Jer. 29:11).
- "I will not leave you orphaned. I'm coming back. In just a little while the world will no longer see me, but you're going to see me because I am alive and you're about to come alive. At that moment you will know absolutely that I'm in my Father, and you're in me, and I'm in you" (John 14:18 MSG).
- "We plan the way we want to live, but only GOD makes us able to live it" (Prov. 16:9 MSG).
- "First pay attention to me, and then relax. Now you can take it easy— you're in good hands" (Prov. 1:33 MSG).
- "I am the Vine, you are the branches. When you're joined with me and I with you, the relation intimate and organic, the harvest is sure to be abundant. Separated, you can't produce a thing. Anyone who separates from me is deadwood, gathered up and thrown on the bonfire. But if you make yourselves at home with me and my words are at home in you, you can be sure that whatever you ask will be listened to and acted upon. This is how my Father shows who he is—when you produce grapes, when you mature as my disciples" (John 15:5–8 MSG).

QUESTIONS FOR GROUP OR PERSONAL STUDY

1. Did you experience a post-decision evaluation? What was it like? What do you wish had happened? Is there a lesson in this for others?

2. Do you recall a friend, relative, or acquaintance with whom you shared your faith? Where was it? When was it? Were there natural bridges of God (that is, relational connections) involved that helped you communicate your faith? How did they help?

3. Do you recall sharing your faith with a stranger? Compare and contrast this experience with your answer to the question above.

4. Do you know someone who changed, apparently because of a praying loved one? How long was the process before the reversal? What toll did the waiting take on the person being prayed for? What toll did the waiting take on the person who prayed? Is there a lesson in this?

5. Recall a time when you prayed for something only to see it accomplished after a long time. What does this tell you about how God works? And what does this tell you about prayer? What does this tell you about you?

INTEGRATION WITH THE BODY OF CHRIST

I'm a spiritual mutt," begins Tim. "I participated in a lot of churches and youth groups before it all came together." It was during his teen years that Tim's life unraveled. His parents grew apart and eventually divorced. "What had begun as experimentation with sex, drugs, and alcohol quickly grew to a destructive lifestyle. Those things became channels for my anger and pain," recalls Tim. "When a family is in distress, a child sometimes exhibits destructive behavior as a way of coping. That was me. Plus, I've always been intellectually oriented. So I immersed myself in the writing of existentialist thinkers such as Franz Kafka, Albert Camus, and Jean-Paul Sartre." But at the same time, there emerged three people who would have an enormous impact upon Tim's life.

The first was a businessman who volunteered with the parachurch organization Young Life. "He listened to my philosophical questioning without judging me. He took me seriously. He didn't waver in his belief in God, but he didn't put down my ramblings either. I saw him one night when I was drunk at a football game. I don't know what it was inside of me that made me do it, but I walked up to him and asked if I could go to his Bible study. He said sure. But

> We need others. We need others to love and we need to be loved by them. There is no doubt that without it, we too, like the infant left alone, would cease to grow, cease to develop, choose madness and even death.
>
> —Leo F. Buscaglia[1]

when I went, the other guys never showed up. Instead, we spent a lot of time talking philosophy, sharing, studying the Bible, and praying. He had just become part of a church planting effort, and he invited me to church. He picked me up so I could go."

There, Tim met the second person who was going to impact his life. "The pastor was an exceptional communicator. What he said really made sense to me and I started to grow in my faith. I now had a faith environment that engaged me deeply on an intellectual and relational level. I started attending regularly, and in December of that year, I realized this was the family I needed."

The third person who impacted Tim was the youth pastor of a nearby church. "He invited me to help with the youth group," he says. "I guess he saw potential in me, more than I saw in myself. You see, even though I was trying to follow Christ, I had temptations I was still dealing with. When he asked me to help with the youth group, I thought, Wow, I better quit smoking dope if I'm going to help with the youth. And I did.

"So my integration with the body of Christ came by three men in three different ways. The first was the businessman who took me seriously but also was very blunt. He did not ridicule my ideas. He explained rationally about Jesus. He also told me the things I needed to hear, like about boundaries and sins I needed to give up. Second, there was this pastor who engaged me intellectually. What he explained about Jesus was not rooted in emotionalism or the moment. He just made sense. Lastly, there was this fun youth pastor who showed me that ministry was not only fun but worth giving up anything for. I got plugged into this particular faith community. Then, when I got married, I became the first youth pastor of the church. I've been integrated into the body of Christ ever since."

Today, Tim Keel pastors a large organic church in midtown Kansas City called Jacob's Well. "Our name reflects what we are," states Tim. The Website explains that "In the New Testament book of John, Jesus encounters a woman who is at the fringes of her culture, a woman with great hunger and great need. Jesus reaches out to her and invites her into his life and kingdom. In so doing she becomes a part of a new community. In the same way, Jacob's Well is striving to be a place—like the biblical Jacob's well—where people who are searching can encounter God and find a place in his kingdom and community and join him in his work in the world."[2]

WAYPOINT CHARACTERISTICS

SIGNS OF TRAVELERS AT WAYPOINT 5

A Hunger for Integration. Integration is an important word when describing incorporation into the body of Christ. Integration comes from the Latin of *integratus*, which means "to work together to make a whole." When a traveler adds her or his complementary gifts to those of others, the traveler senses that he or she is becoming whole. Integration likewise carries the idea that a whole is comprised of many parts, and thus a traveler's skills, talents, and expertise are needed in the effort. And integration carries the idea that though there are many different contributions, each contributor is still autonomous, and they work (Latin *integer*) together for a common and higher good.

Fear of Control and Cloning. Yet there is fear, and oftentimes rightly so, of tyrannical and oppressive communities and cults. The Church has not escaped such blunders. The evil Borg colony, in the television series *Star Trek the Next Generation*, famously intoned, "Resistance is futile; you will be assimilated." People have been leery of repressive and digestive organizations that suck out individuality and manufacture cloned disciples. Media images of religious sects with similarly dressed adherents foster concern over loss of individuality.

The church should not be a community of doppelgangers, for the Scriptures are filled with colorful and diverse stories of Christ's disciples. Seemingly to underscore this, Matthew recorded that among Jesus' ancestors were not only priests, prophets, and kings; but also foreigners, ordinary laborers, and at least one prostitute (Matt. 1:1–17).

The church must therefore strive to overcome the broad brush of popular depictions and explain to the traveler that though the Christian community will correspondingly rebuff sin, a Christian community will also be made up of different social, economic, ethnic, and affinity cultures.[3] While there will be

163

"one body and one Spirit . . . one Lord, one faith, one baptism; one God and Father of all" (Eph. 4:4–6), there will also be varied styles of music, dress, art, language, and emphasis.

The community of faith must also emphasize the priesthood of all believers, whereby accountability and answerability in a faith community holds sin and manipulation in check. Paul admonished the Corinthians as a community to address and mend division (1 Cor. 1:10–17; 3:1–23), settle disputes (1 Cor. 6:1–11), and root out sexual immorality (1 Cor. 5:1–13; 6:12–20).

ACTIONS THAT HELP WAYPOINT 5 TRAVELERS

ACTION 5.1: DIALOGUE THAT CONNECTS TRAVELER AND COMMUNITY

Just as the businessman listened to Tim's spiritual ramblings without criticizing him, travelers at this waypoint need to work out their understandings of God in a loving environment that permits struggling and questioning. This is not a time to censure, nor even a time for in-depth teaching. In-depth teaching can follow at Waypoint 4: Spiritual Foundations. Instead, at Waypoint 5, the traveler and the faith community must enter a warm and mutually respectful dialogue about the responsibilities, expectations, and foundations of a community of faith.

This is also not the time for authoritarian pronouncements or domineering teaching, for travelers are only beginning their voyage into the finer elements of spiritual principles. The best avenue may thus be the so-called Platonic method of communication. The Greek philosopher Plato was known for fostering engaging dialogues between friends.[4] Felix Marti-Ibanez described Plato's method as "an entirely spontaneous form, not as ponderous treatises but in dramatic dialogues between friends . . . He invented the form to make his concepts intelligible to the layman . . . this first attempt to humanize knowledge was warm, personal, fresh and frequently humorous."[5]

Tim's integration with the body of Christ came through a businessman he describes as "a friend who always entered my world and engaged me intellectually, philosophically, and biblically."[6] This businessman serves as a model for a community of faith that will listen, engage, and accept that though Christ is working, he has not yet been fully formed in the traveler.

ACTION 5.2: THE PURPOSES AND CONNECTIONS OF COMMUNITY

Participation in a Christian community fosters unique interpersonal and supernatural connections. There are four elements to this bonding that must be explored further.

A Community of Faith Fosters a Connection of Personal Responsibility. As his parents' marriage dissolved, Tim, in similar fashion to Len Sweet, now was on his own in connecting with God. When a local youth pastor invited Tim to volunteer with a middle school youth ministry, suddenly the magnitude, responsibility, and expectations of a Christian community were driven home. Tim recognized that some sinful habits he had left unchecked must now be jettisoned if he was to minister to youth. In a community, every person is expected to contribute, and at this juncture, travelers will recognize that they must personally take on responsibility, contribute to the common good, and serve others. Paul, speaking to a divided Corinthian church, extoled the varied and complementary gifts that all believers contribute to this common good, saying,

> The way God designed our bodies is a model for understanding our lives together as a church: every part dependent on every other part, the parts we mention and the parts we don't, the parts we see and the parts we don't. If one part hurts, every other part is involved in the hurt, and in the healing. If one part flourishes, every other part enters into the exuberance. (1 Cor. 12:25–26 MSG)

This is the body of Christ. As can be seen from 1 Corinthians 12:25–26, cited above, the New Testament describes the community of faith in Christ as Christ's body on the earth. This is in fact Paul's most common description for a community of faith in Christ.[7] For Paul, the body metaphor conveyed the organic, interrelated, and living nature of the church.[8]

The body of faith fosters a force for good. It is not recommended that a person be recruited for advanced ministry in order to convict of ongoing sin, but this is how it happened for Tim. In most cases, however, this conviction of wrong actions and attitudes will happen through the Platonic dialogue of Action 5.1. Regardless of how it happens, the outcome should be that a faith community grows in good deeds and thus can do more good together than separately.

A Community of Faith is about Much More than Attending Church. At this juncture, a question often arises: Is attending a worship service the same as joining a faith community? This topic can be volatile, due to a Western predilection for equating worship attendance with communal participation. In answering this question, there are several factors to keep in mind.

Modern worship in a church building is a post-New Testament concept. In the New Testament, teaching and worship often took place in homes, small gatherings, or the synagogue. For the first three centuries, small house churches were where many early Christians received their integration into the body of Christ.[9] The modern worship service and the buildings that house them are not wrong or optional. In fact, I shall argue shortly that the worship encounter is necessary. But those who try to require attendance at worship services in church buildings by citing Hebrews 10:25, should note that this Scripture is not referring to church worship services in church buildings. Rather this verse is referring to fellowship in homes.

Both communal and individual worship are expected by God. Yet the Scriptures tell us that God expects corporate worship to result from the moving of his Holy Spirit (Ps. 50:23; Acts 2:42). The Bible tells us that worship should also be conducted personally (Isa. 57:15; John 4:23–24). Thus, attending a church worship service is a venue that can stimulate both corporate and individual prayer. The worship service thus becomes a multifaceted avenue for connecting with God. The biblical words for worship convey this close connection. The Hebrew word *shachah* comes from combining the Hebrew words for "to honor" and "to bow down" and connotes the idea of lying prostrate directly in front of a monarch in respect, reverence, and adulation.[10] The Greek word for worship, *proskuneo*, similarly conveys the idea of drawing close in submission and humility.[11] God longs for these opportunities to connect intimately with us (Ps. 51:7).

A Community of Faith is Needed for Growth and Maturation. The Scriptures stress that God created humans for socialization and fellowship. God's very action in Genesis was to create human beings for fellowship with him (Gen. 2–3) and between one another (Gen. 1:20–24). The intergenerational mentoring mentioned in Titus 2 and the gifts given for the common good mentioned in 1 Corinthians 12; Romans 12; and Ephesians 4 would be impossible to cultivate without a community of kinship.

This is why the church is far more than attendance at a worship service. From the above, it can be seen that attending church services for teaching, personal/corporate worship, mentoring, and prayer is an important endeavor. But the community of faith is much more than worship attendance. The community of faith is an ongoing community of fellow travelers who undertake life's journey together. They rely upon each other to encounter and overcome detours, barriers, and challenges on their journey of life.

A community of faith fosters acceptance. In the faith community, we eat, minister, learn, and grow side by side. A result is that deeper understandings and appreciations can result. John Perkins, an African-American church leader, recalls an example. In the middle of the racist 1970s, whites would often cry out, "John, I love your soul." Perkins knew that God created humans as both soul and body. The soul is the supernatural personality and the body the physical residence of that soul. Yet what his taunters were saying to Perkins was that they wanted to lead him to Jesus without dealing with his body. Perkins famously retorted, "My soul is in a black body. And if you really want to get to my soul, you're going to have to deal with this body."[12] It is in the midst of a community of faith, service, grace, and learning that such chasms can be spanned. The community of faith thus plays a critical role in fostering tolerance. John Stott said that each person is actually "a body-soul-in-community."[13]

A community of faith also fosters mentoring and answerability. Paul noted that the community of faith fosters intergenerational mentoring and accountability, where the older men and women can share insight with younger people (Titus 2). Today, extended families are often scattered, so, the church must become the venue for generations to intersect.[14] It is in such environments that the lessons of the older congregants can be passed down to younger attendees. St. Thomas' Church of Sheffield, England, created an innovative solution to assist local families who do not have biological families nearby. Once a month the church combines, or clusters, three to five small groups.[15] According to former rector Mike Breen, these clusters "create an extended family feel, like the movie *My Big Fat Greek Wedding*."[16] It is in these clusters (numbering between thirty-five and seventy-five people) that congregants at St. Thomas come together once a month to socialize, serve the needy, and grow in Christ. Clusters thus become extended families for many St. Thomas attendees.

> The church must be honest about her strengths, and because she is populated with imperfect human beings, her weaknesses as well.

A Community of Faith Fosters a Supernatural Connection. As a final note, I cannot emphasize too greatly the supernatural connection that is created by integration into the body of Christ. George Ladd points out that in the New Testament, the church is "a fellowship created by the Holy Spirit" (2 Cor. 13:14).[17] It thus has a supernatural genesis, sanction, and permeation. Ladd sums up that "a bond exists between all who are in Christ that is unique and transcends all other human relationships."[18]

ACTION 5.3: THE IMPERFECT COMMUNITY

Despite the advantages I have described, a Christian community is not perfect. And thus, those seeking the perfect community will be disappointed and usually depart. The Church must become authentically realistic in portraying the community of faith. Too often, aggrandizement and exaggeration are employed when inviting newcomers to become a part of our communities. Somewhere in our fears may lurk the notion that if they knew how we really were, they would not join us. But the result will be that the traveler will feel duped, misled, or worse. The Church must be honest about her strengths, and because she is populated with imperfect human beings, her weaknesses as well.

Though they are caught in a spiritual journey and sense a supernatural pull, many people avoid church today because of poor preaching, unfriendly people, music that is too new or too loud or a host of other reasons. Yet when new attendees begin to recognize that the local church is an evolving entity made up of fallible human beings, then tolerance and forbearance begin to emerge.

ACTION 5.4: THE EXCITEMENT, JOY, AND MODERATION OF SERVICE

The reader may have been taken aback by Tim Keel's revelation that he was still smoking marijuana when asked to volunteer with a youth group. It is not advisable that people who are still struggling with such issues be placed in such important ministries. From my conversations with Tim, it was clear that the youth leader did not know of Tim's struggles. But what is clear is that the youth leader exhibited to Tim the fun, excitement, and fulfillment that comes from communal service.

A lack of this enthusiasm may be why so many children of church leaders do not go into the ministry. In my consulting practice, I frequently interview grown children of church leaders. I often find that the reason they eschew ministry is because they see their parents' lack of enthusiasm for the task and the toll it's taken on their marriages. "It burned out my parents and almost ruined their marriage," remembered one grown pastor's kid. "I don't want that to happen to my marriage," she concluded. Concepts such as the seventh day of rest (the Sabbath, Gen. 2:1–3) and the Year of Jubilee (where debts and slavery would be forgiven, Lev. 25:8–25) underscore the importance of resting and taking a break. If an all-powerful God should undertake a Sabbath, and even command his offspring to follow this example (Ex. 31:15; Deut. 5:15), it becomes important for the community of faith to foster such pauses to renew passion.

INTERVIEW WITH TIM KEEL

Author, artist, and founding pastor of Jacob's Well,
Kansas City, Missouri

Whitesel: You chose the name for your church because, as you say on your Website that Jesus encountered a woman who was at the fringes of her culture, and who was in great need. Jesus reached out to her and invited her into his life and kingdom and she became a part of a new community. Why is it important to emphasize community today?

Keel: Churches today are largely collections of individuals that come together because of shared preferences, not community. They prefer a certain type of worship, or a certain type of preaching, or children's ministry, or youth ministry. Churches have become a sort of church mall with a bunch of different stores. You can go from store to store until you find what you want. And if you find something you like, then you pay for it. People are culturally wired to do that. But it kills our souls, because God created us for relationships. God created us for community.

Whitesel: And building these relationships takes time?

Keel: Right! We are a quick-fix, immediate-gratification society. We want things fast. But community takes time; it doesn't happen quickly. People usually stay in a church three years, and that is usually how long it takes for someone to see your brokenness.

Whitesel: So the Church must provide a safe, secure, honest, and ongoing environment for spiritual growth?

Keel: Yes, the Church in the West has been populated by consumers, always trying to find the best church they can. This was not the New Testament Church. The New Testament Church was based upon reliance and trust . . . not the style of music or preaching offered. We are made in the image of God and that means we are made relationally. The invitation to the gospel is an invitation into a community.

QUESTIONS FOR GROUP OR PERSONAL STUDY

1. How have you experienced the church as the body of Christ? When have you seen the productivity that comes from many people working together, each contributing their unique gifts and talents? Do such actions represent Christ better than a building or organization? How so? What will you do in the next six months to better portray the body of Christ to a watching world?

2. Look up the following Scriptures regarding the body of Christ. What does each tell you?

- Romans 7:4
- 1 Corinthians 10:15–17
- 1 Corinthians 12:26–28
- Ephesians 4:11–13

3. Are there needs in your community that are going unmet but that a team of people might be able to address? Is your church doing enough to address these needs? If not, how can you as a church spend more time serving your neighborhood rather than serving organizational issues?

4. St. Thomas' Church in Sheffield, England, combines three to five small groups into clusters to undertake social service in the community. How do you undertake social service? Is it by small groups, individuals, or something else? How effective have you been? Would you have been more effective if you had combined two to three small groups to tackle a social service project? Should you in the future?[19]

SPIRITUAL FOUNDATIONS

I am an example of all that is good with denominationalism and with Christian families," begins Bil. "I guess I didn't experience the things that turn other people off. For example, I didn't experience the squabbling at a deacon meeting that scares people away. And my parents made sure we went to church. Some people get turned off when visiting a church, but my dad made sure we found a church and attended regularly even if the church didn't seem too friendly at first.

"The reality is that my parents were helpful in the way they modeled Christlike living. It fostered in me a spiritual foundation. You see, my dad never turned it off. He didn't change when he came home from church. He was consistent at church and at home. I would regularly see him praying, reading the Bible, and living out Christian principles. I was just a kid picking this stuff up. That was my spiritual formation, in that small close-knit family."

This spiritual formation began to transform Bil's life in middle school. "We had to move. My sister was in high school and this move really affected her. I remember hearing her cry through the door to her room. She really felt alone. But soon I saw her faith in Jesus turn those tears into joy. I saw her faith in Christ sustain her, and I was touched by how Jesus was real to her. And he became real to me.

> You Christians are so unlike your Christ. The materialism of affluent Christian countries appears to contradict the claims of Jesus Christ that say it's not possible to worship both Mammon [money] and God at the same time.
>
> —MOHANDAS GANDHI[1]

"With these examples, I was an easy win. These are the people who formed spiritual foundations in me. My family lived it in front of me every day, and that is the most important element in spiritual formation. It is authentic, consistent, and faithful living in a tight-knit group."

WAYPOINT CHARACTERISTICS

SIGNS OF TRAVELERS AT WAYPOINT 4

The Seasoned Traveler. Bil was a traveler who had grown up amid a community of faith. In fact, because his military family moved frequently, Bil's family became his most basic and consistent faith community. It was here that Bil grew in his spiritual foundations. Though, in this book, I have interviewed leaders who were hurt, discarded, and even ostracized by the church, I also wanted to point out that this is not always the case, nor should it be. Bil's story is a fitting example of a traveler whose spiritual foundations were fostered in the organic environment of a family with a robust spiritual life. By watching how his dad and sister handled spiritual trials, Bil grew in his spiritual foundations.

Unfortunately, not every traveler is blessed like Bil. But through the use of small groups, the larger faith community can create such environments that foster intimacy and spiritual foundations. Therefore, we will look at actions that help travelers at Waypoint 4, and see how these actions best germinate within the accountability and community of a small group.

The Budding Legalist. Travelers at Waypoint 4 can sometimes be so enamored and captivated by the breadth and helpfulness of the good news that they will inadvertently become legalistic and overbearing with their newfound passion. The good news has so many ramifications and remedies for humankind's impiety that once integrated with the body of Christ in Waypoint 5, travelers can now become overbearing in their insistence that the good news be caught by their friends. The result can be backlash. The community of faith must help the traveler understand that the merit of the good news will emotionally energize, and potentially overwhelm, a new disciple. The faith community must also help them remember that this new understanding was patiently, delicately, and graciously revealed by Jesus over time. To assist in grasping this, a new disciple should be introduced to the concept of waypoints. This will help the disciple recognize that others may be earlier on their quest.

The Clone Maker. If people have a sudden conversion or datable conversion, they will often expect their friends to follow the same exact route. It will be important at this waypoint for the faith community to teach new disciples about scriptural rationale for both progressive and sudden conversion.[2]

ACTIONS THAT HELP WAYPOINT 4 TRAVELERS

Spiritual foundations must begin to be laid at this waypoint, but as we shall see, they will continue to mature, expand, and grow throughout the disciple's life. But at Waypoint 4, it is important to understand some foundational beginnings.

ACTION 4.1: EXAMINING WHO JESUS IS

The gospel of Mark provides a fitting story of how Jesus' disciples came to grasp the spiritual foundations of who Jesus is.[3] Let us look at some foundational understandings, along with selected (but not exhaustive) verses from Mark that illustrate how Jesus revealed each to his disciples.

Jesus Is a Wise Teacher. The disciples met Jesus as a great teacher, with powerful lessons about serving others. Selected verses include Mark 2:13–28; 9:33–37, 41; 10:35–45; 12:28–34. This was and is one of the easiest characteristics for people to grasp about Jesus (note the quote by Mohandas Gandhi that began this chapter). But Jesus is more than a great teacher, as we shall see next.

Jesus Is a Miracle Worker. The Jewish people understood supernatural forces, and Jesus demonstrated that he had power over life-destroying powers and illnesses. Selected verses include Mark 3:1–6; 4:35–41; 5:1–43; 6:30–52; 9:14–29; 10:46–52. At Waypoint 4, wayfarers must begin to grasp that Jesus has power over life-destroying powers of illness, addiction, harmful behaviors, behavioral disorders, and everything else.

Jesus Is God in the Flesh. It was easy in New Testament times and also today, for people to believe that Jesus was just a great teacher. And it is somewhat easy to believe that he accomplished great miracles. But when Jesus said he is the Son of God and God in the flesh, some people then and today take exception. Yet Jesus is clear that he is God in the flesh. It is important for the traveler to thoroughly grasp this spiritual foundation: Jesus is more than a great teacher and a miracle worker, but is also God himself. Selected verses include Mark 1:1–11; 8:27–30, 36–38; 9:1–12; 12:35–37; 13:24–37; 14:62.

Jesus Is the Forgiver, Conqueror of Death, and Giver. Jesus forgives our sins; he conquered death; and he gives us the ultimate solution: eternal life. This is a very concise summary of Jesus' work. Selected verses include Mark 2:9–10, 17; 3:23–29; 10:13–16, 31; 11:25; 14:22–26; 16:1–20.

Jesus Sends out Disciples. Jesus called people to carry his message to others. Selected verses include Mark 1:16–20; 2:13–17; 3:13–19; 6:6–13; 8:34–38; 14:27–31; 16:15–20. These verses summarize Jesus' commissions to his followers.

Jesus Requires Holy Living. Jesus also made it clear that spiritual foundations for his disciples included living a life that modeled godly behavior and holy living. Selected verses include Mark 2:17; 7:1–23; 8:34–38; 9:42–50; 10:1–12, 17–31; 11:15–19; 14:37–38. These Scriptures provide a guide for the remainder of the traveler's journey.

ACTION 4.2: A FOUNDATION OF SPIRITUAL FORMATION

After an understanding of who Jesus is comes the essential formation of a healthy and godly spiritual life. It does not come quickly or overnight. As my colleague Jim Dunn likes to say, "Spiritual formation is a process, not a program. It cannot be packaged in a box, book, seminar or special event."[4] It is a process of becoming more like Jesus in thinking and action.

Four things must be remembered about becoming more like Christ:

1. Becoming more like Christ will continue throughout a follower's life. Travelers with Jesus will never stop growing. Waypoints 3 to 0 remind us of this process. To become more like Jesus every day is an ongoing and unfolding progression.

2. Becoming more like Christ means overcoming sins. Sin corrupts, but "if anyone is in Christ, he is a new creation; the old has gone, the new has come!" (2 Cor. 5:17).

3. Becoming more like Christ is not the same as self-improvement. Self-improvement is often directed at bettering a person's own standing, stature, or competency. But being formed more into the image of Jesus means to be a better server of others, not yourself. Returning to our preferences for Mark's succinctness, we see that Jesus exemplified serving others in Mark 2:13–17; 2:18–28; 9:33–37, 41; 10:35–45; 12:28–34.

4. Becoming more like Christ will have noticeable results (that is, the biblical fruit of the Spirit; Gal. 5:22).

ACTION 4.3: A SPIRITUAL FOUNDATION IS MANY SIDED

Like conversion, forming godly living and action takes place over time and in concurrent stages. Jim Dunn created icons to visually represent how this takes place. The plus symbols emphasize that all of these actions must take place concurrently to yield holy living.

FIGURE 4.1

head   heart   hands   habits   holy living

In Figure 4.1, a new disciple of Jesus grows in intellectual (head) and experiential (heart) understandings at the same time he or she serves others (hands). This is similar to Mike Slaughter's story at Waypoint 15 and Dan Kimball's story at Waypoint 13 about how travelers who were not yet Christians were allowed to participate in some service ministries.

In Figure 4.1, a simultaneous action is the development of daily spiritual disciplines that form habits that promote spiritual growth. Such daily habits are, but not limited to, Bible study, prayer, sharing your faith, meditation,[5] and helping others in need. When head, heart, hands, and habits are being fostered concurrently, the traveler is growing with a holistic and multidimensional foundation.

ACTION 4.4: A SPIRITUAL FOUNDATION IS FOSTERED IN SMALL GROUPS

There is a misperception that small groups are a ministry program comprised of home fellowship groups that meet weeknights for church members. While there are such programs, a small group is really "any small group of three to twelve people formally or informally meeting approximately one or more times a month within the church fellowship network."[6] Thus, small groups may include Sunday school classes, Bible studies, leadership committees, classes of any kind, prayer groups, or praise teams, or any kind of church team (ministry, fellowship, or athletic oriented).

Such small groups are where, like for Bil, most spiritual formation takes place. Dietrich Bonhoeffer once said, "The physical presence of other Christians is a source of incomparable joy and strength to the believer."[7] There are three important aspects of small groups that must be kept in mind.

1. Small groups are the best environment to foster spiritual foundations. Even secular researcher Peter Block says that "the small group is the unit of transformation."[8] This is mirrored in Jesus' ministry where he drew to himself a cadre of twelve disciples to mentor and then send out (Mark 3:14; 6:7).

2. Small groups must balance three elements or they will be unhealthy. My friend Mike Breen wrote a book chronicling the growth of the church he pastored into England's largest Anglican congregation.[9] The key was healthy small groups.[10] To help small groups retain their health, Breen emphasized that every small group must operate in three important areas. And he used the icon of a triangle (Figure 4.2) to help congregants maintain balance among these three important elements of every small group.

FIGURE 4.2

THE TRIANGLE

- UP: every small group must have a worship, Word, and prayer component where it connects upward with God.

- IN: every small group must have an inward component where it builds up each attendee through prayer, encouragement, assistance, scriptural application, and so forth.
- OUT: every small group must be actively involved in reaching out and serving others.[11]

3. Small groups must multiply to include most of your attendees. A lack of enough small groups continues to be one of the two most prevalent weaknesses I observe in churches today.[12] Complete a chart to see if it has enough small groups for the size of its congregation.[13]

ACTION 4.5: IT INCLUDES SUDDEN AND PROGRESSIVE CONVERSION

A solid base of spiritual foundations must include an understanding of both progressive and sudden conversion. As noted above, travelers will tend to assume all others will undergo the same type of conversion that they experienced. On one hand, if travelers have a sudden conversion, they will usually begin to engage their friends, trying to persuade them to undergo the same sudden experience. On the other hand, if the new disciple has gone through a progressive or sacramental conversion, they may scoff at a friend who undergoes a more sudden experience.

In addition, at this waypoint, the new disciple is often an effective communicator of the good news to his or her friends. These natural "bridges of God" over which the good news travels are numerous and wide.[14] But if the new disciple tries to manipulate the process or suggest one route across a bridge is preferable to all others, the disciple may squander his or her affect upon others.

INTERVIEW WITH BIL CORNELIUS

Author and pastor of Bay Area Fellowship, Corpus Christi, Texas

Whitesel: You talked about how your parents modeled and fostered a spiritual foundation in you. What resulted?

Cornelius: It helped me see that living for Jesus was just a natural thing you do. It was not some fake thing you do on Sunday. Christianity should be authentic.

Whitesel: Can you give me an example?

Cornelius: When I was in college, I realized people who need Jesus are not going to be comfortable at most churches. I had joined a church and they asked me to take over an existing Bible study, but I told them I wanted to have a Bible study that the fraternity guys down the hall would want to attend. Because the Bible study was for college students, they let me gear it toward unchurched people like the frat boys down the hall. It was more uncultivated than we could do in church. And it went from fifty attendees to three hundred in three years.

Whitesel: It sounds like you utilized the bridges of God to create an environment that unchurched fraternity members could relate to.

Cornelius: Yes. It dawned on me that church environments were stopping growth because they had become an alien church culture to most people. We sing melodies they don't relate to and use terminology they don't understand. So while in seminary, I went to the church growth movement section in the library. I cataloged each book and decided to read them all by graduation. I devoured the whole section. They formed the basics of my understanding of how a church can foster spiritual foundations and touch people with Christ's love and the good news. It's eleven years and sixty-five hundred people later.

Whitesel: You noted that Bay Area Fellowship is running sixty-five hundred in attendance. How do you ensure that spiritual foundations are emphasized in such a large church?

Cornelius: It doesn't matter the size, the principles are the same. It's done in small groups. My family was my small group. But not everyone has the kind of family I had. Therefore, at Bay Area Fellowship, we get attendees into small groups as fast as we can. These small groups connect with God and his Word, fellowship with each other—and don't forget this: They serve others. You learn a lot about Christ in small groups, but you learn more about being Christ when you are serving.

QUESTIONS FOR GROUP OR PERSONAL STUDY

1. Do you have a small group where you regularly receive encouragement, fellowship, and accountability? Regardless of your answer, list five benefits of such a group. Then answer the following questions:

   - If you do not have a group, do these benefits outweigh the difficulty in finding such a group? What will you do about this?
   - If you do have such a group, what will you do to help multiply such groups so more people can experience this environment? Write one paragraph about how your group could use one of the ideas below for small group multiplication:
     - *Seeding a Small Group.* This means creating a small group by sending out or "seeding," three to four people from your group to begin a new group. The sending group remains intact, except for the three to four members that will start the new group.
     - *Sponsoring a Small Group.* Here, an existing small group prays for and invites people to a new small group. The existing small group does not attend the new small group, but it helps promote, initiate, and support the establishment of a similar small group.
     - *Dividing to Make Two Small Groups.* Sometimes small groups have run their course, and they may need to end. Instead of ending a group, they often can be reconstituted into two small groups.[15]

2. Are your small groups balanced in the three elements of the triangle: UP-IN-OUT? Reread the section on the triangle. Then look at your small groups' monthly activities and fill in the following chart.

   - Time spent in UP (worship, prayer, studying the Word) each month in your small groups: _____ hours.
   - Time spent in IN (community, sharing, fellowship, serving others within the church) each month in your small groups: _____ hours.

- Time spent in OUT (serving others outside of the church) each month in your small groups: _____ hours.

Is there a balance? If not, what will you do to balance each of these important elements of a healthy small group? Write two to three sentences about your plans to balance each area.

3. What did Bil Cornelius mean when he said, "You learn a lot about Christ in small groups, but you learn more about being Christ when you are serving"? Are you learning more about Christ or being Christ? In which area are you deficient? Write four steps that can be accomplished in the next three weeks to correct your weakness in either area.

INNER-LIFE GROWTH

In a small Sunday school class, nestled among the hills of West Virginia, Stan had just given his life to Christ. He was seven years old. He was excited. And he was a little scared. But as sure as he knew he had encountered the living Christ, Stan also knew he was called to be a pastor. As with any adolescent, the full impact of that decision did not come to bear on Stan until years later, in another class.

Evelyn McFarland took great interest in the youth of her Sunday school class. She encouraged each to choose a life verse and suggested they quote it daily. "I was fourteen, and chose Psalm 19:14," recalls Stan. "And every day for the past forty-four years, I've quoted that verse every morning—in fact, it became part of a personal growth pattern." Through this daily discipline, a West Virginia teen began his preparation for ministry.

> Leadership and learning are indispensable to each other.
> —JOHN F. KENNEDY[1]

By age seventeen, Stan was a high school junior and pastoring a small church in Newark, Ohio. "There was a real fright factor in that," he says. "I'd never conducted a funeral, wedding, given Communion, anything. But I learned by doing what I saw others doing." Hands-on learning experiences were now added to his devotional emphasis on Psalm 19:14. "I had to have my devotional life together to survive. I realized right then and there that you not only need hands-on experiences, but you also need a daily devotional and prayer life. Even today, I still meditate on Psalm 19:14, pray the Lord's

Prayer, cup my hands to God, and say 'I can't do this; you've got to help me.' And he does!"

At the age of twenty, Stan was joined on the staff by a twenty-four-year-old college friend named John. Both John and Stan were influenced by a book that suggested balancing both practical and spiritual sides of leadership. "The book was *Spiritual Leadership* by J. Oswald Sanders," Stan recalls. "It changed me because it was so practical and so spiritual at the same time. I learned that spiritual growth needs to be accompanied by learning from the lives of others. I immersed myself in the Bible and in learning from the examples of other Christian leaders. To this day, I read three books a week. Sanders' book created not only a real love for reading in me but also a love for learning about leadership."

Another key experience occurred when Stan, John, and three friends jumped into a beat-up station wagon and headed to Virginia for a leadership conference. Stan remembers that "it was a super-conference, with all the best church leadership minds. It was a defining moment for me, because I realized that you reach out with multiple ministries at the same time. That revolutionized the ministry of John and myself. Six months after that conference, our church had increased to over 275 attendees each week. John and I were fired up, and we've never looked back."

Stan Toler and John Maxwell became nationally known authors and speakers on leadership. "But I never lost what I learned in those early years," says Stan. "I keep a record of every sermon I've preached, and I've now preached over ten thousand. But I've never forgotten what I learned about focusing on Scriptures like Psalm 19:14 way back in Mrs. McFarland's Sunday school class, or about hands-on experiences in that small church in Ohio, or how you can learn from great leaders. I've come to understand that learning is something that requires regular discipline, a heart knowledge—which, for me, is Psalm 19:14—hand-on opportunities to fail and succeed, and an insatiable appetite to learn from leaders who have gone before."

WAYPOINT CHARACTERISTICS

SIGNS OF TRAVELERS AT WAYPOINT 3

The Informal Trainee. Here, a traveler is usually invited, recruited, or sometimes just stumbles into a local ministry. This is hands-on training, and most likely the predominant form of training in the majority of churches. Here, a person learns by watching others, which is sometimes called "imitation modeling."[2] Whether by watching another lead a Sunday school class, greet visitors, visit shut-ins, or help the needy, basic learning occurs through observation, trial, error, and modification. Most churches do this well, at least with long-standing members with sufficient social status in the organization. The strategic key for most churches is to recognize that new travelers can be ready for informal and hands-on training.

The Formal Trainee. A traveler at this stage is also interested in gaining ministry knowledge through a formal process. This process can be via college, seminary, conferences, or seminars. The trainee will often exhibit an insatiable passion for additional learning. Due to such enthusiasm, local church leaders can sometimes become wary, fearing that trainees are not getting what they need from the local church. And sometimes this may be the case. Churches cannot offer expertise in all areas of training. Thus, church leaders must recognize that an appetite for more knowledge is a good thing. Leaders must encourage trainees to further their education even if it means departing the local context.

The Heart Trainee. This is training that takes place within the heart of the person. The development is inward, where the trainee grows in sensitivity to others, reaching out beyond his or her comfort zone, and employs moral decision making. Heart training is nurtured through a biblical understanding of leadership, where scriptural illustrations and standards of leadership emerge. Creeds, doctrines, and dogma have their role, too, at this juncture. But it is primarily the living out of biblical principles in the life of the trainee that is taking place. Challenges are often encountered at this stage as well. J. Robert Clinton describes this waypoint as a place were God is "doing some growth testing."[3]

ACTIONS THAT HELP WAYPOINT 3 TRAVELERS

ACTION 3.1: FOSTER INFORMAL TRAINING

Churches often worry about allowing novices to engage in hands-on ministry too soon, especially those travelers who have just completed Waypoint 4. A common opinion is that travelers need time to "get to know the way we do things here." Yet one of the most prevalent and productive methods to foster leadership is to encourage hands-on training.

Foster Hands-on Training and Expect Failures. Volunteers must be permitted to roll up their sleeves and engage in actual ministry. Jesus exemplified this when he sent out the twelve disciples (Matt. 10:1–42; Mark 6:6–13) along with thirty-six teams of two (Luke 10:1–24). And he knew they were not fully ready for everything they would encounter. Since Jesus is all-knowing (1 Sam. 2:3; 1 Chron. 28:9; John 16:30), he knew his disciples would flounder at times. And Jesus chose not to prevent this. For example, Jesus knew beforehand that the disciples would not be able to cast out the demons they encountered (Matt. 17:16–19). Yet Jesus used this failure to teach them about the additional preparation needed in prayer, faith, and fasting (Matt. 17:20–21; Mark 9:29). Because Jesus let them flounder and fail,

Too often new volunteers are abandoned when previous volunteers think they are now relieved of their duty and free to depart. But nothing could be further from the truth. New volunteers need an extended time to learn the wealth of knowledge that previous leaders have accumulated.

lessons learned would not be forgotten. Therefore, allowing a person to be involved in hands-on ministry, and even to make some initial missteps, can drive home a lesson.

Foster Apprenticeship and Mentoring. In the above biblical story, Jesus did not leave his disciples without advice or follow up. Jesus beckoned his disciples to live with him (Matt. 4:18–20; 8:20), to travel with him (Mark 1:16–20), to watch him as he ministered (Mark 1:29–45), report back to him (Matt. 17:16–19), and to be accountable to him (Mark 6:30; Luke 9:10). This gave his disciples informal learning opportunities—an ingredient that many churches underutilize. Too often new volunteers are abandoned when previous volunteers think they are now relieved of their duty and free to depart. But nothing could be further from the truth. New volunteers need an extended time to learn the wealth of knowledge the previous leaders have accumulated. Returning to our example above, Jesus spent months with his disciples before and after he sent them out. And even then, the disciples' mistakes dogged their mission.

Such training can be fostered by both apprenticeship and mentoring. Apprenticeship is training for a specific task, while mentoring trains a leader in a range of ministries. For example, a newly graduated seminarian might be mentored in preaching, delegation, worship, etc. This would be an example of mentoring, for the seasoned leader works with the novice in a broad range of duties.

MENTORING: THE TWO RULES FOR FOSTERING IT

Organically Link Experienced Leaders and New Leaders. This means the mentors and trainees should have a great deal in common, not just job descriptions. If feasible, leaders of similar backgrounds, cultures, and affinity groups should be linked, because communication and connection is best fostered when social and cultural barriers are minimal. For example, a young assistant pastor might best mentor a youth pastor, rather than requiring the senior pastor to mentor the youth pastor. Though youth pastor and senior pastor are involved in similar pastoral functions, the cultural gaps between a middle-aged senior pastor and a twenty-something youth pastor may be too great.

Communicate Both Ways. The mentoring process must include clear and candid communication that goes back and forth between the mentor and the trainee. If communication is only one way, primarily from the experienced leader downward, the trainee will not be able to question for clarification, indigenize for their local context, or evaluate for improvement. If this occurs, communication will cease and frustration will ensue.

APPRENTICESHIP

Apprenticeship, on the other hand, is a more focused action than mentoring. Apprenticeship means focusing on one specific job. For example, a Sunday school teacher might recruit an apprentice and groom them to be their replacement. To foster apprenticeship, there are also two fundamental rules to follow.

Require Job Descriptions for All Professional and Lay Positions. Job descriptions should include

- The number of hours customarily required each week to adequately undertake these duties;
- The leadership hierarchal structure, that is, to whom the leader reports and those individuals the leader oversees;
- A detailed description of the task, including paragraph-long examples describing exceptional work, adequate work, and unacceptable work;
- A reminder that an updated version of the job description is required to be submitted when a person resigns from a job.

Require a Designated Apprentice for All Jobs. In today's fluid and flexible culture, jobs will change and workers will depart. Thus, for continuity, it is necessary for all leaders to train their replacement, even if the leader does not intend to leave in the foreseeable future. Thus, an apprenticeship strategy should

- Be required throughout an organization, and be acknowledged by those who are being led, as well as by all leaders;
- Allow the apprentice to lead (under the supervision of the leader) at least 25 percent of the time;
- Allow the apprentice to attend and receive the same training as the senior leader.

ACTION 3.2: FOSTER FORMAL TRAINING

Churches over 125 in attendance should create a leadership development and training program.[4] There are three elements that are essential for fostering holistic leadership training.

Element 1: Educate the Mind. Leadership training in a local church often takes place one night a week, with churches offering courses on leadership, volunteerism, management, and so forth. Too often churches confuse leadership training with theological or historical training, neglecting the former and accenting the latter. While good training has elements of each, remember that the trainee is struggling with hands-on application. Thus, a sizable portion of educating the mind should deal with the principles of application. It is also important to host a question and answer time for application clarification.

Element 2: Educate the Hands. The focus of most church leadership training is head knowledge, but this can be inadequate, for hands-on doing is needed too. Remember the story of Len Sweet at Waypoint 6? Len had burgeoning head knowledge about Christianity and Christ, but not until he was forced into a ministry experience did God's power impact his life. Thus, training should not be only about theory or case studies, but it should require the leader to be actively participating in ongoing ministry. And the trainee should be reporting back the results on a regular basis. This forces the trainee to learn in the field as did the twelve disciples and the thirty-six teams of two who reported back to the master the results for clarification, adjustment, and improvement in ministry.

Element 3: Educate the Heart. As will be noted in the next section, educating a heart to be sensitive to God's nudging, guidance, and correction is critical for effective leadership. Research suggests that formal training often results in less spirituality in a trainee's life.[5] Thus, to offset the potential to over emphasize head and hand knowledge, a formal training program should include devotionals, meditation, ministry focus verses, and spiritual formation.

These three elements must also be equally balanced. Due to the urgent nature of ministry, education of the hands can often dominate. At other times, educating the mind can rule. Yet because supernatural intervention is needed in leadership development, it is educating the heart that is most critical to the process. Let us therefore investigate this area more closely.

ACTION 3.3: FOSTER HEART TRAINING

Training the heart involves three additional factors.

Factor 1: Prepare for Failure. The trainee must expect challenges and difficulties, and prepare to meet them with prayer, fasting, mediation, reflection, and persistence. When fallible human beings are involved, some failure becomes normal. As the disciples learned (Matt. 17:16–21), God may use failure as a teaching moment to drive home a lesson for future encounters.

Factor 2: Prepare for Maltreatment. Ministering for a living God involves what Jesus described as a spiritual struggle between good and evil (Matt. 4:1–11). Thus, maltreatment, harassment, and even bullying are not absent in ministry but expected. Heart training must emphasize that maltreatment is to be anticipated, and a traveler must be prepared for it through prayer, fasting, and meditation.

Factor 3: Prepare Biblically. The Scriptures are the font from which illustrations and insights leap. To be effective, a leader must grow in scriptural knowledge as he or she grows in practical knowledge. To ignore or pay little heed to biblical wisdom is to relinquish the leadership journey to becoming success driven, personality driven, or history driven. All three of these drives pale in comparison to Jesus' mandate to be driven by a love of God and his compassion for his creation (Matt. 22:37–40).

INTERVIEW WITH STAN TOLER

Pastor, author of over seventy books, international speaker,
and executive director of the Toler Leadership Center

Whitesel: You seem to have been influenced by three things: heart training via a disciplined devotional and prayer life, hands-on ministry where you learned by trial and error, and learning from and with others. Much of this seems self-directed. Is that true?

Toler: That is exactly it. I learned as a child that you had to have a regular devotional life, a life verse, and a regular time to think about them. From Mrs. McFarland's Sunday school class, I took away an understanding that you have to be disciplined and devoted to learning. No one will do it for you.

Whitesel: In forty-four years of ministry, what has changed?

Toler: I think God uses different tools at different times. There are things that come along for seasons, and then they are less effective. John and I had a transportation ministry to help the poor get a ride to church. Today with gas prices and insurance considerations, you have to change your methodology.

Whitesel: What changes do you see that excite you?

Toler: There are many. We live in an exciting technological world with new ways to communicate the good news faster and better. I have people text-messaging me as I am preaching. I can stay in contact with people better than ever.

Whitesel: What else has changed since you began your ministry?

Toler: Forty-four years ago, we had flannelgraph and a filmstrip projector to teach people. I remember that some churches considered those things controversial. If people can just grasp that God uses different methodology but the message must never change, then I think because of advances in technology, we've got more potential to help people with inner-life growth than ever before. Bob, for ministry opportunity and outreach, we're living in the most exciting days I've seen in my lifetime!

QUESTIONS FOR GROUP OR PERSONAL STUDY

1. Does your church have a training program for volunteers? What are/were its strengths? What are/were its weaknesses? What percentage of your attendees are involved in it? Do you need to resurrect or improve it? If so, describe what an improved training program would look like. Share your results with other leaders for modification, improvements, and feedback.

2. Does your church utilize or have you utilized job descriptions? Are the elements mentioned in this chapter included? Which were missing? Knowing what you know now, how could you reintroduce job descriptions so that they accomplish their task of creating apprenticeships?

3. Do you have stories of leadership mentoring to share? If so, share a story of what happened when mentoring went poorly. Then share what happened when mentoring went well. What did you learn? How would you undertake mentoring differently in the future?

4. How well does your church do the following? Give an example of each and then honestly assess the balance. What must you do to balance these areas of learning? Create four steps toward bringing each into balance.

- Educate the mind
- Educate the hands
- Educate the heart

5. Share a story about how others have helped you foster one of the three types of knowledge below.

- Head knowledge
- Hand knowledge
- Heart knowledge

MINISTRY EMERGENCE

Though not yet three-years-old, Sally climbed onto the piano bench and began pounding out a song. Then she added words, and much to her mother's surprise, Sally began to weave a song describing God's restoration of a destroyed world. "The song's beginning was very ominous," remembers Sally. "The music began dark and sad because humans had done such evil to the world. But then the music turned cheerful, and I played very lightly. I began singing about how God was restoring happiness and joy to the world. I like the word *emergence*," continues Sally, "for from a very young age I had a sense of an emerging divine presence and a special gifting to make him known."

By the time she was a teenager, Sally carried a camera wherever she went. "I wanted to use pictures to tell stories of how God works. I looked for God's divine activity in everyday life. I felt it was through artistic gifts that I was created to share God's message."

Sally's artistic bent shaped her writing as well. In church one Sunday, the worship leader said, "In

> So remember, every picture tells a story, don't it.
>
> —ROD STEWART AND RON WOOD[1]

worship, we should encounter God." So, "I began reporting on what God was doing during worship in my life and in the lives of others. God united my artistic gifts with my writing talents. The result was a book called *Worship Evangelism* about how people are reencountering God through worship. But my journey is really about telling God's story through artistic expression. I want to bring to people a hope in God. And I want to help people see his subtle but obvious presence," Sally reflects.

WAYPOINT CHARACTERISTICS

SIGNS OF TRAVELERS AT WAYPOINT 2

Travelers May Experiment with a Variety of Ministries. At this juncture, travelers may yearn to try their hand at numerous ministries that seasoned travelers may feel are unsuitable for them. But some experimentation—within spiritual, moral, and theological boundaries—must be allowed. This is because travelers must learn to discern the difference between spiritually empowered gifts and those that have their genesis in human aspiration. The importance of personal spiritual confirmation will be explored under Action 2.4.

Travelers May Focus too Narrowly on One Ministry. While some travelers will try many ministry options, others will focus too narrowly, smitten with the first Spirit-empowered ministry they experience. The community of faith must encourage the traveler to see God's diverse matrix of gifts as well as realize that all ministry requires a mixture of gifts. A leader's unique assortment of gifts is what has been called a "gift-mix."[2] This mixture may be received in different proportions and in different strengths. Rarely do Christians have just one gift, for God's creation is customarily a wonderful synthesis of diversity. Sally Morgenthaler most likely has a gift mix of encouragement, artist, and prophecy.[3] These might just be the most noticeable ones, for God's creation is customarily comprised of a splendid array of elements. The community of faith must encourage wayfarers to not just focus on the first gift that emerges in their ministry, but to continue to explore God's endowment for their lives.

ACTIONS THAT HELP WAYPOINT 2 TRAVELERS

At this waypoint, traits, abilities, skills, or behaviors can become supernaturally empowered by the Holy Spirit as manifestations or gifts of the Holy Spirit.[4] It is important to note that these can be understood as gifts or manifestations. Theologian James D. G. Dunn observes that they are gifts because they are given, and manifestations because they attest to the reality of the unseen giver.[5] And according to the Scriptures, these are given to all Christians:[6] "Now to *each one* the manifestation of the Spirit is given for the common good" (1 Cor. 12:7); "But to *each one* of us grace has been given as Christ apportioned it" (Eph. 4:7); "*Each one* should use whatever gift he has received to serve others, faithfully administering God's grace in its various forms" (1 Pet. 4:10, emphases mine).

At this waypoint, the leader now "recognizes that part of God's guidance for ministry comes through establishing ministry priorities by discerning gifts."[7] Discerning or determining a leader's gift-mix can take place through the following four actions.

ACTION 2.1: LEARN ABOUT YOUR GIFTS

The route toward discovering a leader's gift matrix begins with a study of the gifts in the Scriptures. Romans 12; 1 Corinthians 12; and Ephesians 4—along with secondary gift lists in 1 Corinthians 7:13–14; Ephesians 3; and 1 Peter 4—describe approximately twenty-five gifts of the Holy Spirit. Yet because none of the gift lists are complete in themselves, it is reasonable to conclude that there may be other plausible gifts if they can be scripturally verified.[8] Therefore, I have listed an additional gift of "artist" that is not mentioned in the main gifts lists, but which appears to have attestation in Scripture and church history.

Figure 2.1 is an annotated expansion of the list the reader first encountered at Waypoint 11.[9]

FIGURE 2.1		
Gift	**Explanation**	**Scripture**
Administration	Effective planning and organization	1 Cor. 2:28; Acts 6:1–7
Discernment	Distinguish between error and truth	1 Cor. 12:10; Acts 5:1–11
Encouragement	Ability to comfort, console, encourage, and counsel	Rom. 12:8; Heb. 10:25; 1 Tim. 4:13
Evangelism	Building relationships that help travelers move toward a personal relationship with Christ	Luke 19:1–10; 2 Tim. 4:5
Faith	Discerning with extraordinary confidence the will and purposes of God	1 Cor. 12:9; Acts 11:22–24; Heb. 11; Rom. 4:18–21
Giving	Cheerfully giving of resources without remorse	Rom. 12:8; 2 Cor. 8:1–7; 9:2–8; Mark 12:41–44 *continued*

Gift	Explanation	Scripture
Hospitality	Creating comfort and assistance for those in need[10]	1 Pet. 4:9; Rom. 12:9–13; 16:23; Acts 16:14–15; Heb. 13:1–2
Intercession	Passionate, extended, and effective prayer	James 5:14–16; 1 Tim. 2:1–2; Col. 1:9–12; 4:12–13
Knowledge[11]	To discover, accumulate, analyze, and clarify information and ideas that are pertinent to the well-being of a Christian community	1 Cor. 2:14; 12:8; Acts 5:1–11; Col. 2:2–3
Leadership	To cast vision, set goals, and motivate to cooperatively accomplish God's purposes	Luke 9:51; Rom. 12:8; Heb. 13:17
Mercy	To feel authentic empathy and compassion accompanied by action that reflects Christ's love and alleviates suffering	Rom. 12:8; Matt. 25:34–36; Luke 10:30–37
Prophecy[12]	Providing guidance by explaining and proclaiming God's truth	1 Cor. 12:10, 28; Eph. 4:11–14; Rom. 12:6; Acts 21:9–11
Helps	Investing time and talents in others to increase others' effectiveness	1 Cor. 12:28; Rom. 16:1–2; Acts 9:36
Service[13]	A tactical gift that identifies steps and processes in tasks	2 Tim. 1:16–18; Rom. 12:7; Acts 6:1–7
Pastor	Long-term personal responsibility for the welfare of spiritual travelers	Eph. 4:1–14; 1 Tim. 3:1–7; John 10:1–18; 1 Pet. 5:1–3
Teaching	Communicating relevant information that results in learning	1 Cor. 12:28; Eph. 4:11–14; Rom. 12:7; Acts 18:24–28; 20:20–21
Wisdom[14]	To have insight into applying knowledge	1 Cor. 2:1–13; 12:8; Acts 6:3, 10; James 1:5–6, 2 Pet. 3:15–16
Missionary	Using spiritual gifts effectively in a nonindigenous culture	1 Cor. 9:19–21; Acts 8:4; 13:2–3; 22:21; Rom. 10:15
Miracles	To perform compelling acts that are perceived by observers to have altered the ordinary course of nature	1 Cor. 12:10, 28; Acts 9:36–42; 19:11–20; 20:7–12; Rom. 15:18–19; 2 Cor. 12:12
Healing	To serve as human intermediaries through whom it pleases God to restore health	1 Cor. 12:9, 28; Acts 3:1–10; 5:12–16; 9:32–35; 28:7–10
Tongues[15]	Various explanations of this gift include (a) to speak to God in a language the speaker has never learned or (b) to receive and communicate an immediate message of God to his people.[16] Another option is that this can mean an ability to speak a foreign language and convey concepts across cultures.	1 Cor. 12:10, 28; 14:13–19; Acts 2:1–13; 10:44–46; 19:1–7 *continued*

Gift	Explanation	Scripture
Interpretation	To make known a message of one who speaks in tongues[17] or it can mean "those who help build bridges across cultural, generational and language divides"[18]	1 Cor. 12:10, 30; 14:13, 26–28
Voluntary Poverty	To renounce material comfort and luxury to assist others	1 Cor. 13:1–3; Acts 2:44–45; 4:34–37; 2 Cor. 6:10; 8:9
Celibacy	To remain single with joy and not suffer undue sexual temptation	1 Cor. 7:7–8; Matt. 19:10–12
Martyrdom[19]	Ability to undergo suffering for the faith even to death, while displaying an attitude that brings glory to God	1 Cor. 13:3
Below is a gift that is not mentioned directly in the New Testament gift lists, but which is seen at other junctures in the Scriptures and Church history.		
Artist[20]	The ability to communicate God's message via artistic mediums	1 Chron. 5; Pss. 33:3; 42:8; 74:21; 149:1; 150; Col. 3:16; Eph. 5:19

ACTION 2.2: FIND A NEED

The next step is to look for a need that must be filled. The Scriptures say that "to each one the manifestation of the Spirit is given for the common good" (1 Cor. 12:7), so that "each one should use whatever gift he has received to serve others" (1 Pet. 4:10). Since the purpose is "the common good" and to "serve others," areas in need of service become a required starting point. Therefore, the community of faith must help wayfarers begin their discovery process not with the leader, or with the gifts, but with the needs of others that beg to be filled.

ACTION 2.3: TEST YOUR GIFTS

Ray Stedman said, "You discover a spiritual gift just like you discovered your natural talents."[21] Gift discovery often continues with testing various gifts that can meet the needs identified in Action 2.2. There are certainly some gifts that do not lend themselves to experimentation, such as the gift of martyrdom, but for most gifts, researching and testing is a way to discover your gifts.

Since the purpose is "the common good" and to "serve others," areas in need of service become a required starting point. Thus, the community of faith must help wayfarers begin their discovery process not with the leader, or with the gifts, but with the needs of others that beg to be filled.

Still, sometimes a need is so vital that experimentation is not recommended. In such cases, there are spiritual gift questionnaires that can assist a wayfarer. Most of these questionnaires are based upon the work of Richard Houts.[22] Many denominational offices have theologically distinct versions available as well.

However, I have noticed that gift inventories are often given without subsequent follow-up or exploration. Churches often require congregants to take such inventories but do little with the results. Such inventories will only help if they are followed by testing, where under the supervision of a trained mentor, people put their perceived gift into practice.

ACTION 2.4: EXPECT CONFIRMATION

A Supervisor Should Give Confirmation. Because all ministry involves human souls and spiritual destinies, it is critical that all testing be supervised. James Dunn points out that Paul encouraged supervision in Corinth to prevent overindulgence in the more unusual gifts.[23]

The Person Exercising the Gift Should Expect Confirmation. God gives good gifts to his children (Matt. 7:11), and while exercising in giftedness, leaders should sense an anointing in their work. Findley Edge labels this the "eureka" factor because a person senses that "this, really, is what [he or she] had rather do for God than anything else in the world."[24]

The Recipient Should Give Confirmation. Testing should not be done in an autocratic or detached manner, but in close partnership with the recipient. This is called "action research," for it signifies research that is conducted with the active involvement of recipients and their input. Recipients are not guinea pigs, but rather souls formed in God's image. As such, recipients possess valuable feedback for the ministers.

The Community of Faith Should Give Confirmation. When a leader operates with a God-given gifting, one that has been given "for the common good" (1 Cor. 12:7) and "to serve others" (1 Pet. 4:10), then the community of faith should perceive and appreciate that common good as well as the appropriateness of that service.

INTERVIEW WITH SALLY MORGENTHALER

Author, speaker, artist, and innovator

Whitesel: Do you think you have the gift of artist? Or is there another gift you sense working here?

Morgenthaler: Yes, from an early age I felt I had the gift of artist. But I also feel like other gifts are operating too. Maybe I have the gift of encouragement. People have told me I have the ability to counsel and comfort them. Or, it could be a prophetic gift, for I sense that God has created me to explain his truth. It's an emerging mixture, and it's hard to describe.

Whitesel: So you describe the understandings of these giftings as emerging?

Morgenthaler: That's right. I am not conceptually orientated, but more sensory and intuitive. Thus *emergence* is a better term for me, because from a very young age, I had a sense of an emerging divine presence and a special gifting to make God known.

Whitesel: And this divine presence has expressed itself in a mixture of giftings?

Morgenthaler: Yes. I feel God gave me artistic gifts to unite my other giftings. Whether writing a song at the piano, photographing God's world, or writing a book, my purpose has been to encourage people and make God's truth real to them. God has used my art to sort of bind together my gifts into the ministry I have today.

QUESTIONS FOR GROUP OR PERSONAL STUDY

1. Look at the chart of gifts in this chapter. Which gifts to you think you possess? How have you experienced confirmation? Look at the four areas of confirmation and tell if and when you experienced confirmation in each category.

   - A supervisor's confirmation
   - Your inner confirmation

- The recipient's confirmation
- The community of faith's confirmation

2. Choose three of the gifts (from the chart in this chapter) based on someone you know that exemplifies each. What gave you the impression that they possess that gift? Do they know that have the gift? How might they serve as a model for others with this gift?

3. Fill out a Houts Questionnaire (obtain one online, from a denominational source, a book, or a parachurch resource) and answer the following:

- Does it bring your spiritual gifts into focus?
- What about the results surprise you?
- What doesn't surprise you?
- Would taking this questionnaire earlier in your leadership development have proven beneficial?
- Why or why not?

IMPACT EMERGENCE

The pastor was an old, bald dude," remembers Larry. "At least that's what I thought at seventeen-years-old. But there was something different about him that I'd never seen in a pastor before. He was real. He didn't seem like a pastor, he seemed like himself. I didn't know that was possible. Today, we'd say he was authentic. His authenticity rocked my world, changed my view of ministry, and changed the course of my life."

Larry had become a Christian the year before and had faithfully attended a very traditional church. "Nothing about the church resonated with me personally or culturally," recalls Larry. "Though it did seem to make the folks my grandparents' age pretty happy. From the moment I got saved, I knew I'd been called to serve God—but I just knew it wouldn't be as a pastor like I saw in this church because pastors weren't real to me; they seemed more like actors and role players."

It wasn't long afterward that a friend took Larry to a growing church nearby. "The pastor wasn't cool. But he was comfortable in his skin. As I heard him teach and relate to people, I was stunned. It was my first 'authenticity sighting,' and the first time I realized I could be me and still be used of God. I didn't have to conform to cliché images and roles that would fit me as poorly as Saul's armor fit David."

> Seek out that particular mental attribute which makes you feel most deeply and vitally alive, along with which comes the inner voice which says, "This is the real me," and when you have found that attitude, follow it.
>
> —WILLIAM JAMES[1]

That night, Larry sensed God's call to the pastorate. "I never wavered after that. A new vision began to emerge. God still had a lot to clean up in my life, but for the first time, I realized it was sin that he wanted to get rid of, not me."

Today, Larry has the opportunity to mentor pastors across North America. "But there is one thing I always tell them," emphasizes Larry. "And that is to lose themselves in Christ but not to lose themselves in the role of being a pastor. Jesus will use the personality and gifts he gave you. And he didn't slip any in there by mistake. The same thing holds true for growing a church. That same authenticity sighting set me on a course of building the kind of church I'd want to attend rather than photocopying the ministry of another church. After all, it's the only church I'm gifted and prepared to lead."

Today Larry Osborne is a prolific writer, a teaching pastor at a mega-church, and mentor to thousands of pastors and leaders. But he states, "My ministry began with that first authenticity sighting. I saw for the first time that God wanted me to be true to who he had made me to be."

WAYPOINT CHARACTERISTICS

SIGNS OF TRAVELERS AT WAYPOINT 1

Regular People are Leaders Too. Leaders at this waypoint often become increasingly aware they are normal with all the faults, idiosyncrasies, and quirks that come with being human. As leaders negotiate this waypoint, they become increasingly approachable as well as honest about their shortcomings. For example, at the height of the controversy over Rick Warren's participation at the inauguration of President Barak Obama, Warren was interviewed by NBC's Ann Curry. During their dialogue about whether homosexuality is determined by biology or experience, Warren replied, "Well, just because it seems natural doesn't mean it's best for you or society. I'm naturally inclined to have sex with every beautiful woman I see. But that doesn't mean it's the right thing to do . . . I think that's part of maturity. I think it's part of delayed gratification. I think it's part of character."[2] The question noticeably took aback his interviewer, but such candor has led to Warren's influence. Leadership researcher

Michael Kernis describes authenticity as an "unobstructed operation of one's true, or core, self in one's daily enterprise."[3]

They Lead the Kind of Ministry They Would Want to Join. Emerging leaders at Waypoint 1 see ministry as natural, enjoyable, and influential. They feel ministry is not something they are required to do, but something they are fortunate to do. They take pleasure in ministry because they are doing what they enjoy. And their sense of enjoyment inspires others to join them. Thus, they do not clone ministry or try to imitate others, for they are true to themselves; and any ministry they lead must be a ministry they take pleasure in doing. As they seek to become more like Christ, they cultivate ministry based upon what seems organic and natural to them. They break with tradition, but not theology, to foster ministry that is more updated, relevant, and satisfying.

ACTIONS THAT HELP WAYPOINT 1 TRAVELERS

A route to authentic leadership in a four-lane world. Too often emerging leaders think they must emulate or copy a successful leader. Yet this ignores the wonderful complexity and diversity of God's creation. God has created an amazing array of diverse personalities, experiences, and environments. Therefore, Waypoint 1 travelers must resist the prefabricated, four-lane highway laid before them by others, and opt for an indigenous and authentic route to leadership that is comprised of six actions.[4]

ACTION 1.1: AUTHENTIC LEADERSHIP IS BASED ON DISCOVERING STRATEGIC, TACTICAL, AND OPERATIONAL TRAITS

Traits are personality qualities that each person is born with or develops. Northouse states, "All of us are born with a wide array of unique traits and many of these traits can have a positive impact on leadership. It also may be possible to modify or change some traits."[5] Traits are thus part of each person's unique personality and history. There are many ways to describe leadership traits,[6] but the three most inclusive and helpful are strategic, tactical, and operational leadership traits.[7]

Strategic traits are found in big-picture people who often see the future better than they see the present. Labeled *strategic leaders*, they are motivated by vision and tend to be the senior leaders in our churches. Speaking from the perspective of a strategic thinker, Theodore Hesburgh, the president emeritus of the University of Notre Dame, said, "The very essence of leadership is that you have to have vision. You can't blow an uncertain trumpet."[8] While this is true, the trumpet sound will do little to rally the troops if the vision has not been organized by tactical leaders.

Tactical leaders complement strategic leaders because they're skilled in the art of organizing, allocation, analysis, planning, evaluation, and adjustment. Tactical leaders wait for the strategic leaders to set the direction via a vision; then they go to work, making step-by-step plans

> A strategic leader's dreams are brought about by the tactical leader's goals and deadlines.

to bring about this vision. Unfortunately, tactical leaders are often missing in our churches because their work with numbers and analysis is sometimes seen as detached or profane. But they are the critical link for bringing about realistic, supportable, and measurable plans. Diana Scharf Hunt, speaking as a tactical leader, famously intoned, "Goals are dreams with deadlines."[9] Another way to say this is that "a strategic leader's dreams are brought about by the tactical leader's goals and deadlines."

Operational leaders lead skilled teams and small groups on critical assignments. And they lead through the close relationships they develop. Typically leading a small group of individuals, they "have an immediate, urgent, and vital task to perform. They may not see where their efforts fit into the bigger picture, but they are the masters of relational leadership."[10] Operational leaders are the most numerous leaders in our churches. They lead Bible studies, teach Sunday school classes, head up committees, host small gatherings, lead worship teams, and organize ushers. They lead through relationships.

To summarize, strategic leaders lead by vision; tactical leaders lead by planning; and operational leaders lead by relationship. Which are needed? All three! Therefore, authentic leaders today do not try to copy someone else's traits. They know they're unique and that strategic, tactical, and operational leaders complement one another.

ACTION 1.2: AUTHENTIC LEADERSHIP IS BASED ON DISCOVERING THE ABILITIES YOU ENJOY AND THOSE YOU DON'T

A leadership ability is a proficiency, learned from experience, that a leader enjoys doing. If traits are what you naturally do, then abilities are what you enjoy doing. Authentic leadership is based upon a leader finding a job where he or she can do enjoyable things. Osborne credits the growth of the church he leads to staying true to his ability to enjoy being flexible and diverse. As a result, his church hosts multiple worship services at multiple times and locations. This dispersion of worship venues is true to his leadership ability for variety, convenience, and localization. Osborne has developed a leadership style and system that is natural, genuine, and appreciated.

A variety of experiences, both good and bad, makes leaders who he or she become. Fred Luthans and Bruce Avolio say that authentic leadership development (ALD) "is essentially something that happens both across one's life span and in unexpected negative or positive moments. These critical ALD moments may occur in any setting or circumstance. Moments that matter for ALD may happen while growing up, at social gatherings, at work, in the gym, on a bike trail, or in a church, temple, or mosque."[11] Thus, authentic leaders expect a variety of experiences through which they recognize they are good at some things and not so good at other things. Authentic leaders do not try to copy or fabricate something that is not authentic for them. Instead, they stick with things they have discovered that they do well, and they work in teams with those who complement their abilities.

> Authentic leaders do not try to copy or fabricate something that is not authentic for them. Instead, they stick with things they do well and work in teams of people who complement their abilities.

ACTION 1.3: AUTHENTIC LEADERSHIP IS BASED ON DEVELOPING SKILLS AND TEAM LEADERSHIP

Skills are specific and precise competencies for undertaking a task.[12] A skill may be casting a vision, developing a budget, organizing a team, or playing a musical instrument. Skills can be learned, but the best skills are those that are based upon traits (what you naturally do) and abilities (what you enjoy doing).

Authentic leaders recognize they have certain skills, but surround themselves with those who have skills that complement theirs. If leaders have little interest in creating budgets or fiscal planning, then they will surround themselves with those who have such skills. Thus, the authentic leader recognizes that authentic leadership is based upon teamwork and partnership. Authentic leaders recognize that they do not have all the skills needed for a task, and thus they industriously build teams to create the collage of skills necessary for a complex task. In fact, research has shown that this is a hallmark of authentic leadership, for such a leader "gives priority to developing associates to be leaders. The authentic leader is true to him/herself and the exhibited behavior positively transforms or develops associates into leaders themselves."[13]

ACTION 1.4: AUTHENTIC LEADERSHIP IS BASED ON HONESTY ABOUT WEAKNESSES

Authentic leadership recognizes that all people, including leaders, are in the process of becoming more Christlike, but they're not there yet. Therefore, authentic leaders exhibit the following behaviors.

Understands Trait Weaknesses. Oftentimes leaders may have been born with certain traits that make them insecure, overconfident, jealous, angry, or a host of other characteristics. For example, insecurity may result in a leader not delegating authority for fear of an insurrection. One pastor told me, "It is hard to give others too much responsibility. If I do, they could replace me." Again, authentic leaders understand their inherent shortcomings and surround themselves with those who can provide support and accountability.

Moral and Ethical in Behavior. Researchers have found that authentic leaders have a high ethical standard to which they hold themselves.[14] For example, I have a personal standard to not ride alone in a car with a female passenger who is not my wife or one of my daughters. Once, while in Pensacola, Florida, I was unable to rent a car due to my expired driver's license. Unknown to me, the pastor sent his female secretary to pick me up. I explained to her my personal guidelines, and she graciously drove back to the church so that the male pastor could return to pick me up. While such guidelines are not required by my university, I do so to set an ethical benchmark. Such actions, higher than required, are often undertaken by leaders because of their desire to acknowledge the invasive and pervasive power of temptation. In addition, authentic leaders recognize if they have a moral weakness, and are not coy or secretive about it. Still, they do not wear their weakness on their sleeve as a badge of shame or pity. Instead, they acknowledge their areas of weaknesses to spouses, pastors, and accountability parties. Through openness and honesty, authentic leaders create a team to help them avoid moral and ethical failures.

Rise above Physical Weaknesses. Scott Schmieding is a cancer survivor who pastors a growing church in Baton Rouge. Several years ago, Scott was diagnosed with tongue cancer. Eventually losing his tongue, he writes how faith helped him muster the physical and emotional strength to take on cancer.[15] Though his vocal cords were damaged by the surgery, and his new "tongue" consisted of repurposed abdominal muscle, Scott learned to speak again and returned to preaching—even though he was told his speech would be distracting and difficult to understand. Though his enunciation is affected, his listeners have become accustomed to his articulation. Scott saw the loss of his ability to speak as a setback to preaching ministry. But he also knew his fight would "be a spiritual help to those experiencing the ups and downs of cancer—that it will feed peoples' faith to help them fight the disease." The authentic leader sees physical weakness as another obstruction on the journey that will be met and surmounted with God's help.

Through prayer, support, discipline, accountability, and even avoidance, authentic leaders surround themselves with help to ensure they will not fail.

ACTION 1.5: AUTHENTIC LEADERSHIP IS BASED ON REGULAR EVALUATION

Authentic leaders do not shy away from evaluation; they relish it. They regularly ask others to give them input and advice.[16] Luthans and Avolio tell the story of Dr. Martin Luther King, Jr., who, in response to the Birmingham bombings, "went to the privacy of a bedroom and summoned a diversity of opinions—from a Jew, a white person, an elderly person, a woman, and a close male confidant, more or less in that order. This moment symbolized . . . Dr. King's constant attention to getting a diverse input from everyone and building a broad coalition of supporters, regardless of race, religion, age or gender."[17]

This moment symbolized . . . Dr. King's constant attention to getting a diverse input from everyone and building a broad coalition of supporters, regardless of race, religion, age or gender.

Larry Osborne said, "Leaders get isolated. I call it being sucked into the middle of the organization and away from the people on the edges . . . I try to rub shoulders with people on the fringe by being accessible . . . And on weekends I walk around among our thirteen worship venues. That way I can see for myself what's happening, plus I learn a great deal by talking to people in the corridors and halls."[18] Larry also reads every prayer request card and every suggestion card filled out at Sunday services. "I see each comment or prayer request with my own eyes. I handle it. I touch it. We're too large for me to know everyone, but with these 'fast feedback loops' I can get to know the needs of people on the fringe, not just the middle."[19]

ACTION 1.6: AUTHENTIC LEADERSHIP IS BASED ON COMPANIONSHIP FOR THE JOURNEY

In Osborne's story, we see that authentic leaders can inspire other leaders to be themselves. Subsequently, following an authentic leader is uncomplicated, for the leader's route is predictable. Leadership researchers Chan, Hannah, and Gardner state, "When followers are able to accurately infer that their leader is authentic, their working relationship with the leader becomes more manageable. Because leaders who are true to themselves are predictable, followers spend less time and energy trying to anticipate what such leaders' next moves will be."[20]

Thus, authentic leaders are often accompanied by a cadre of followers who have willingly and cheerfully joined them on the trek. These followers are not spiritual androids devoid of sense or judgment. Rather, they are companions and equals on the journey, inspired by the honesty, organic traits, abilities, skills, and challenges of one another. Such personal integrity, honesty, and truthful relationships "lead to unconditional trust on the part of their followers."[21]

INTERVIEW WITH LARRY OSBORNE

Author, mentor, and teaching pastor of North Coast Church with four campuses and twenty-three worship venues

Whitesel: You were uncomfortable with a formulaic image of church pastors being too slick, too professional, too caught up in imitating someone else, but you had embarked on this journey with Jesus Christ. How do you explain that?

Osborne: The Church is still his bride even though she may not be very good looking at times. Back then, many churches were embracing culture more than the Bible. And the pastors I knew seemed to have a handshake that was a little too warm and a hug that was a little too long. But despite that, I knew I needed to go to church. So I did.

Whitesel: You said that an "authenticity sighting" helped you overcome this cultural barrier and launched you into ministry. Can you explain this?

Osborne: Authenticity simply means you are genuine. For me, an authenticity sighting is seeing someone who is real, not polished or slick. That old, bald pastor was the first pastor I'd ever seen who fit the bill. All the others acted like pastors, if you know what I mean. And that certainly wasn't me. I didn't want any part of that.

> The church is still his bride even though she may not be very good looking at times.

Whitesel: Was this authenticity sighting a waypoint in your ministry?

Osborne: It's been the GPS for my ministry. It has guided me since. It helps me remember that it's God who decides if anyone comes to my church. All I can control is my obedience, faithfulness, and authenticity. Crowds, if there are any, are his job. And I tell you, that takes all the pressure of ministry off.

Whitesel: Could people misinterpret this, thinking that you are saying people don't need to repent or turn from their sins?

Osborne: Oh, I hope not. We obviously still have to grow in our character, faithfulness, and obedience, but we can do that and still be who we are. Too often, we think we have to have a certain type of personality, drive or to be a pastor. Faithfulness and obedience called for huge changes in my life, but I didn't have to change who I am.

Whitesel: Is North Coast Church an authenticity sighting for people today?

Osborne: I sure hope so. I will tell you this: every pastor who makes a mark and virtually every pastor who helps shape the future is someone who broke the traditions and paradigms of what the church should look like. They all did things to reach people that the church was not accustomed to doing. I'm not talking about doing sinful things. I'm talking about using methods that the church was hesitant to embrace. For instance, when we embraced video venues where the worship is live but the sermon is broadcast via live video feed, people said, "You can't do that!" Yet we did, and God used it to bring many people to the Lord. In fact, every creative thing we've done has been out of the ordinary. That's what has made it creative. We didn't violate God's good news, but we were true to ourselves rather than the stereotype images of what a church should be and do.

Whitesel: Is there a last thought you want to pass along to pastors?

Osborne: Yes, I always tell pastors to pastor the church you would want to attend. It is the only church you will enjoy pastoring. And it's the only church you will pastor well.

QUESTIONS FOR GROUP OR PERSONAL STUDY

1. When have you had an "authenticity sighting" where you observed someone doing ministry so naturally that it impacted you? In what ways did it change you? And are you as authentic today or has some of that authenticity deteriorated?

2. What does your ideal ministry look like (one you would want to join)? Describe this ministry in three paragraphs. In the first paragraph, describe the ministry context (location, culture, etc.). In the second paragraph, describe the leadership team that would lead this ministry. In the third paragraph, describe the impact this ministry would have and upon whom.

3. Are you a strategic, tactical, or operational leader? Reread Action 18.1. Analyze yourself and your leadership team through the lens of these three traits. Is there a balance? Which leadership traits are missing or under-represented in the leadership team?[22]

4. How honest are you about your shortcomings, weaknesses, and temptations? Without being gratuitous or shocking, answer honestly: Are there shortcomings, weaknesses, and temptations that you would like friends or colleagues to help you overcome?

5. How often and honestly do you get input from others about your leadership? List four examples in the past two weeks. Are these examples sufficient? Do you need more or fewer such evaluative experiences?

6. Do coworkers and volunteers feel you are true to yourself and predictable? Ask five coworkers or volunteers for their candid opinions and write a paragraph on each person's evaluation. Write a final paragraph regarding a plan to become more predictable in your leadership.

CONVERGENCE

Tony was eighteen, and though he didn't feel qualified, the impassioned plea of his pastor led him to volunteer to teach a junior high Sunday school class. "To paraphrase what others have said, 'Some come to their calling through grace, some via a slow process, but I had my calling thrust upon me,'" recalls Tony. "I didn't really come to a point where I said, 'This is what I should be doing.' But situations developed that required me to experiment with my gifts. And the gifts I was good at, I stuck with."

Tony always had an intellectual bent, and soon found himself teaching at an Ivy League school. And similar to his experience as a teenager, Tony's gifts opened doors he had not imagined. "I was teaching sociology at the University of Pennsylvania, and I developed a style of dialogue

> This is the true joy in life—being used for a purpose recognized by yourself as a mighty one; the being thoroughly worn out before you are thrown on the scrap heap; the being a force of Nature instead of a feverish, selfish little clod of ailments and grievances complaining that the world will not devote itself to making you happy.
>
> —George Bernard Shaw[1]

with my secular students that made them very receptive to Jesus. It was in that context that I realized I had a gift to teach apologetics." Tony's skill to frame difficult concepts in easy to digest intellectual morsels has been called "organic intellectualism."[2]

"It was that ability that opened doors for me to speak. I didn't look for these opportunities. They came to me. So I prayed and accepted many."

Books soon followed. "I fell into these roles. And if I did them well, I stuck with them."

Yet the purpose of Tony's giftings did not come into focus until a trip to the Dominican Republic. "It was one of the most heart-wrenching experiences I've had," recalls Tony. "I was standing on the edge of a grass landing strip near a small village, waiting for a small plane to pick me up and take me back to the city. I was there to oversee the work my students were doing in meeting the very desperate needs of the villagers. I was looking at the sky to spot the Piper Cub, and a woman came to me holding a little child. The child's stomach was swollen because of worms and malnutrition. The child's hair was rust color from malnutrition. It was evident the child was near death.

"To my amazement, she thrust the child at me and said, 'Take my baby! Don't let my baby die! If you take my baby, he will live. But if he stays here, he will die!' I tried to explain why I couldn't take her baby, but she kept begging. I was relieved when the plane landed, but she followed me to the plane. I ran to it, climbed into the cockpit, and closed the Plexiglas door. She ran to the side of the plane, banging on the door and banging on the fuselage. Over the roar of the engine, I could hear her pleading, 'Take my baby. Please, take my baby!' Gradually the plane pulled away from her and then took off. I was shaken, and halfway back to the capital city, I heard Jesus saying to me, 'I was hungry and you gave me nothing to eat, I was thirsty and you gave me nothing to drink, I needed clothes and you did not clothe me, I was sick and in prison and you did not look after me . . . I was that child, and you did not take me in.'

"Should I have done something? I should have addressed that need somehow! From that moment on, I resolved to never fly away from people in need if I could help. That changed the focus of my gifts. I went from being primarily a speaker and writer to being someone who would use his gifts to stimulate people to respond to the needs of the poor and the oppressed." Somewhere in the air over the Dominican Republic, Tony found the focus of his gifts. Today, Tony Campolo challenges millions of people all over the world to respond to God's love by combining personal discipleship, evangelism, and social justice.

WAYPOINT CHARACTERISTICS

SIGNS OF TRAVELERS AT WAYPOINT 0[3]

Ministry Is Maximized.[4] Because leaders are working from their gifts and strengths and not from areas in which they are not gifted, ministry is maximized. And the recognition of this maximized ministry gains widespread attention. Yet the key for the leader is that his or her gifts are focused. Consequently, leaders are often very vocal about staying with the gifts they are given and not moving into other areas where they do not have gifts, despite their allure. The leader then maximizes effectiveness because God-given gifts and not fluctuating opportunities form the basis for their ministry.

Wayfarers Recognize that God Is the Navigator, but Marvel that God Chose Them. Tony Campolo's life highlights the importance of the unexpected blessings that can occur from teen years onward. Leaders who reach convergence recognize these divine occasions are the result of God's grace, generosity, and benevolence. Subsequently, leaders entering convergence often feel humble, fortunate, and a bit bewildered by God's liberality.

Being and Spiritual Authority Form the True Power Base for Mature Ministry.[5] Though leaders who reach this waypoint are usually afforded opportunities they did not expect, true Waypoint 0 leaders react with modesty, trustworthiness, and faithfulness. They guard their reputation, their focus, and their authority. It is not surprising that such leaders understand that they possess only some of the gifts needed for leadership. So they surround themselves with leaders who possess complementary gifts and are good at raising up such leaders whom insecure leaders might regard as competition. Though maximization of ministry usually results in growth of reputation, distinction, and authority, the leader at convergence accepts these with humility and fidelity.

ACTIONS THAT HELP WAYPOINT 0 TRAVELERS

ACTION 0.1: FREE FROM GIFTS YOU DO NOT POSSESS

First of all, the faith community must overcome the pastor-must-do-it-all mindset. The church as a community must not shirk her responsibility as the agency through which the world will be served. The pastor, despite all of his or her gifts, does not possess all the gifts required for the healthy ministry of a church. Paul reminded the Corinthian church of this: "Each person is given something to do that shows who God is: Everyone gets in on it, everyone benefits. All kinds of things are handed out by the Spirit, and to all kinds of people!" (1 Cor. 12:7 MSG). And Peter said, "Each one should use whatever gift he has received to serve others, faithfully administering God's grace in its various forms" (1 Pet. 4:10).

The world will be hopelessly underserved if only professional leaders do the serving. Jesus repeatedly delegated his authority to ordinary disciples, sending them out with instructions to carry his ministry into the needy communities.

- Delegating to the Twelve. "Jesus now called the Twelve and gave them authority and power to deal with all the demons and cure diseases. He commissioned them to preach the news of God's kingdom and heal the sick. He said, 'Don't load yourselves up with equipment. Keep it simple; you are the equipment. And no luxury inns—get a modest place and be content there until you leave. If you're not welcomed, leave town. Don't make a scene. Shrug your shoulders and move on.' Commissioned, they left. They traveled from town to town telling the latest news of God, the Message, and curing people everywhere they went" (Luke 9:1–6 MSG).
- Delegating to the thirty-six teams of two (see Luke 10:1–24). Jesus "sent them ahead of him in pairs to every town and place where he intended to go. He gave them this charge: 'What a huge harvest! And how few the harvest hands. So on your knees; ask the God of the Harvest to send harvest hands. On your way! But be careful—this is hazardous work . . . The one who listens to you, listens to me. The one who rejects you, rejects me. And rejecting me is the same as rejecting God, who sent me'" (Luke 10:1–16 MSG).

- Delegating to all followers. "God authorized and commanded me to commission you: Go out and train everyone you meet, far and near, in this way of life, marking them by baptism in the threefold name: Father, Son, and Holy Spirit. Then instruct them in the practice of all I have commanded you. I'll be with you as you do this, day after day after day, right up to the end of the age" (Matt. 28:19 MSG).

ACTION 0.2: FREE TO GIVE YOUR BEST

Leaders Discover the Focus of Their Gifts. Clinton says at this waypoint that the leader "ministers out of what they are."[6] Leadership is organic, rising from the unique gift-mix of the individual, coupled with the authority they have been given, as well as the focus of their ministry. Tony Campolo, by his own admission, is "a person who runs in super-high gear." But he doesn't use that energy to run in different directions. He could easily be producing scholarly apologetic books in addition to motivating Christians to serve the needy. But the experience in the plane above the Dominican Republic galvanized Tony's many gifts into a single-minded focus. Leaders at the convergence waypoint recognize their gifts can take them in many directions, but they also recognize that God desires to unite these gifts toward a single purpose or focus.

Leaders Stay Focused on Scriptural Ideals. With success can come an inordinate dependence on human-derived insight. And while humans can reflect godly principles, for the converging leader, the Scriptures provide an ongoing foundation of reflection, meditation, and inspiration. The situation is similar to the one Timothy experienced as the young leader of a growing and contentious church. Paul stressed that Timothy must refocus his ministry on the gifts he had received, and in doing so, Paul reminded Timothy of the foundational role of Scripture:

But don't let it faze you. Stick with what you learned and believed, sure of the integrity of your teachers—why, you took in the sacred Scriptures with your mother's milk! There's nothing like the written Word of God for showing you the way to salvation through faith in Christ Jesus. Every part of Scripture is God-breathed and useful one way or another—showing us truth, exposing our rebellion, correcting our mistakes, training us to live God's way. Through the Word we are put together and shaped up for the tasks God has for us. (2 Tim. 3:14–17 MSG)

Leaders Model an Organic and Progressive Leadership Experience. Finally, the converging leader recognizes that varied experiences, failures, gifts, colleagues, and undeserved opportunities have led them to where they are. They do not take credit themselves, for not only have they been blessed, but they have stumbled as well. I made many mistakes in my early years of ministry, even being blamed for some I did not make. But these learning experiences, both those that were deserved and those that were unjustified, equipped me to be a better trainer of pastors. My journey (the good, the bad, and the groundless) has shaped my understanding of and advice to young pastors today. After twenty years of ministry, time has been an advocate and defender. But all of my experiences have added knowledge and leadership to my journey.

INTERVIEW WITH TONY CAMPOLO
Speaker, author, sociologist, pastor, and social activist

Whitesel: Tony, you talk about how your focus changed aboard that airplane. Can you describe the new focus?

Campolo: Bob, I can explain that focus by telling you what I want on my gravestone. When they drop me in the hole and throw the dirt on my face, I hope my gravestone will read: "There were two hundred young men and women who committed themselves to serving the poor in the name of Christ, because of Tony's ministry."

Whitesel: What changed?

Campolo: My preaching, my teaching, my writing—they all changed. I cannot do any of that today without pleading with people to meet the needs of the poor, the ill, and the oppressed. My books took on more of a missiological tone calling people to commit their lives to missionary service. I'm seventy-five now. I was forty then, halfway through life. I am thankful that Christ allowed me to discover the focus for my gifts at that midpoint. It's amazing what can happen when your gifts become focused.

Whitesel: How has your thinking changed about your gifts?

Campolo: I've learned two things. First, stick with just the gifts you were given. Second, I also learned that you have to discover God's focus for those gifts. Because of that experience in the Dominican Republic, my focus shifted from being a scholarly apologist to being a pleader on behalf of Christ for Christians to meet the needs of the poor and oppressed. It's part of the evangelism process. And it's my part.

QUESTIONS FOR GROUP OR PERSONAL STUDY

1. Are you running in many different directions with your gifts? Complete the questionnaire (Figure 0.1) on the next page to help you track any emerging convergence of your spiritual gifts and your ministry. Discuss the results with two friends.

2. Do you surround yourself with leaders who complement and offset your gifts by bringing new perspectives or ideas you have not considered? Or do most of your leaders mirror your thoughts and perspectives? After you have answered these questions, ask two friends who are outside of your leadership circle these same two questions. What insights did you gain? And what will you do about them?

3. What lessons have you learned from your failures? Are they more or less helpful with your mentoring of other leaders? (There is no right answer here.) Do you often want to shirk from discussing the lessons learned from failures because they are embarrassing? Is this good or bad? And how will you help others avoid your leadership failures?

FIGURE 0.1

Are You Converging? (Circle the answers that best describe your feelings.)		
	Unfocused Spiritual Gifts	**Focused Spiritual Gifts**
At the end of the day:	You feel tired and worn out.	You feel tired, but it is a good tired. You feel you have used the gifts you enjoy and that you made a positive impact.
Understanding of your spiritual gifts:	You do not see clearly how your various spiritual gifts complement one another.	You see that your spiritual gifts form a complementary matrix where each one builds upon the other.
Your coworkers and friends:	They rely upon you to get things done. You have to constantly take the initiative.	They complement you, having strengths where you have weaknesses. You form with other leaders an inter-reliant team.
Serving Jesus:	It is something that must be done, and you labor at doing it.	It is a joy and a blessing. You feel tired but more so, inspired.
The needy and oppressed:	Their situation is the result of a fallen world. You despise the forces that have imprisoned them, and meeting their needs is laborious and painstaking.	They are made in the *imageo Dei*, God's image, and you love them and what Christ can do for them more than you despise the forces that put them there.
The Church:	Is comprised of a petty alliance of dissenters, critics, and culturally captive advocates. Playing politics is necessary to lead them.	Is an errant yet beloved community for whom Christ died. As a fellowship of the cross, they help the leader and each other overcome the obstacles and detours of the journey.
The future:	The pastor will labor in ministry until death or burnout (the former is preferred).	The pastor will journey through the trials and triumphs of ministry, and in the end, mirror Shaw's description of Bunyan's Christian: "This is the true joy in life—being used for a purpose recognized by yourself as a mighty one."[7]

AFTERWORD

As the reader has noticed, the journey of the good news never ends. It just leads to more responsibility. Successfully traversing a waypoint only affords the trekker an opportunity to help others navigate that same waypoint. My friends and colleagues have contributed their personal stories for this purpose.

To provide a clearer map of this route, I have written an important companion book titled *Waypoint: Navigating Your Spiritual Journey* (Indianapolis, Ind.: Wesleyan Publishing House, 2010). The companion volume is designed to help the person who is presently struggling with the obstacles, challenges, and detours of this spiritual road. This companion book is for non-Christians, new Christians, and Christian leaders alike. If you know of people on this journey, *Waypoint: Navigating Your Spiritual Journey* is the roadmap they have been seeking.

This companion book provides an agenda for

Anyone who sets himself up as "religious" by talking a good game is self-deceived. This kind of religion is hot air and only hot air. Real religion, the kind that passes muster before God the Father, is this: Reach out to the homeless and loveless in their plight, and guard against corruption from the godless world.

—JAMES 1:26–27 (MSG)

each of the weeks—a course that can be used in Sunday school, small groups, leadership committees, or Bible studies. In this course, travelers will share their experiences, help others, and make an impact on their communities.

For more information on either the companion book or the course, see http://www.Waypoints-Book.com.

In this appendix, we shall investigate two popular ways to describe this journey. First we will look at the Engel Scale. We will see that for all of its attractiveness and durability, it is weak in its depiction of the discipleship that occurs.

To address these weaknesses, we will look at Robert Clinton's phases of leadership development. Clinton's stages are helpful for describing the process from new Christian to ministry effectiveness, but lack a robust explanation of the pre-discipleship journey.

Therefore, I weave together these two important descriptions, updating them for a contemporary milieu, and renaming them to help retention and navigation.

EVANGELISTIC EFFECTIVENESS IS MISSING

"Ministry effectiveness must be evaluated and not simply assumed." Thus intoned a social scientist by the name of James Engel as he assessed North American church health. As the author of dozens of journal articles on business strategy, Engel had been taken aback by the cavalier attitude Christians held toward evaluation. His concerns were echoed by Fuller Seminary professor Donald McGavran, who argued that his term *church growth*, while valid, had come to mean something unintended: attendance growth. McGavran therefore sought, unsuccessfully, to supplant the term *church growth* with the more accurate phrase *effective evangelism*, because this emphasized effectiveness over bulk.[1]

When teaching business students, Engel stressed it was not size but effectiveness that was the key. A large organization could be as unhealthy as a small one. Thus, effectiveness, not mass, was the goal. And though Engel believed that God wanted all persons to know him, this did not precluded evaluating exactly which methodologies God was using at the time.[2] Engel's actions were mirrored by Eddie Gibbs, who stated that "the intentions of God do not set aside the need for careful evaluation."[3]

McGavran sought, unsuccessfully, to supplant the term *church growth* with the phrase *effective evangelism,* because this emphasized effectiveness over bulk.

Engel developed a scale of spiritual decision that did not reply upon statistics or ratings but tracked progress. He celebrated that there was a point when "a new disciple was born" but felt the church had become ineffective by placing too much emphasis upon the point of decision.[4] He saw churches overly fixated upon altar calls, prefabricated explanations of the good news, and celebrations of the new birth.[5] Engel (and I), sees nothing wrong with such celebration, only that in many churches, the celebration clouds the fact that there are waypoints that lead to a spiritual decision, and subsequent waypoints that lead to maturity.

When euphoria steals our attention from requisite follow-through, the dilemma becomes analogous to a newborn child who is left at the hospital after the initial elation of the parents wanes. All parents will tell you that the journey gets more complex and complicated after birth, and you'd better be prepared. And so it is with new births in Christ. In both parenting and discipling, there are waypoints ahead, and each one will require a new set of skills.

ELASTIC PARENTING IN WORD AND DEED

In previous writings, I described how the pattern of parenting is a helpful and biblical leadership metaphor in part because of elasticity.[6] By elastic, I mean that a parent must stretch and adjust methods as a child matures without changing the parent's underlying principles. So, too, must the church adjust its ministry (but not its principles) as the new person grows in Christ. If the church does not adjust its methods, the maturing disciple may go elsewhere in search of a spiritual home that can help him or her with the next stage in the spiritual journey. Such partings undercut a church's effectiveness and interrupt the consistency that young disciples need.

Consider an example: Grace Church might be skilled in helping community residents with a clothing shelf and food bank. But at the same time this church may be weak in explaining the fundamentals of the good news. This can occur because Grace Church feels benevolent and compassionate deeds are the primary way they express the good news. This is sometimes called "evangelism in deed," where the deed is seen as reflecting the love of Christ. And it certainly can and should. However, such a church can be weak in its explanation of the tenets of the good news. Skill in explaining the tenets of the good news is sometimes called "evangelism in word," where teaching about the words of Christ form a church's primary thrust of the good news.[7]

We saw in the introduction that both of these actions—charitable deeds (the cultural mandate), and explaining the biblical Word (the evangelistic mandate)—are part of our good news. But a church that majors on one mandate and only minors on the other mandate risks creating missing links in the traveler's journey. If a parent did not adapt his or her parenting style as the child grows into teen years, that teenager might leave home complaining of still being treated as a child. And so it happens in similar fashion in our churches.

> Most churches focus on a narrow band of the journey and give lip service to the rest. This must change.
>
> We are forcing new disciples to break-reestablish, break-reestablish, and break-reestablish relationships just to continue on their spiritual path.

There is nothing wrong when churches divide this process, with some churches focusing on the good news in deed and other churches focusing on the good news in word.[8] Ron Sider and his colleagues have even suggested practical strategies for creating partnerships between such congregations.[9]

But a problem emerges when we look at this from the viewpoint of the wayfarer. Travelers begin to make friends with those helping them on their journey, only to find that once they travel to another waypoint, they must break ties with former friends and seek to penetrate a new community. This forces wayfarers to continually cut ties and repeatedly seek a new community that can facilitate the next stage of their journey.

The problem is exacerbated because churches often find it challenging to offer ministry at more than a few waypoints. So, most churches just don't make the effort. A result is that most churches focus on a narrow band of the journey and give lip service to the rest. This must change. If it does not, then for the convenience of church workers, we are forcing new disciples to break-reestablish, break-reestablish, and break-reestablish relationships just to continue on their spiritual journey.

An even more worrisome outcome is that when severing relationships with one congregation and initiating relationships with another, wayfarers may drop out of the journey. The person who exits a congregation often feels as if he or she is betraying friends.[10] The result is that relationships are rent, and looking back becomes painful.

The answer begins by creating a map of how the good news travels, one that depicts the direction, waypoints, and progress of the journey. Once churches grasp this visual depiction with its many waypoints, churches can either encourage a disciple to move on, or the congregation can decide to expand its ministry into adjacent waypoints and beyond.[11]

ENGEL'S SCALE

To visualize this process, Engel began with what he called "the Great Commission in common dress"[12] and viewed this as a process of stages. Let us look briefly at each stage (Figure A.1) in what Engel labeled "a model of spiritual decision processes"[13]:

-8: A person at this stage might label themselves an agnostic, knowing there is a god but not knowing who that god is.

-7: Here a person becomes aware of good news about God (the gospel) through the deeds, words, and testimony of Christians or others.

-6: A deepening awareness of the fundamentals of this good news could include the traveler experiencing charity, forgiveness, graciousness, reciprocity, and so on. This could be exemplified in acts of mercy, sacrifice, or justice, which fulfill the Great Commandment (Mark 12:31) to "love your neighbor as yourself" (sometimes called the "cultural mandate"). A sizable portion of people today may be in this realm, appreciating the good deeds of Christians but not moving into the next stage (-5) where they grasp the personal implications of the good news.

FIGURE A.1

Engel's Stages of Spiritual Decision[14]

-8 Awareness of supreme being; no knowledge of gospel
-7 Initial awareness of gospel
-6 Awareness of fundamentals of gospel
-5 Grasp of implications of gospel
-4 Positive attitude towards gospel
-3 Personal problem recognition
-2 Decision to act
-1 Repentance and faith in Christ
New Birth: A New Disciple Is Born
+1 Post-decision evaluation
+2 Incorporation into body
+3 Conceptual and behavioral growth
+4 Communion with God
+5 Stewardship

-5: This indicates the person understands the personal requirements of the good news. Here is where major disconnects may occur, when people see good deeds but fail to grasp that the good news has requirements and obligations upon the hearer. Jesus noted this many times, for instance, when he said, "Take my yoke upon you and learn from me, for I am gentle and humble in heart, and you will find rest for your souls. For my yoke is easy and my burden is light" (Matt. 11:29–30).

-4: The person develops a positive view of the gospel. Again, because of what was noted above, many unchurched people today probably reside in a realm between -7 and -4.

-3: Here a person recognizes a personal deficiency, incapable of being addressed without divine interaction and assistance.

-2: A person makes a decision to act and reach out for supernatural assistance to address the deficiency.

-1: A person recognizes having not lived up to God's standards, and that only by faith in Jesus Christ and his death on our behalf can we escape the penalty of our sins.

New Birth: God creates an intersection between the spiritual and physical worlds, and a new person is born (John 3:3–8).

+1: Here, the person reviews what has happened and whether the decision was worth the effort or the emerging criticism. Some, after reevaluating their decision, lapse back to -3 or -4 with either a decision not to act, or to reevaluate their positive attitude toward the good news.

+2: If forward progress occurs, a person will seek out a support network of fellow Christians, fulfilling the admonition of Hebrews 10:24–25, to "consider how we may spur one another on toward love and good deeds. Let us not give up meeting together . . . but let us encourage one another."

+3: Here, spiritual growth is observed in faith and action. In Acts 2:42–47, we observe three types of church growth that should emerge: growth in maturity (growing in passion for the Bible, fellowship, and prayer), growth in unity (growing in harmony with others), and growth in service (growing in service to others both inside and outside of the church).[15] Engel places traditions associated with new birth, such as adult baptism or confirmation, in this stage.[16]

+4: At this point, Engel clouds the picture a bit, referring to this stage as communion with God "through prayer and worship."[17] Though he acknowledges that this happens earlier too, by stressing it here Engel gives the unintended impression that supernatural encounter mostly flourishes later.[18]

In fact, here there is a weakness in the Engel Scale: It is stronger and more descriptive of the pre-birth process than of the post-birth journey. If both aspects of the journey should be balanced as Engel suggests,[19] then further waypoints must be added to the upper realms of the Engel Scale to make it truly holistic.

CLINTON'S PHASES

J. Robert Clinton from Fuller Seminary focused on the phases of the journey after new birth (Figure A.2). Though other authors have offered similar process models,[20] Clinton's is one of the best organized and defined. In addition, Clinton emphasizes that these phases overlap and are indigenized for each person.[21] Let us look briefly at each of what Clinton calls "Six Phases of Leadership Development."

I. SOVEREIGN FOUNDATIONS

Clinton suggests this phase begins in the period before new birth. Clinton sees God imbuing his creation with certain personality characteristics that after new birth will correlate to spiritual gifts. During this phase, God is preparing a leader through experiences and character traits.[23]

FIGURE A.2

Clinton's Six Phases of Leadership Development[22]

I. Sovereign Foundations
New Birth: A New Disciple Is Born
II. Inner-Life Growth
III. Ministry Maturation
IV. Life Maturation
V. Convergence
VI. Afterglow

NEW BIRTH: A NEW DISCIPLE IS BORN

Between phases I and II, Clinton sees "an all-out surrender commitment, in which the would-be leader aspires to spend a lifetime that counts for God."[24] Here, Engel does offer more depth as he charts the minute, but important, mental steps that lead up to a surrender commitment. Therefore, Engel's preparatory steps to this experience will contribute more robustly to our way-point approach.

II. INNER-LIFE GROWTH

In this phase, Clinton describes the mentoring and modeling that the new Christian experiences. Clinton neglects Engel's insights regarding the post-birth evaluation, yet Clinton adds to our understandings the influence of both informal apprenticeships and formal training.[25]

III. MINISTRY MATURATION

This phase occurs as disciples sense ministry is increasingly becoming a focus of their life. The disciples become motivated to explore ministry options and spiritual giftings.[26] At this juncture, Clinton offers the most satisfying insights, pointing out that much of the growth in new disciples is self-directed, meaning they must take it upon themselves to look for opportunities to volunteer, minister to others, and evaluate effectiveness. Ministry is thus often organic, unpaid, and unscripted.[27] Though Clinton notes that "most people are anxious to bypass Phase II and get on with the real thing—Phase III, ministry,"[28] in hindsight, Phase II can be very satisfying because all options are possible and hope abounds.

IV. LIFE MATURATION

Here, Clinton offers a critical insight into the powerful synergy that is unleashed when disciples finds ministries that correspond to their gifts. Ministry priorities are also established during this phase, which Clinton describes as a phase of "mature fruitfulness."[29]

V. EVERYTHING CONVERGES

In this phase, personality, training, experience, gifts, and geographical location converge to release ministry that is not only effective but also widely appreciated. Clinton points out that not all disciples reach this stage, but by just defining the stage, Clinton gives us a mental picture of God's potential for the individual. "Ministry is maximized," sums up Clinton.[30]

VI. AFTERGLOW

This is a phase when a person's ministry is so influential over such an extended period of time that the person enjoys the afterglow of effective ministry. Though an end that should be considered, Clinton notes that few get there. But travelers should not be discouraged or surprised, for the Scriptures are replete with examples of saints who never attained (at least in this life) afterglow.

Clinton provides an interesting roadmap toward the growth of influential and effective leadership, even if the higher phases are often not realized in this lifetime. It is in the phases of leadership development that Clinton bests Engel.[31]

A NEW ROADMAP FOR A NEW ERA

Engel's and Clinton's scales provide helpful visual reminders in a world increasingly comfortable and dependent upon symbols and icons.[32] But both Engel and Clinton are still rooted in a modernist world where inflexible stages and lock-step phases rob the journey of outreach of its elastic and local flavor.

Who would want to blindly follow someone else's travelogue and not experience surprises, scenic byways, and flexibility en route?

A new postmodern era is emphasizing the importance of learning through experience, not just from books.[33] These are people who want to experience the journey, not just live vicariously through someone else's diary. For these people, a new roadmap is needed, a map that draws from the best of Engel and Clinton, but one that also emphasizes how each traveler experiences the journey uniquely. This new map must emphasize that there are common waypoints that each traveler will encounter, though at different times and with different facets. Our new map must focus less on stages and phases, and instead concentrate on the natural experiences that the traveler will encounter on the journey.

To begin to chart this new route, let us see how (in Figure A.3) both Engel and Clinton contribute insights but on different segments of the journey.

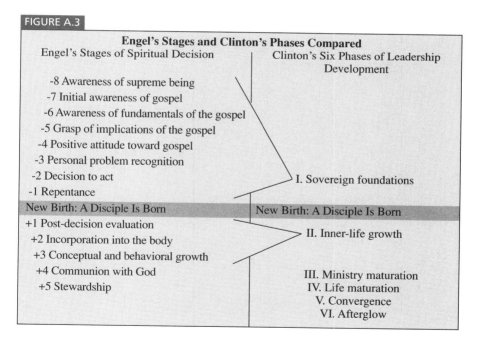

FIGURE A.3

Engel's Stages and Clinton's Phases Compared

Engel's Stages of Spiritual Decision	Clinton's Six Phases of Leadership Development
-8 Awareness of supreme being	
-7 Initial awareness of gospel	
-6 Awareness of fundamentals of the gospel	
-5 Grasp of implications of the gospel	
-4 Positive attitude toward gospel	
-3 Personal problem recognition	
-2 Decision to act	I. Sovereign foundations
-1 Repentance	
New Birth: A Disciple Is Born	New Birth: A Disciple Is Born
+1 Post-decision evaluation	
+2 Incorporation into the body	II. Inner-life growth
+3 Conceptual and behavioral growth	
+4 Communion with God	III. Ministry maturation
+5 Stewardship	IV. Life maturation
	V. Convergence
	VI. Afterglow

As seen in Figure A.3, both scales have their strong points. By combining the two, taking out some overlap, updating terminology, and focusing on the process rather than static stages or phases, a new roadmap can emerge that is more attuned to today's traveler. Therefore to provide a more elastic and organic alternative, I suggest that the stages and phases become less prominent, and they be replaced with moveable waypoints that give a general understanding of where one is within a certain segment of the journey. Figure A.4, then, is a new scale, born from the above, but with emphasis upon indigenous waypoints for tracking the traveler's progress.[34]

FIGURE A.4

WAYPOINTS

16	No awareness of a supreme being
15	Awareness of a supreme being, no knowledge of the good news
14	Initial awareness of the good news
13	Awareness of the fundamentals of the good news
12	Grasp of the implications of the good news
11	Positive attitude toward the good news
10	Personal problem recognition
9	Decision to act
8	Repentance and faith in Christ
7	NEW BIRTH
6	Post-decision evaluation
5	Incorporation into the body
4	Spiritual foundations (conceptual and behavioral growth)
3	Inner-life growth (deepening communion with God)
2	Ministry emergence (spiritual gifts emerge)
1	Impact emergence (life influences others)
0	Convergence (experience, gifts, and influence converge into a life of integrity and inspiration)

NOTES

INTRODUCTION

1. Lesslie Newbigin, *The Gospel in a Pluralistic Society* (Grand Rapids, Mich.: Eerdmans Publishing, 1989), 183.
2. Esther de Waal, *Seeking God: The Way of St. Benedict* (Collegeville, Minn.: Liturgical Press, 2001), 69.
3. J. Gresham Machen, *New Testament: An Introduction to Its History and Literature* (Edinburgh, UK: Banner of Truth Trust, 1976), 338–354.
4. Billy Graham, *Peace with God: The Secret of Happiness* (New York: Thomas Nelson, 1953, 2000), 237.
5. Donald A. McGavran and C. Peter Wagner, *Understanding Church Growth* (Grand Rapids, Mich.: Eerdmans Publishing, 1970), 25.
6. Arthur F. Glasser, "Confession, Church Growth, and Authentic Unity in Missionary Strategy," in Norma A. Horner, ed., *Protestant Crosscurrents in Mission* (Nashville: Abingdon Press, 1968), 178–221.
7. C. Peter Wagner, *Church Growth and the Whole Gospel: A Biblical Mandate* (New York: Harper & Row, 1981), 13.
8. Lewis A. Drummond, *Reaching Generation Next: Effective Evangelism in Today's Culture* (Grand Rapids, Mich.: Baker Books, 2002), 179.
9. C. Peter Wagner, *Frontiers in Missionary Strategy* (Chicago: Moody Press, 1971), 37.
10. John Stott, ed., *Evangelism and Social Responsibility: An Evangelical Commitment* (Lausanne Committee for Evangelism and the World Evangelical Fellowship, 1982), 23.
11. Donald B. Kraybill, *The Upside-Down Kingdom* (Scottdale, Pa.: Herald Press, 1978, 2003), 19–20.
12. Ronald J. Sider, *Rich Christians in an Age of Hunger: A Biblical Study* (Downers Grove, Ill.: InterVarsity Press, 1977), 22.
13. For more on the emergence of the historical divide between social and evangelistic action, see Roger Finke and Rodney Stark's meticulous look at church growth in America, titled *The Churching of America 1776–2005:*

Winners and Losers in Our Religious Economy (Piscataway, N.J.: Rutgers University Press, 2005). For the reader seeking a more concise overview, see Wilbert R. Shenk, *Changing Frontiers of Mission* (Maryknoll, N.Y.: Orbis Books, 2005), 22–24.

14. Bob Whitesel, *Inside the Organic Church: Learning from 12 Emerging Congregations* (Nashville: Abingdon Press, 2006).

15. Ibid., 37.

16. McGavran and Wagner, *Understanding Church Growth*, 395.

17. David L. McKenna, ed., *The Urban Crisis* (Grand Rapids, Mich.: Zondervan, 1969), 138.

18. James F. Engel and Wilbert Norton, *What's Gone Wrong With the Harvest?: A Communication Strategy for the Church and World Evangelism* (Grand Rapids, Mich.: Zondervan, 1975), 35.

19. Richard Peace, *Conversion in the New Testament: Paul and the Twelve* (Grand Rapids, Mich.: Eerdmans Publishing, 1999). Peace offers a helpful examination of Mark's account of the twelve disciples and their conversionary experiences. Peace argues that they were not converted while traveling with Jesus as members of his apostolic band but that Mark's gospel is organized in part to underscore that they "were brought step-by-step to the experience of repentance and faith," 12.

20. Ibid., 309.

21. de Waal, *Seeking God*, 69.

22. Lesslie Newbigin, *The Gospel in a Pluralistic Society* (Grand Rapids, Mich.: Eerdmans Publishing, 1989), 183.

23. Shenk, *Changing Frontiers of Mission*, 28.

24. Eddie Gibbs and Ryan Bolger, *Emerging Churches: Creating Christian Community in Postmodern Cultures* (Grand Rapids, Mich.: Baker Academic, 2005), 149.

25. Eddie Gibbs, *Church Next: Quantum Changes in How We Do Ministry* (Downers Grove, Ill.: InterVarsity Press, 2000), 22–27.

26. Whitesel, *Inside the Organic Church*, xvi–xvii.

27. Gibbs and Bolger, *Emerging Churches*, 149.

28. Brian McLaren, "The Method, the Message, and the Ongoing Story," in *The Church in Emerging Culture: Five Perspectives*, Leonard Sweet, ed., (Grand Rapids, Mich.: Zondervan, 2003), 214–215. For a critique of McLaren's perspective see Martin Downes, "Entrapment: The Emerging Church Conversation and the Cultural Captivity of the Gospel," in Gary L. W. Johnson and Ronald N. Gleason, eds., *Reforming or Conforming: Post-Conservative Evangelicals and the Emerging Church*, (Wheaton, Ill.: Crossway Books, 2008), 224–243.

29. Jim Wallis, *God's Politics: Why the Right Gets It Wrong and the Left Doesn't Get It* (New York: HarperOne, 2006), 66.
30. Though familiar to the New Testament hearer, this term would be strangely unique because it was rarely used as a verb, i.e.: "to evangelize."
31. Alan Richardson, *A Theological Word Book of the Bible* (New York: Macmillan Publishers, 1950), 100.
32. Robert Louis Stevenson, "Travels with a Donkey in Cevennes: An Inland Voyage" in *Selected Writings* (New York: Random House, 1947), 957.
33. Stott, *Evangelism and Social Responsibility*, 25.
34. Howard A. Snyder, *The Community of the King* (Downers Grove, Ill.: InterVarsity Press), 101.
35. Wagner, *Church Growth and the Whole Gospel*, 52.
36. Snyder, *The Community of the King*, 102.
37. Engel and Norton, *What's Gone Wrong With the Harvest?*.
38. James F. Engel, *Contemporary Christian Communications, Its Theory and Practice* (Nashville: Thomas Nelson, 1979), 223. For a more thorough analysis and comparison, see the appendix of this book.
39. J. Robert Clinton, *The Making of a Leader: Recognizing the Lessons and Stages of Leadership Development* (Colorado Springs, Colo.: NavPress, 1988). For a more thorough analysis and comparison, see the appendix of this book.
40. Graham, *Peace with God*, 133. (At other times, Graham depicts this process as a series of the phases, cf. Sterling W. Huston, *Crusade Evangelism and the Local Church* [Minneapolis, Minn.: World Wide Publishers, 1984], 52–54.)
41. Graham, *Peace with God*, 133.
42. Steps, stages, and phases depict an inflexible process of fixed dimensions. In similar fashion, the term *mile marker* provides a poor metaphor. All of these appellations suffer from a lack of flexibility and elasticity. This may be the result of modern conventions, where processes are erroneously thought to follow in lock-step fashion and predictability. To embrace such inflexibility would be akin to embracing the erroneous scientific management of Frederick Taylor, where fabrication and consistency were desired. (For a valuable analysis of scientific management and its inflexibility, see Daniel Boorstin, *The Americans: The Democratic Experience* [New York: Vintage Books, 1974]). A more supple and postmodern description (which I prefer) is that of a *waypoint*, which does not occur at regular intervals, but rather calculates the traveler's current position on the route.
43. Billy Graham in *Peace with God* states this well when he says, "It is the Holy Spirit who brings about this conviction. Actually, repentance cannot

take place unless first there is a movement of the Holy Spirit in the heart and mind" (146). It is this movement in heart and mind that the journey metaphor used in this book will seek to chart.

44. James D. G. Dunn points out that the involvement of the Holy Spirit in the birth of the Church, as well as in new disciples, is seen by John as an example of how the Holy Spirit is involved in many facets of the evangelistic journey. Dunn notes, "His spirit may be experienced in many diverse ways, both in non-rational ecstasy and through the mind, both in experiences of dramatically effective power and in compulsion to serve" in *Jesus and the Spirit: A Study in the Religious and Charismatic Experience of Jesus and the First Christians as Reflected in the New Testament* (Philadelphia, Pa.: Westminster Press, 1975), 357–58.

45. To learn more about the importance of cultures and how to grow indigenous and organic ministries, see my other books: *Preparing for Change Reaction: How to Introduce Change in Your Church* (Indianapolis, Ind.: Wesleyan Publishing House, 2007) and *Inside the Organic Church: Learning from 12 Emerging Congregations* (Nashville: Abingdon Press, 2006).

46. Churches might counter this argument by saying, "But we are effective at one waypoint, why should we try to create ministry in areas in which we are not good?" This is an argument rooted in a common misperception regarding management theory—that organizations should focus on doing only one thing well. In the business world, an organization does not want to engage in too many disparate fields. However, if that business can enter a field that builds upon a field they already do well, then that becomes a good strategy. For instance, a company that builds homes will find that if it can add a realtor business, it can capitalize on the business generated before and after the house is built. The firm becomes more competitive because it covers more of the fields related to its purpose. So, too, the Church becomes more holistic and helpful if it helps people on more waypoints on the journey of evangelism.

47. Such partnerships often organically develop in churches that have been planted by a mother congregation. Often an offspring congregation is more effective in meeting the needs of the disenfranchised, because the offspring is less administratively distant and nearer to the need. However, as travelers move along the journey of good news, they may find they are in need of ministry that only the mother congregation can provide. In such scenarios, the connection between the daughter and the mother congregations often allows wayfarers to shift to the mother congregation in a relatively smooth manner.

48. Researchers have suggested that an emphasis upon social concerns has, in the past, led some evangelicals to become more liberal in theology and less evangelical in methodology (Ed Stetzer, address given to American

Society for Church Growth [La Mirada, Calif.: Biola University, Nov. 14, 2008]). However, understanding the journey of outreach can assist in halting this digression by emphasizing the direction and waypoints of this journey of good news. An immunization against this malady might be of greater use and familiarity with a waypoint model where the progress of the human condition is highlighted by waypoints that are not the ends of the journey but merely markers toward an ultimate convergence.

49. The Greek word commonly used for church in the New Testament, *ekklesia*, indicates a *community* or *assembly* that is called out for joint action. See William F. Arndt and F. Wilbur Gingrich, *A Greek-English Lexicon of the New Testament and Other Early Literature* (Chicago: University of Chicago Press, 1959), 240–241.

50. Still, the mandates are two parts of the same process. Engel, however, makes a persuasive argument that Wagner (*Evangelical Missions Quarterly*, vol. 12 [July, 1976], 177–180) separates too greatly the cultural mandate from the evangelistic mandate (*Contemporary Christian Communications*, 66–68). Engel argues from Scripture and from practicality that it is a "grave missiological error" to separate the cultural mandate from the evangelical mandate at all. It is toward recoupling these mandates that metaphors of a journey and waypoints are employed.

51. Donald A. McGavran, *Effective Evangelism: A Theological Mandate* (Phillipsburg, N.J.: Presbyterian and Reformed Publishing, 1988), 17.

52. Engel, *Contemporary Christian Communications*, 66.

WAYPOINT 16

1. C. S. Lewis, *Surprised by Joy: The Shape of My Early Life* (New York: Harcourt Brace & Co., 1956), 111.

2. Richard V. Peace has written extensively on the process of evangelism. Some of his most helpful writings include "Conflicting Understandings of Christian Conversion: A Missiological Challenge," in *International Bulletin of Missionary Research*, vol. 28, No. 1; "Holy Conversation: The Lost Art of Witness" in *Word and World*, vol. 22, no. 3, 2002; "Harry and the Evangelicals" in *Religion in the News*, Spring 2002; *Holy Conversation: Talking About God in Everyday Life* (Downers Grove, Ill.: InterVarsity Press, 2006); and *Conversion in the New Testament: Paul and the Twelve* (Grand Rapids, Mich.: Eerdmans Publishing, 1999).

3. Christopher Hitchens, *God Is Not Great: How Religion Poisons Everything* (New York: Twelve-Hachette Book Group, 2007), 160.

4. William T. Cavanaugh, *The Myth of Religious Violence: Secular Ideology and the Roots of Modern Conflict* (Oxford, UK: Oxford University Press, 2009).

5. Barry A. Kosmin and Ariela Keysar, *The American Religious Identification Survey (ARIS) 2008* (Hartford, Conn.: Program on Public Values, 2009).

6. See, for example, Paul's admonition to the Corinthian church, whose zeal had mutated into ostentatious and brazen immorality and status seeking (1 Cor. 1–14).

7. An example could be Marjoe Gortner (see the film on his life titled, *Marjoe*, which won a 1972 Academy Award for best documentary feature).

8. Bertrand Russell's essay "Why I Am Not a Christian" in *Why I Am Not a Christian and Other Essays on Religion and Related Subjects* (New York: Simon & Schuster, 1965) might be an example of this perspective.

9. C. Peter Wagner, *Your Spiritual Gifts Can Help Your Church Grow* (Ventura, Calif.: Regal Books, 1979), 120.

10. Michael Griffiths, *Cinderella's Betrothal Gifts* (Littleton, Colo.: OMF Books, 1978), 36.

11. Alastair Davidson, *Antonio Gramsci: Towards an Intellectual Biography* (Atlantic Highlands, N.J.: Humanities Press, 1977).

12. Lewis, *Surprised by Joy*. See also the critical analysis of Lewis' change in John Beversluis's *C. S. Lewis and the Search for Rational Religion* (New York: Prometheus Books, 2007).

13. For a glimpse of George MacDonald's influence upon C. S. Lewis, see Lewis's compilation of 365 selections of MacDonald's writings in *George McDonald* (New York: HarperOne, 2001).

14. Review of *Mere Christianity* in *Library Journal* (New York: Reed Publications, 2001), retrieved from http://www.christianbook.com/mere-christianity-c-s-lewis/9780060652920/pd/2926X.

15. Lewis was influenced by fantasy writer George McDonald, who often framed spiritual lessons in fantastic dream worlds. For the development of the connection between these two organic intellectuals, see C. S. Lewis's stepson's account: Douglas H. Gresham, *Jack's Life: The Life Story of C. S. Lewis* (New York: B&H Publishing, 2005), 126–142.

16. Lewis, *Surprised by Joy*, 111.

17. New Testament theologian Everett F. Harrison points out that the name "Christian" or "little Christs" originated among non-Christians who were describing the followers of Christ, in *Acts: The Expanding Church* (Chicago: Moody Press, 1975), 185. Thus the use of this term underscores the importance of social modeling, for Christians were first labeled such because non-Christians noted that followers of Christ were acting in the same selfless and gracious ways that Christ himself exhibited.

18. Christopher Hitchens, *The Portable Atheist: Essential Readings for the Nonbeliever* (Cambridge, Mass.: Da Capo Press, 2007), 136.

19. David Kinnaman and Gabe Lyons, *unChristian: What a New Generation Really Thinks about Christianity . . . and Why It Matters* (Grand Rapids, Mich.: Baker Books, 2007), 71.

20. Again, placing too much emphasis upon the conversion event and not an equal emphasis upon helping the person navigate the route to that waypoint and beyond, can lead to an infatuation with new birth numbers and not travelers you are helping on the journey.

21. This Scripture addresses the problem with truth telling that the Jewish people were having in regard to oaths. Though directed here toward truthfulness in oath giving, the principle God requires of truth telling is evident.

22. This may be indicative of church cultures that live like they have nothing to fear from God's displeasure or retribution. Christians often take advantage of people not part of the Church ignoring that God loves these people too and died for them (John 3:16). And because they are made in God's image (Gen. 1:26–27), he longs to restore his relationship with them (Matt. 23:36–38).

23. For more insight on Lewis's conversion, which took place in stages and in conversation with his Christian colleagues, J. R. R. Tolkien and Victor "Hugo" Dyson, see George Sayer, *Jack: A Life of C. S. Lewis* (Wheaton, Ill.: Crossway Books, 2005), 217–226.

24. Lewis, *Surprised by Joy*, 111.

WAYPOINT 15

1. A prayer attributed to Teresa of Avila, Ronald Rolheiser, *A Holy Longing: The Search for a Christian Spirituality* (New York: Doubleday Religion, 1999).

2. Barry A. Kosmin and Ariela Keysar, *The American Religious Identification Survey (ARIS) 2008* (Hartford, Conn.: Program on Public Values, 2009).

3. Ibid., i.

4. Adapted from Abraham H. Maslow, *Motivation and Personality*, 2nd ed. (New York: Harper & Row, 1970), 300–394; and Abraham H. Maslow, *The Farther Reaches of Human Nature* (New York: Viking Press, 1971), 300.

5. The church's enthusiasm for primarily meeting belongingness and love needs sheds light on how churches grew during the post-World War II economic expansion. The Builder Generation (b. 1945 and before) was basking in unrivaled prosperity and a church-friendly milieu. Thus, tactics that meet belongingness and love needs, such as membership classes and assimilation standards, were touted. (See Roger Finke and Rodney Starke, *The Churching of America 1776–2005: Winners and Losers in*

Our Religious Economy [Piscataway, N.J.: Rutgers University Press, 2005] as well as additional factors discussed in Laurence Iannacone's 1994 essay "Why Strict Churches Are Strong" in *American Journal of Sociology* [Chicago: University of Chicago Press, 1994], vol. 99, no. 5, 1180–1211).

6. Francis Brown, S. R. Driver, and Charles A. Briggs, *A Hebrew and English Lexicon of the Old Testament* (Oxford, UK: Clarendon Press, 1974), 338.

7. See "Missteps with Staff Influence" in my book *Growth By Accident, Death By Planning: Missteps with Staff* (Nashville: Abingdon Press, 2004), 17–29.

8. For more about the dynamics of "group polarization effect," see Nancy Kogan and Michael A. Wallach, *Risk Taking: A Study in Cognition and Personality* (New York: Holt, Rinehart and Winston, 1964) and David G. Myers and S. J. Arenson, "Enhancement of Dominant Risk Tendencies in Group Discussion," in *Psychological Reports*, vol. 30 (Missoula, Mont.: Ammons Scientific, Ltd., 1972), 615–623.

9. For guidelines in hosting effective focus groups, see "How to Conduct A Focus Group" in my and Kent R. Hunter, *A House Divided: Bridging the Generation Gaps in Your Church* (Nashville: Abingdon Press, 2000), 152–155.

10. Ideas and examples for partnering can be found in Ronald J. Sider and others, *Linking Arms, Linking Lives: How Suburban Partnerships Can Transform Communities* (Grand Rapids, Mich.: Baker Books, 2008). Though this book is largely about partnering suburban churches with urban ones to create an economy of scale and scope, the dynamics of partnership that are discussed can be relevant for all churches seeking to expand their coverage of waypoints.

11. Donald A. McGavran and C. Peter Wagner, "A Universal Fog" and "The Facts Needed" in *Understanding Church Growth* (Grand Rapids, Mich.: Eerdmans Publishing, 1970), 76–120.

12. Donald A. McGavran, *Effective Evangelism: A Theological Mandate* (Phillipsburg, N.J.: Presbyterian and Reformed Publishing, 1988).

13. Though there may be some who misperceive the focus of the church growth movement, there is a growing cadre of scholars who understand that the church growth movement is viable, but needs to be more holistic in its theology and application. I am one such person. I agree with my colleagues in "The Gospel and Our Culture Network" who point out that the church growth movement has been weak in engaging postmodern culture. And I concur with Gailyn Van Rheenen that the church growth

movement has been weak in determining effective strategy. My upcoming editorship and contributions to *Foundations of Church Administration* (Kansas City, Mo.: Beacon Hill Press, 2010), as well as this book address this strategy link. Finally, I am especially in agreement with Howard Snyder and his critique that the church growth movement has been too narrow in its perception of the kingdom of God. This current book is written to put forth a more holistic emphasis upon the journey of the kingdom news. Gary McIntosh has done a great service by sorting out these perspectives in his seminal book *Evaluating the Church Growth Movement* (Grand Rapids, Mich.: Zondervan 2004).

14. Whitesel and Hunter, *A House Divided*, 207–221.
15. James W. Carey, "The Origins of Radical Discourse on Cultural Studies in the United States," in *Journal of Communication*, vol. 33 (Hoboken, N.J.: Wiley-Blackwell, 1983), 313. See also James W. Carey, *Communication as Culture: Essays on Media and Society* (Oxford, UK: Taylor & Francis, 2008).
16. For examples of evaluation tools that can measure each church growth metric, see Whitesel and Hunter, "Measuring Four Types of Growth" in *A House Divided*, 207–221.

WAYPOINT 14

1. Donald A. McGavran and C. Peter Wagner, *Understanding Church Growth* (Grand Rapids, Mich.: Eerdmans Publishing, 1970), 25.
2. Ronald J. Sider, *Rich Christians in an Age of Hunger: A Biblical Study* (Downers Grove, Ill.: InterVarsity Press, 1977).
3. About, "The Lausanne Movement," http://www.lausanne.org/about.html.
4. An anonymous member of the "Consultation on the Relationship between Evangelism and Social Responsibility" quoted by John Stott, *Evangelism and Social Responsibility: An Evangelical Commitment* (Grand Rapids, Mich.: Lausanne Committee for World Evangelism, 1982), 23.
5. For more information on the EVLN paradigm and the church, see Bruno Dyck and Frederick A. Starke, "The Formation of Breakaway Organizations: Observations and a Process Model" in *Administrative Science Quarterly* (1999) 44:792–822. The EVLN paradigm was first introduced by Albert O. Hirschman, *Exit, Voice and Loyalty* (Cambridge, Mass.: Harvard University Press, 1970). While much of the research looks at how the EVLN paradigm affects organizational members, its principles can also apply to stakeholders who are considering linking with an organization.
6. C. S. Lewis, "Christian Apologetics" in *God in the Dock: Essays on Theology and Ethics* (Grand Rapids, Mich.: Eerdmans Publishing, 1994), 101.

7. Alister E. McGrath, *A Brief History of Heaven* (Hoboken, N.J.: Wiley-Blackwell, 2003), 166–169. McGrath also points out that worship should reflect heaven on earth and "for this reason that the place of Christian worship is of such importance in connection with Christian understandings of heaven."
8. Alan Deutschman, "Change or Die" in *Fast Company Magazine* (New York: Fast Company, 2007), Dec. 19.
9. To gain a mental picture of the magnificence and splendor of Eden, see John Milton's masterpiece, *Paradise Lost* (New York: Penguin Classics, 2003).
10. Sider, *Rich Christians in an Age of Hunger*, 84.
11. Walter Brueggemann, *Living Toward a Vision: Biblical Reflections on Shalom* (New York: United Church Press, 1982), 15–16.
12. Ronald J. Sider and others, *Linking Arms, Linking Lives: How Urban-Suburban Partnerships Can Transform Communities* (Grand Rapids, Mich.: Baker Books, 2008), 53.
13. Howard Snyder, *The Problem of Wineskins: Church Structure in a Technological Age* (Downers Grove, Ill.: InterVarsity Press, 1975), 39.
14. McGavran and Wagner, *Understanding Church Growth*, 25.
15. For more information on the Church of the Nazarene's Good Samaritan Churches initiative, see http://www.ncm.org/min_goodsam.aspx.
16. Donald Miller and Tetsunao Yamamori, *Global Pentecostalism: The New Face of Christian Social Engagement* (Los Angeles: University of California Press, 2007).

WAYPOINT 13
1. Tim Cahill, *Road Fever* (New York: Vintage Books, 1992), vii.
2. Barry A. Kosmin and Ariela Keysar, *The American Religious Identification Survey (ARIS) 2008* (Hartford, Conn.: Program on Public Values, 2009), 3–8.
3. Richard Peace makes a well-supported argument that the conversion of the twelve disciples was a slow turning process (unlike Paul experienced). This would support the idea that travelers at Waypoint 6 and higher can participate significantly in the community of faith, as Jesus' disciples did with him. See *Conversion in the New Testament: Paul and the Twelve* (Grand Rapids, Mich.: Eerdmans Publishing, 1999), 253–281.
4. Larry Norman (1972), *Dialogue* (musical performance), Explo 72, Dallas, Texas.
5. For more about cultures, subcultures, and how to spot the differences, see "The North American Cultural Mix" in my *Preparing for Change Reaction: How to Introduce Change in Your Church* (Indianapolis, Ind., Wesleyan Publishing House, 2007), 49–71.

6. Translating between cultures is an ongoing and complex endeavor. The four principles noted are a brief codification of translation theory. For additional insights, see Lynne Long, ed., *Translation and Religion: Holy Untranslatable (Topics in Translation)* (Bristol, UK: Multilingual Matters Limited, 2005), and Eugene A. Nida and Charles R. Taber, *The Theory and Practice of Translation* (Boston, Mass.: Brill Academic Publishers, 2003).

7. This process if often called "dynamic equivalence." Eugene Nida, *Message and Mission* (New York: HarperCollins, 1960), 139–140. Dynamic equivalence describes a phrase that is equal to another phrase, hence the word *equivalence.* And it indicates a term that has some elasticity, meaning that it conveys varied aspects of an entity. A prized pig has a dynamic equivalence with a treasured lamb for the hearer can picture in their mind the many actions and incidents that accompany raising a pig or a lamb. Though Nida preferred the term *functional equivalence* to dynamic equivalence because function carried the idea of effective equivalence (1960:194), I prefer *dynamic equivalence* for it conveys that our translated words must carry imagery of the original term, with all of the original's elasticity, animation, and metamorphosis.

8. Ed L. Miller, *Questions that Matter: An Invitation to Philosophy* (New York: McGraw-Hill, 1996), 199.

9. Eddie Gibbs, *I Believe in Church Growth* (Grand Rapids, Mich.: Eerdmans Publishing, 1981), 120.

10. I noted in an earlier book (*Inside the Organic Church: Learning From 12 Emerging Congregations* [Nashville: Abingdon Press, 2006]), that many postmodern young people are drawn to iconography, liturgy, and mystical terminology because it puts back into the church some of the mystery that many churches have abandoned. However, emerging churches that use such ancient images and language are careful to explain its ancient meaning in modern terms. See, for example, the use of and explanation of the icons called Directions© at Mars Hill Church in Grandville, Michigan (21–30); the use icons labeled Lifeshapes© by St. Thomas' Church in Sheffield, UK (1–12); and the use of updated *lectio divina* in pan-Wesleyan churches in *Listening to God Through 1 & 2 Peter* by Tim Guptill (Kansas City, Mo.: Beacon Hill Press, 2006).

WAYPOINT 12

1. Susan Sontag, *Styles of Radical Will* (New York: Macmillan Publishers, 2002), 75.

2. Lauren Winner explains this dream in *Girl Meets God: A Memoir* (New York: Random House, 2003).

3. The Mitford novels are a popular series of fictional novels about spirituality and relationships written by Jan Karon.
4. Barry A. Kosmin and Ariela Keysar, *The American Religious Identification Survey (ARIS) 2008* (Hartford, Conn.: Program on Public Values, 2009), i.
5. Roger Finke, "Religious Deregulation: Origins and Consequences," in *Journal of Church and State*, vol. 32 (1990), 609–626; Roger Finke and Rodney Stark, *The Churching of America, 1776–1990: Winners and Loser in Our Religious Economy* (Piscataway, N.J.: Rutgers University Press, 1992).
6. Darrell L. Guder, ed. *Missional Church: A Vision for the Sending of the Church in North America* (Grand Rapids, Mich.: Eerdmans Publishing, 1998), 2.
7. This codified list of patterns within a post-Christian worldview was adapted from a list conceived by James F. Engel in 1979. The reader will notice that Engel had his pulse on permutations in culture at an early juncture. For a fuller explanation of Engel's cultural analysis, see James F. Engel, *Contemporary Christian Communications, It's Theory and Practice* (Nashville: Thomas Nelson, 1979), 74–76. For expanded lists of postmodern behaviors, ideas, and products, see "Understanding North American Culture" in Darrel L. Guder, ed., *Missional Church: A Vision for the Sending of the Church in North America* (Grand Rapids, Mich.: Eerdmans Publishing, 1998), 37; Eddie Gibbs and Ryan Bolger, *Emerging Churches: Creating Christian Community in Postmodern Cultures* (Grand Rapids, Mich.: Baker Academic, 2005), and my *Inside the Organic Church: Learning From 12 Emerging Congregations* (Nashville: Abingdon Press, 2004), xxviii–xxxiii.
8. Richard Peace labels the lost art of compassion the "lost art of witness," but his article is essentially about the interpersonal dialogue of the good news that results from companionship or community. Because Peace is writing for a Christian audience in the journal *Word and World:* "Theology for Christian Ministry," his labels are valid. But because I am attempting to translate these concepts for a post-Christian environment I have chosen to translate "the lost art of witness" as the "lost art of companionship," since companionship conveys not only accompaniment but also engagement. For more information see Richard Peace, "Holy Conversation: The Lost Art of Witness" in *Word and World*, vol. 22, no. 3 (Saint Paul, Minn.: Word and World Publishers, 2002), 255–263.
9. Norman L. Geisler and Paul K. Hoffman, eds., *Why I Am a Christian: Leading Thinkers Explain Why They Believe* (Grand Rapids, Mich.: Baker Books, 2006).

10. Gary Poole, *How Does Anyone Know God Exists?* (Tough Questions series) (Grand Rapids, Mich.: Zondervan, 2003).

11. Lee Strobel, *The Case for Christ: A Journalist's Personal Investigation of the Evidence for Jesus* (Grand Rapids, Mich.: Zondervan, 1998), 19–130.

12. J. B. Phillips, *The Ring of Truth: A Translator's Testimony* (Vancouver, BC: Regent College Publishing, 2004).

13. F. F. Bruce, *The New Testament Documents: Are They Reliable* (Downers Grove, Ill.: InterVarsity Press, 1997), 32.

14. Kathryn L. Ludwigson, "Postmodernism: A Declaration of Bankruptcy" in *The Challenge of Postmodernism: An Evangelical Engagement*, David S. Dockery, ed. (Wheaton, Ill.: Bridgepoint Books, 1995), 281–292.

15. James Emery White, "Evangelism in a Postmodern World" in *The Challenge of Postmodernism: An Evangelical Engagement*, David S. Dockery, ed. (Wheaton, Ill.: Bridgepoint Books, 1995), 359–373.

16. J. B. Phillips, *Your God is Too Small: A Guide for Believer and Skeptics Alike* (New York: Touchstone Publishing, 2004).

17. Richard Stearns, *The Hole in Our Gospel: The Answer That Changed My Life and Might Just Change the World* (Nashville: Thomas Nelson, 2009).

18. Randy Alcorn, *Money, Possessions, and Eternity* (Carol Stream, Ill.: Tyndale House Publishers, 2003).

19. Shane Claiborne, *The Irresistible Revolution: Living as an Ordinary Radical* (Grand Rapids, Mich.: Zondervan, 2006).

20. C. S. Lewis, *God in the Dock: Essays on Theology and Ethics* (Grand Rapids, Mich.: Eerdmans Publishing, 1994).

21. Normal L. Geisler, *Christian Apologetics* (Grand Rapids, Mich.: Baker Academic, 1988). This book will be helpful at all stages, but even more so at this one. A classic and comprehensive treatise, it may be a bit difficult for the casual reader, but it is filled with well-conceived insights.

22. N. T. Wright, *Simply Christian: Why Christianity Makes Sense* (New York: Harper & Row, 2006).

23. Norman Geisler and Paul K. Hoffman, eds., *Why I Am a Christian: Leading Thinkers Explain Why They Believe* (Grand Rapids. Mich.: Baker Books, 2007).

24. Pamela Binnings Ewen, *Faith on Trial* (New York: B&H Publishing, 1998).

25. Lee Strobel, *The Case for Christ: A Journalist's Personal Investigation of the Evidence for Jesus* (Grand Rapids, Mich.: Zondervan, 1998).

26. Timothy Keller, *The Prodigal God: Recovering the Heart of the Christian Faith* (Boston, Mass.: Dutton Adult, 2008).

27. Kosmin and Keysar, *American Religious Identification Survey (ARIS) 2008*, i.

28. Peace, *Word and World:* "Holy Conversation: The Lost Art of Witness," 257.

29. Geisler and Hoffman, *Why I Am a Christian*, 87–104.

30. Fr. Benedict Groeschel, *Tears of God: Persevering in the Face of Great Sorrow or Catastrophe* (Fort Collins, Colo.: Ignatius Press, 2009).

31. Paul E. Little, *Know Why You Believe* (Downers Grove, Ill.: InterVarsity Press, 2008).

32. John Eldridge, *Epic: The Story God is Telling* (Nashville: Thomas Nelson, 2007).

33. Geisler and Hoffman, *Why I Am a Christian*, 221–238, 239–262.

34. Strobel, *The Case for Christ*, 131–190.

35. Paul E. Little, *How to Give Away Your Faith* (Downers Grove, Ill.: InterVarsity Press, 2008).

36. Philip Yancey, *The Jesus I Never Knew* (Grand Rapids, Mich.: Zondervan, 1996).

37. Geisler and Hoffman, *Why I Am a Christian*, 197–220.

38. F. F. Bruce, *The New Testament Documents: Are They Reliable* (Downers Grove, Ill.: InterVarsity Press, 1997).

39. J. P. Moreland, "Why I Have Made Jesus Christ Lord of My Life," in Norman L. Geisler and Paul K. Hoffman eds., *Why I Am a Christian: Leading Thinkers Explain Why They Believe* (Grand Rapids, Mich.: Baker Books, 2006).

40. Brad Kallenberg, *Life to Tell: Evangelism for a Postmodern Age* (Grand Rapids, Mich.: Baker Books, 2002).

41. Brent Curtis and John Eldredge, *The Sacred Romance: Drawing Closer to the Heart of God* (Nashville: Thomas Nelson, 1997).

42. Billy Graham, *Peace with God* (Garden City, N.Y.: Doubleday Publishing, 1953).

WAYPOINT 11

1. Ralph Waldo Emerson, retrieved from http://www.brainyquote.com/quotes/keywords/god_10.html.

2. Michael Franzese, *Quitting the Mob* (New York: HarperCollins, 1992); *Blood Covenant: The Michael Franzese Story* (New Kensington, Pa.: Whitaker House, 2003); *The Good, the Bad, and the Forgiven* (Vista, Calif.: Outreach, 2008); *I'll Make You an Offer You Can't Refuse: Insider Business Tips from a Former Mob Boss* (Nashville: Thomas Nelson, 2009).

3. David A. DeCenzo and Stephen P. Robbins, *Fundamentals of Human Resource Management*, 6th ed. (Hoboken, N.J.: Wiley-Blackwell, 2006), 122–139.

4. Peter G. Northouse, *Introduction to Leadership: Concepts and Practice* (Thousand Oaks, Calif.: Sage Publications, 2009), 2–3.

5. Adapted from the United Methodist Church's *Explore Your Spiritual Gifts* (http://www.umc.org/site/c.lwL4KnN1LtH/b.1355371/k.9501/Spiritual_Gifts.htm, 2009); Jack W. MacGorman's *The Gifts of the Spirit* (Nashville: Broadman Press, 1974); Kenneth C. Kinghorn's *Gifts of the Spirit* (Nashville: Abingdon Press, 1976); and C. Peter Wagner's *Your Spiritual Gifts Can Help Your Church Grow: How to Find Your Gifts and Use Them to Bless Others* (Ventura, Calif.: Regal Books, 1994). For an extended discussion of these gifts, see Waypoint 2.

6. For this gift, there are several interpretations: Donald Gee, *Concerning Spiritual Gifts* (Springfield, Mo.: Gospel Publishing House, 1972) and Wagner, *Your Spiritual Gifts Can Help Your Church Grow.*

7. Here again there are several perspectives: Gee, *Concerning Spiritual Gifts* and Kinghorn, *Gifts of the Spirit.*

8. Varied perspectives exist here as well: Gee, *Concerning Spiritual Gifts*; Kinghorn, *Gifts of the Spirit*; and Wagner, *Your Spiritual Gifts Can Help Your Church Grow.*

9. For varied interpretations, see Wagner, *Your Spiritual Gifts Can Help Your Church Grow* and Gee, *Concerning Spiritual Gifts.*

10. The United Methodist Church, "Explore Your Spiritual Gifts," http://www.umc.org/site/c.lwL4KnN1LtH/b.1355371/k.9501/Spiritual_Gifts.htm, 2009.

11. For the classical Pentecostal viewpoint, see Wagner, *Your Spiritual Gifts Can Help Your Church Grow*, 256–257.

12. For another viewpoint of this and other gifts see the United Methodist Church's definitions in "Explore Your Spiritual Gifts," http://www.umc.org/site/c.lwL4KnN1LtH/b.1355371/k.9501/Spiritual_Gifts.htm, 2009.

13. A person who has a spiritual gift should "expect confirmation from the Body" according to Wagner, *Your Spiritual Gifts Can Help Your Church Grow,* 123–124.

WAYPOINT 10

1. O. J. Simpson, http://www.famousquotesandauthors.com/topics/self_reliance_quotes.html.

2. Psychological research on rejection is still in its infancy. However, the most exhaustive look at this malady is in a volume edited by Mark R. Leary, *Interpersonal Rejection* (Oxford, UK: Oxford University Press, 2006).

3. R. F. Baumeister and M. R. Leary, "The Need to Belong: Desire for Inter-personal Attachments as a Fundamental Human Motivation," in *Psychological Bulletin*, 117 (1995), 497.

4. William McDougall, *An Introduction to Social Psychology*, 23rd ed. (London: Methuen and Co., 1937), 373.

5. Despondency often manifests itself via one of two avenues. First, it can bring on social withdrawal. This is because people feel that the future is so bleak they can only count on themselves for survival. This will often result in run-ning away from friendships and responsibilities. Second, the person may become suicidal, seeing no potential gain or improvement in their situation.

6. Though depression often results from rejection or despondency, depres-sion can result from a host of other maladies as well. The reader should not infer that because a person is depressed the reason is solely rejection or despondency. The reader should probe further with a depressed indi-vidual and assist him or her to seek professional help. Depression is mentioned here to acquaint the reader with possible behaviors that way-farers at Waypoint 10 might exhibit.

7. American Psychiatric Association, *Diagnostic and Statistical Manual of Mental Disorders DSM-IV-TF*, 4th ed. (Arlington, Va.: American Psy-chiatric Association, 2000), 345–427.

8. There are a number of good resources for assisting people who are bat-tling depression. A successful technique pioneered by Albert Ellis called "rational emotive behavior theory" suggests replacing negative behaviors with positive ones. See William J. Knaus, *The Cognitive Behavioral Workbook for Depression: A Step-by-step Program* (Oakland, Calif.: New Harbinger Publications, 2006) and William Backus and Marie Chapian, *Telling Yourself the Truth: Find Your Way Out of Depression, Anxiety, Fear, Anger, and Other Common Problems By Applying the Principles of Misbelief Therapy* (Minneapolis, Minn.: Bethany House, 2000).

9. Psychologists often label excessive self-confidence as the "overconfi-dence effect," which has been shown to be prevalent in varied professions. B. Fischoff, "Judgment and Decision Making," in *The Psy-chology of Human Thoughts*, R. J. Sternberg and E. E. Smith, eds. (Cambridge, UK: Cambridge University Press, 1988).

10. Peter G. Northouse, *Introduction to Leadership: Concepts and Practice* (Thousand Oaks, Calif.: Sage Publications, 2009), 2.

11. F. F. Bruce, *New Testament History* (New York: Doubleday Publishing, 1971), 32–40.

12. For the background and context of Francis Thompson's poem "The Hound of Heaven," see John R. W. Stott, *Why I am a Christian* (Downers Grove, Ill.: InterVaristy Press, 2004), 15.

13. Northouse, *Introduction to Leadership*, 2–3.

14. C. Peter Wagner, *Your Spiritual Gifts Can Help Your Church Grow: How to Find Your Gifts and Use Them to Bless Others* (Ventura, Calif.: Regal Books, 1994).

15. Ibid., 255. Scriptures that describe the "gift of mercy" include: Matthew 20:29–34; 25:34–40; Mark 9:41; Luke 10:33–35; Acts 16:33–35; 11:28–30; Romans 12:8.

WAYPOINT 9

1. A pseudonym for an actual soldier who communicated with Shane Claiborne.

2. Shane Claiborne, foreword to Christopher L. Heuertz, *Simple Spirituality: Learning to See God in a Broken World* (Downers Grove, Ill.: InterVarsity Press, 2008), 12.

3. C. F. Walter Bosing, *The Complete Paintings of Bosch*, rev. ed. (Cologne, Ger.: Taschen Books, 2000), 14.

4. James F. Engel, *Contemporary Christian Communications: It's Theory and Practice* (Nashville: Thomas Nelson, 1979), 210.

5. Rainer's research found that "a significant number of the unchurched told us that their first reason for visiting a church was a crisis," *Surprising Insights from the Unchurched* (Grand Rapids, Mich.: Zondervan, 2001), 169.

6. "A person who is captive to self navigating . . . can never please God." Engel, *Contemporary Christian Communications*, 211.

WAYPOINT 8

1. C. S. Lewis, *The Great Divorce* (New York: Harper & Row, 1945), 75.

2. James F. Engel, *Contemporary Christian Communications: It's Theory and Practice* (Nashville: Thomas Nelson, 1979), 211.

3. An excellent book that biblically and historically examines the rationale and requirements of God's holiness is Keith Drury's aptly titled *Holiness for Ordinary People* (Indianapolis, Ind.: Wesleyan Publishing House, 1983). See especially the chapter "It's Everywhere" for a biblical examination of the scope of holiness.

4. Lewis, *The Great Divorce*, 75.

5. Donald A. McGavran, *The Bridges of God: A Study in the Strategies of Missions* (Eugene, Ore.: Wipf and Stock Publishers, 1955).

6. For a concise and helpful overview of the three primary approaches to exploring conversion, psychological, sociological, and physiological, see Engel, *Contemporary Christian Communications*, 206–210.

7. William James, *The Varieties of Religious Experience* (London: Longmans Publishing, 1902), 114.
8. Engel, *Contemporary Christian Communications*, 211.
9. Ibid.
10. Ibid., 210.
11. Ibid., 211.
12. Ibid.
13. Faith means "to trust, to (have) confidence in God" (William F. Arndt and F. Wilbur Gingrich, *A Greek-English Lexicon of the New Testament* [Chicago: University of Chicago Press, 1957], 668–670). And repentance indicates "the idea of turning" to be in line with these realities (Richard Peace, "Conflicting Understandings of Christian Conversion: A Missional Challenge" in *International Bulletin of Missionary Research,* vol. 28, No. 1, 8). I touch on these in more detail in Waypoint 7, yet here it is important to note that faith and repentance regarding Reality 1 and Reality 2 will result in faith in Reality 3.
14. Arndt and Gingrich, *A Greek-English Lexicon of the New Testament*, 301.
15. Various forms of declaration are often exhibited at this juncture. And declaratory actions that accompany conversion are as diverse as cultures. On one hand in modernist societies shaped by education, a testimony might be expected. While on the other hand, in postmodern environs influenced by action, serving others might be anticipated. For more on the behavioral differences between modernist and postmodernist cultures and their impact upon explaining the good news, see *Preparing for Change Reaction: How to Introduce Change in Your Church* (Indianapolis, Ind.: Wesleyan Publishing House, 2007), 49–7 and *Inside the Organic Church: Learning from 12 Emerging Congregations* (Nashville: Abingdon Press, 2004), xxiii–xxxiii; and Bob Whitesel and Kent Hunter, *A House Divided: Bridging the Generation Gaps in Your Church* (Nashville: Abingdon Press, 2000), 13–81.
16. Engel, *Contemporary Christian Communications*, 211.
17. Ibid.

WAYPOINT 7

1. Richard Peace, "Conflicting Understandings of Christian Conversion: A Missiological Challenge," in *International Bulletin of Missionary Research*, vol. 28, No. 1, 8.
2. William F. Arndt and F. Wilbur Gingrich, *A Greek-English Lexicon of the New Testament and Other Early Literature* (Chicago: University of Chicago Press, 1957), 668–670.

3. Ibid., 301.

4. Richard Peace, *Conversion in the New Testament: Paul and the Twelve* (Grand Rapids, Mich.: Eerdmans Publishing, 1999), 7–11.

5. For more on manipulative conversion, see Flo Conway and Hi Siegelman, *Snapping America's Epidemic of Sudden Personality Change* (Philadelphia, Pa.: Lippincott Williams & Wilkins, 1978). For an overview of the New Testament milieu of conversion, and varieties of conversion in secular life, see A. D. Nock's classic historical treatise *Conversion: The Old and the New in Religion from Alexander the Great to Augustine of Hippo* (Baltimore, Md.: John Hopkins University Press, 1933).

6. Robert Jay Lifton, *Thought Reform and the Psychology of Totalism: A Study of "Brainwashing" in China* (New York: W. W. Norton & Co., 1961).

7. For examples of the range and variety in Christian conversionary experiences, see Hugh T. Kerr and John M. Mulder, eds., *Conversions: The Christian Experience* (Grand Rapids, Mich.: Eerdmans Publishing, 1983).

8. Quoted by Jacob W. Heikkinen, "Conversion: A Biblical Study," in *National Faith and Order Colloquium*, World Council of Churches, June 12–17, 1966, 1.

9. Arndt and Gingrich, *A Greek-English Lexicon of the New Testament*, 301.

10. Peace, "Conflicting Understandings of Christian Conversion," 8.

11. Ibid.

12. Arndt and Gingrich, *A Greek-English Lexicon of the New Testament*, 668–670.

13. Peace, "Conflicting Understandings of Christian Conversion," 8.

14. Charles Kraft, "Christian Conversion as a Dynamic Process," in *International Christian Broadcasters Bulletin* (Colorado Springs, Colo.: International Christian Broadcasters, 1974), second quarter; Scot McKnight, *Turning to Jesus: The Sociology of Conversion in the Gospels* (Louisville, Ky.: Westminster John Knox Press, 2002); Richard Peace, *Conversion in the New Testament: Paul and the Twelve*, 6; "Conflicting Understandings of Christian Conversion"; and Lewis R. Rambo, *Understanding Religious Conversion* (New Haven, Conn.: Yale University Press, 1993).

15. Peace, *Conversion in the New Testament: Paul and the Twelve*, 6.

16. Peace, "Conflicting Understandings of Christian Conversion," 8–9.

17. Donald Miller's analysis of the results of crusade evangelism in the Harvest Crusades with evangelist Greg Laurie discovered that only about 10 percent of the decisions for Christ resulted in long-term changes in personal behavior (*Reinventing American Protestantism: Christianity in the new Millennium* [Berkeley, Calif.: University of California Press, 1997],

171–172). However, Sterling Huston's earlier research on the Billy Graham Crusades suggested the results were six times this (Sterling W. Huston, *Crusade Evangelism and the Local Church* [Minneapolis, Minn.: World Wide Publishers, 1984]). Whether these discrepancies were the result of tactics, cultures, samples, or eras remains to be researched. The answer may lie somewhere in between. The ambiguity of these results begs further analysis by researchers.

18. Rambo, *Understanding Religious Conversion*, 165.

19. Charles Kraft introduced terminology to distinguish the different types of people that experience sudden conversion or progressive conversion. On the one hand, Kraft saw that people who undergo radical and sudden conversion are usually "first-generation Christians" who previously had only been moderately influenced by Christian principles. On the other hand, Kraft saw "second-generation Christians" as those who were raised in Christian homes and in which "there may be little or no behavioral change evident as a result of the conscious decision to personally affirm one's commitment to the Christian community in which one has been practicing since birth" (Charles Kraft, "Christian Conversion as a Dynamic Process," *International Christian Broadcasters Bulletin*, 8.) While the terms *first-* and *second-generation Christians* have been widely used, these terms cause some problems. First, Paul's conversion was certainly radical and sudden (Acts 9), yet he had been practicing a devout lifestyle (Acts 23:6). So in Kraft's paradigm, he should have had a more progressive experience. In addition, McKnight's story does not fit with Kraft's paradigm, for in the interview that concludes this chapter, McKnight states that he underwent a radical behavioral change in a progressive sequence. Thus, the value of Kraft's insights may be that there are numerous ways that conversion is encountered and that whether a person is a first- or second-generation Christian has some, though limited, effect. Instead, the emphasis should be upon the fluid role of the Holy Spirit in individualizing conversion to each traveler, for as John 3:7 states:

> So don't be so surprised when I tell you that you have to be "born from above"—out of this world, so to speak. You know well enough how the wind blows this way and that. You hear it rustling through the trees, but you have no idea where it comes from or where it's headed next. That's the way it is with everyone "born from above" by the wind of God, the Spirit of God. (MSG)

20. Peace, *Conversion in the New Testament*, 4.

21. Ibid., 10. Some may argue that progressive conversion as described in Mark was necessitated because the Holy Spirit had not yet been given at the day of Pentecost. While this is a valid critique, Lewis Rambo's research suggesting that most conversion is progressive (Rambo, *Understanding Religious Conversion*, 165) may indicate that both examples are valid.

22. McKnight, *Turning to Jesus*, 5.

23. Ibid., 7.

24. Quoted by Jacob W. Heikkinen, "Conversion: A Biblical Study," in *National Faith and Order Colloquium*, World Council of Churches, June 12–17, 1966, 1.

25. Arndt and Gingrich, *A Greek-English Lexicon of the New Testament*, 301.

26. McKnight, *Turning to Jesus*, 1.

27. Arndt and Gingrich, *A Greek-English Lexicon of the New Testament*, 301.

28. Richard Peace, "Holy Conversation: The Lost Art of Witness" in *Word and World: Theology for Christian Ministry,* vol. 22, no. 3, 255–263.

WAYPOINT 6

1. Woody Allen, http://www.quotationspage.com/quote/51.html.

2. For a postmodern inclination to prefer biblical narratives, see my research in *Inside the Organic Church: Learning from 12 Emerging Congregations* (Nashville: Abingdon Press, 2004).

3. Billy Graham, *Just As I Am: The Autobiography of Billy Graham* (New York: HarperOne, 2007), 31.

4. Dietrich Bonhoeffer, *The Cost of Discipleship* (New York: Macmillan Publishers, 1966) and Eberhard Bethge, ed., *Letters and Papers from Prison* (New York: Macmillan Publishers, 1972).

5. Marvin Andrew McMickle, "Adam Clayton Powell Sr.," in *An Encyclopedia of African American Christian Heritage* (Valley Forge, Pa.: Judson Press, 2002).

6. For more on the influence that Abyssinian Baptist Church and its pastor Adam Clayton Powell Sr. had on Dietrich Bonhoeffer, see J. Deotis Roberts, *Bonhoeffer and King: Speaking Truth to Power* (Louisville, Ky.: Westminster John Knox Press, 2005), 46–47.

7. Charles Kraft, *Christianity in Culture* (Maryknoll, N.Y.: Orbis Books, 1979), 116–146.

8. Eddie Gibbs, *I Believe in Church Growth* (Grand Rapids, Mich.: Eerdmans Publishing, 1981), 120.

9. Donald A. McGavran and C. Peter Wagner, *Understanding Church Growth* (Grand Rapids, Mich.: Eerdmans Publishing, 1970), 395.

WAYPOINT 5

1. Leo F. Buscaglia, *Love: What Life Is All About* (New York: Ballantine Books, 1996), 55.
2. Jacob's Well, http://jacobswellchurch.org.
3. For more about cultures and how Christ redeems some aspects of cultures while condemning elements that run counter to God's requirements, see "The Character of a Culture" in my book *Preparing for Change Reaction: How to Introduce Change in Your Church* (Indianapolis, Ind.: Wesleyan Publishing House, 2007), 58–71.
4. Plato's method of engaging and teaching was different from that of his mentor and mouthpiece Socrates. Socrates tendered difficult questions to his pupils so they could mull over the topic in their own minds before arriving at a conclusion. Socrates' questions could be biting at times, especially when he detected an error in the logic of his pupil. Because of such piercing questions of the Athenian political scene, Socrates came to be known as the "gadfly" or "stinging fly" of Athens (Plato, *Apology*, James J, Helm ed. [Mundelein, Ill.: Bolchazy-Carducci Publishers, 1997], 57).
5. Felix Marti-Ibanez, *Tales of Philosophy* (New York: Clarkson Potter, 1964), 31.
6. Tim Keel, personal correspondence with the author, June 18, 2009.
7. George Elton Ladd, *A Theology of the New Testament* (Grand Rapids, Mich.: Eerdmans Publishing, 1974), 545.
8. For more on the organic nature of the church, see my book, *Inside the Organic Church: Learning from 12 Emerging Congregations* (Nashville, Abingdon Press, 2006), xxiv–xxxviii.
9. Ladd, *A Theology of the New Testament*, 532.
10. Francis Brown, S. R. Driver, and Charles Briggs, *A Hebrew and English Lexicon of the Old Testament* (Oxford, UK: Clarendon Press, 1974), 1005.
11. William F. Arndt and F. Wilbur Gingrich, *A Greek-English Lexicon of the New Testament* (Chicago: University of Chicago Press, 1957), 723.
12. John Perkins, *A Call to Wholistic Ministry* (St. Louis, Mo.: Open Door Press, 1980), 43–44.
13. John R. W. Stott, *Christian Mission* (Downers Grove, Ill.: InterVarsity Press, 1975), 30.
14. I have suggested that a healthy model for most churches will be a multi-generational structure, and I have described seven steps for growing a multi-generational church in Bob Whitesel and Kent R. Hunter, *A House Divided: Bridging the Generation Gaps in Your Church* (Nashville: Abingdon Press, 2001).

15. Bob Whitesel, "The Perfect Cluster: For Young Adults, St. Tom's, Sheffield Creates Extended Families, And Everyone Knows Where They Fit" in *Outreach Magazine*, vol. 4, issue 3 (Vista, Calif.: Outreach Inc., 2005), 112–114.

16. Mike Breen, personal conversation with the author, Sheffield, UK, May 20, 2004.

17. Ladd, *A Theology of the New Testament*, 543.

18. Ibid.

19. If this interests you, download the following book: Bob Hopkins and Mike Breen, *Clusters: Creative Midsized Missional Communities* (Sheffield, UK: 3D Publishing, 2007) from http://www.3dministries.com/store/Products/Clusters—Creative-Mid-Sized-Missional-Communities-Download_3010.aspx.

WAYPOINT 4

1. Mohandas Karamchand Gandhi, as quoted by William Rees-Mogg in *The Times* (London, 4 April 2005). Gandhi is referring to the statement of Jesus in Luke 16:13, which says, "No servant can serve two masters. Either he will hate the one and love the other, or he will be devoted to the one and despise the other. You cannot serve both God and Money."

2. See the earlier chapter titled "Waypoint 7: New Birth" to review the differences between sudden conversion and progressive conversion.

3. Though other Gospels and Epistles provide fitting examples as well of the spiritual foundation for the wayfarer, to keep the scriptural references from becoming too vast, I will limit the references to the gospel of Mark. This was done for two reasons. First, Mark provides the most concise rendering of Jesus' ministry and thus is a suitable and comprehensive overview for a new disciple. Second, the author, Mark, underscores the progressive nature of the disciples' belief. For a thorough examination of Mark in relationship to the conversion of the disciples, see Richard Peace, *Conversion in the New Testament: Paul and the Twelve* (Grand Rapids, Mich.: Eerdmans Publishing, 1999), 105–281, 319–329.

4. Jim Dunn, *The Process of Spiritual Formation*, letter to the author, nd.

5. Meditating on God's Word or on his work in our lives is often a way to focus on God's goodness in a hectic and hostile world. Richard Foster has said, "The detachment from the confusion all around us is in order to have a richer attachment to God. Christian meditation leads us to the inner wholeness necessary to give ourselves to God freely." Richard Foster, *The Celebration of Discipline: The Path to Spiritual Growth* (New York: HarperOne, 1988), 21.

6. Bob Whitesel, *Growth By Accident, Death By Planning: Missteps with Staff* (Nashville: Abingdon Press, 2004), 139–140.
7. Dietrich Bonhoeffer, *Life Together*, trans. John W. Doberstein (New York: Harper & Row, 1954), 19.
8. Peter Block, *Community: The Struggle of Belonging* (San Francisco: Berrett-Koehler Publishers, 2008), 95.
9. Mike Breen first proposed the triangle in *Outside In: Reaching Unchurched Young People Today* (Bletchley, UK: Scripture Union Publishing, 2003) and later developed the triangle and accompanying icons into a discipleship tool called "LifeShapes." For more information, see Mike Breen and Walt Kallestad, *The Passionate Church: The Art of Lifechanging Discipleship* (Colorado Springs, Colo.: Cook Publications, 2005). For an overview of the LifeShapes icons, see my book, *Inside the Organic Church: Learning from 12 Emerging Congregations* (Nashville: Abingdon Press, 2006), 6–8.
10. Paddy Mallon wrote a probing look at the rise of St. Thomas' Church to England's largest Anglican congregation: *Calling a City Back to God* (Eastbourne, UK: Kingsway Publishers, 2003).
11. Sometimes the OUT or "outreach" element of small groups is the most difficult to foster. Some small groups are effectively closed to outsiders, often because the small group has shared personal challenges and they eschew the idea of sharing these too publicly. Thus, a small group, even without realizing it, may not make newcomers feel welcome. And this may be permissible for small groups with attendees struggling with personal and confidential life issues. Still, these groups should be engaged in some outreach in order to maintain a healthy balance of three small group elements. If they do not maintain this balance, they can become self-centered rather than altruistic. Mike Breen's congregation in Sheffield, England, overcame this problem by combining three to five small groups into an outreach and service "cluster." See Breen and Bob Hopkins, *Clusters, Midsized Missional Communities* (Sheffield, UK: Anglican Church Planting Initiatives, 2008). These clusters range in size from thirty-five to seventy-five people and provide a good-sized force for social service ministries. In addition, Breen found that clusters that met once a month were better venues for reaching out to newcomers and helping them find a suitable small group. When three to five small groups are clustered, the newcomer can participate in the cluster and through relationships, discover which small group is best for them. Breen also said, "People don't feel they lost their friends when they start a new small group, and some members of their group leave to help start it. They still

see each other in the monthly cluster meetings, and thus they don't feel like they've lost their former small group friends." (Mike Breen, personal conversation, Sheffield, UK, June 10, 2009).

12. In addition to not having enough small groups, the other weakness that undermines healthy churches today is not having robust prayer ministries. Toward fostering prayer ministry see Whitesel, "Missteps with Prayer" in *Growth By Accident, Death By Planning*, and Bob Whitesel and Kent R. Hunter, "Step 7: Mobilizing Your Church for Transgenerational Prayer," *A House Divided: Bridging the Generation Gaps in Your Church* (Nashville: Abingdon Press, 2001). Also see Elmer Towns' exhaustive study on the correlation between church growth and vibrant prayer in *Praying the Lord's Prayer for Spiritual Breakthrough* (Ventura, Calif.: Gospel Light Publications, 1997); *How to Pray When You Don't Know What to Say: More Than 40 Ways to Approach God* (Ventura, Calif.: Regal Books, 2006); and *Prayer Partners: How to Increase the Power and Joy of Your Prayer Life by Praying with Others* (Ventura, Calif.: Regal Books, 2006).

13. I have a proposed chart in my book, *Growth By Accident Death By Planning*, 142–143.

14. For more on the importance of the "bridges of God," see Donald A. McGavran, *The Bridges of God: A Study in the Strategies of Missions* (Eugene, Ore.: Wipf and Stock Publishers, 1955).

15. The division method of small group proliferation is not recommended unless there is a growing feeling among small group participants that the group is nearing the end of its life cycle. Some small groups can last for years or even decades because they provide a needed accountability and community for people struggling with life issues. For instance, small groups dealing with addictive behavior or health issues may exist for many years because these issues often a long time to address. In addition, older members of a congregation may need long-lasting small groups because they find the stability they need in a small group environment. For instance, aging congregants will usually be experiencing increasing instability in their finances and health, and many of their family and friends may be moving away or dying. Thus, for seniors, the small group environment of a Sunday school can provide the reliable community and fellowship that they need to replace the loss of these in other areas. Therefore, it is not advisable to divide or abruptly end these types of groups. Instead, it is a better strategy to allow such small groups to multiply through sponsorship or sending just a few members out to plant a new group. Both of these strategies allow small groups to participate in multiplication without disbanding a needed small group.

WAYPOINT 3

1. This quote is from a speech prepared for delivery in Dallas, the day of his assassination, November 22, 1963, from Nelle Connally and Mickey Herskowitz, *From Love Field: Our Final Hours with President John F. Kennedy* (New York: Rugged Land, 2003), 180.
2. J. Robert Clinton utilizes the term "imitation modeling" for this training model. It is described in greater detail in J. Robert Clinton, *Leadership Emergence Patterns: A Self-study Manual for Evaluating Leadership Selection Processes* (Altadena, Calif.: Barnabas Resources, 1984).
3. J. Robert Clinton, *The Making of a Leader: Recognizing the Lessons and Stages of Leadership Development* (Colorado Springs, Colo.: NavPress, 1988), 31.
4. Churches under 125 in adult attendance primarily function as one large, extended family. These networks, sometimes called "clusters" (Bob Hopkins and Mike Breen, *Clusters: Creative Midsized Missional Communities* [Sheffield, UK: 3D Ministries, 2007]) or "sub-congregations" (Bob Whitesel and Kent R. Hunter, *A House Divided: Bridging the Generation Gaps in Your Church* [Nashville: Abingdon Press, 2001], 13–29) conduct most of their training via informal networks (Bob Whitesel, *Growth By Accident, Death By Planning: Missteps with Staff* [Nashville: Abingdon Press, 2004], 109–120).
5. Whitesel, *Growth By Accident, Death By Planning*, 121–123; Roger Finke and Rodney Stark, *The Churching of America 1776–2005: Winners and Losers in Our Religious Economy* (Piscataway, N.J.: Rutgers University Press, 2005); Roger Finke and Kevin Dougherty, "The Effects of Professional Training: The Social and Religious Capital Acquired in Seminaries," in *Journal for Scientific Study of Religion* 41 (2002), 103–120.

WAYPOINT 2

1. Rod Stewart and Ron Wood, "Every Picture Tells a Story," album by the same title (Los Angeles: Polygram Records, 1971).
2. J. Robert Clinton, *The Making of a Leader: Recognizing the Lessons and Stages of Leadership Development* (Colorado Springs, Colo.: NavPress, 1988), 32.
3. See the definitions and scriptural explanation of these gifts in Figure 2.1.
4. Leadership scholar Peter Northouse describes traits, abilities, skills, and behaviors as the basic building blocks of leadership (*Introduction to Leadership: Concepts and Practice* [Thousand Oaks, Calif.: Sage Publications, 2009], 2–3). *Traits* are inherent and endowed qualities; *abilities* are aptitudes developed by experience; *skills* are methods for carrying out leadership; and

behaviors are what leaders do with traits, abilities, and skills. Northouse makes a persuasive argument that all leaders develop these elements of leadership. First Corinthians 12:7; Ephesians 4:7; and 1 Peter 4:10 appear to indicate that such predilections take on supernatural vigor when empowered by the Holy Spirit.

5. James D. G. Dunn, *Jesus and The Spirit: A Study in the Religious and Charismatic Experience of Jesus and the First Christians as Reflected in the New Testament* (Philadelphia: Westminster Press, 1975), 205–209.

6. I am indebted to Eddie Gibbs for this comparative structure from *I Believe in Church Growth* (Grand Rapids, Mich.: Eerdmans Publishing, 1981), 325.

7. Clinton, *The Making of a Leader*, 32.

8. C. Peter Wagner holds that witnessing a gift in use in the body of Christ verifies its legitimacy (*Your Spiritual Gifts Can Help Your Church Grow: How to Find Your Gifts and Use Them to Bless Others* [Ventura, Calif.: Regal Books, 1994], 67). I disagree with Wagner here, who embraces a too-open-ended approach to spiritual gifts. I find Wagner's viewpoint interesting and possibly supportable if there is spiritually mature verification (see 1 Cor. 12–14). However, this may be forcing the text to express too much from silence. I see the lack of comprehensive nature in the three gift lists suggesting other biblically verifiable gifts, but not going so far as to support just any gift that appears in the Church. For more on a scriptural three-criteria assessment of spiritual gifts, see Dunn, *Jesus and the Spirit*, 293–297.

9. Adapted from the United Methodist Church's *Explore Your Spiritual Gifts* (http://www.umc.org/site/c.lwL4KnN1LtH/b.1355371/k.9501/Spiritual_Gifts.htm, 2009); Jack W. MacGorman's *The Gifts of the Spirit* (Nashville: Broadman Press, 1974); Kenneth C. Kinghorn's *Gifts of the Spirit* (Nashville: Abingdon Press, 1976); and C. Peter Wagner's *Your Spiritual Gifts Can Help Your Church Grow*. Note that the list tendered here is not definitive, nor exhaustive. Rather, it is a codification of the above gift inventories and designed to provide a holistic list for Christian communities seeking to help travelers at Waypoint 2. For a chart of the gifts correlated with their biblical attestations, see George Elton Ladd, *A Theology of the New Testament* (Grand Rapids, Mich.: Eerdmans Publishing, 1974), 534–535.

10. The gift of hospitality is often primarily associated, though erroneously, with church assimilation programs such as hosting newcomer tables, greeting church visitors, etc. However, when the Scriptures discuss the gift of hospitality, something more radical and basic is indicated by the

context. For example, Peter admonishes the church in 1 Peter 1:9 to offer hospitality in scenarios where grumbling might be the normal reaction. The context of Peter's admonition (1 Pet. 1:1–11) indicates that Peter is talking about giving hospitality not only to the Christians, but also to those who heap abuse upon Christians. Such radical hospitality means meeting what Maslow described as physiological and safety needs before that person is ready to have their needs met for belongingness and love met (Abraham H. Maslow, *Motivation and Personality*, 2nd ed. [New York: Harper & Row, 1970], 300–394; and *The Farther Reaches of Human Nature* [New York: Viking Press, 1971], 300).

11. This is a gift for which there are several interpretations. Assemblies of God writer Donald Gee sees the gift of knowledge as a supernatural forth-telling (Donald Gee, *Concerning Spiritual Gifts* [Springfield, Mo.: Gospel Publishing House, 1972]. Others, like Wagner (*Your Spiritual Gifts Can Help Your Church Grow*), take a less supernatural route, noting that "those who have this gift are superior learners" (p. 190). It is not my intention to side with one interpretation over the other, for readers from various backgrounds and theology will use this book. Therefore, this book is designed to describe the gifts from varying perspectives, to allow the reader to embrace the interpretation that best fits his or her understanding, tradition, and theology.

12. Here again are several perspectives. For examples of the differences see Gee's *Concerning Spiritual Gifts* and Kenneth C. Kinghorn's *Gifts of the Spirit* (Nashville: Abingdon Press, 1976).

13. The gift of service is sometimes attached too exclusively to administrative tasks (*Your Spiritual Gifts Can Help Your Church Grow*, 258) when, in the context of verses such as 2 Timothy 1:16–18, the gift of service indicates organizing to meet the needs of all others. Thus, the gift of service should not be primarily a service to the church, but equally indicate serving the needs of those outside the church.

14. This is another gift that has a more supernatural tenor in Gee's *Concerning Spiritual Gifts*. Kinghorn (*Gifts of the Spirit*) and Wagner (*Your Spiritual Gifts Can Help Your Church Grow*) see the gift of wisdom differently, as those possessing insight and perception into problems and solutions.

15. See the United Methodist Church's definition in "Explore Your Spiritual Gifts," http://www.umc.org/site/c.lwL4KnN1LtH/b.1355371/k.9501/Spiritual_Gifts.htm, 2009.

16. Regarding this gift, see Wagner's *Your Spiritual Gifts Can Help Your Church Grow* for a charismatic viewpoint and Gee's *Concerning Spiritual Gifts* for a classical Pentecostal viewpoint.

17. The charismatic and classical Pentecostal viewpoints are best described by Wagner in *Your Spiritual Gifts Can Help Your Church Grow*, 256–257.
18. For another viewpoint of this and other gifts, see the United Methodist Church's definitions in "Explore Your Spiritual Gifts," http://www.umc.org/site/c.lwL4KnN1LtH/b.1355371/k.9501/Spiritual_Gifts.htm, 2009.
19. For the stories of five missionary martyrs, see Wagner, *Your Spiritual Gifts Can Help Your Church Grow,* 62–63.
20. Some authors list craftsmanship and music as gifts of the Holy Spirit (see Christian A. Schwarz, *The 3 Colors of Ministry* [St. Charles, Ill.: ChurchSmart Resources, 2001], 157), but these designations are actually subcategories of artist. To use these subcategories ignores the important Scriptural attestations to the Old Testament artisans who worked in varied crafts and mediums. Thus, for a more holistic understanding, "artist" better sums up this categorical gift. Needless to say, Sally Morgenthaler's story illustrates the various permutations of what may be an artistic gifting.
21. Ray Stedman, *Body Life* (Ventura, Calif.: Regal Books, 1972), 54.
22. Richard Houts originally published his thoughts in *Eternity Magazine* (Philadelphia, Pa.: Evangelical Foundation, 1976). He also penned the *Houts Inventory of Spiritual Gifts: A Self-assessment Instrument to Help Ascertain Your Ministry Gift, or Gifts, and the Related Opportunities for Christian Service* (Pasadena, Calif.: Fuller Evangelistic Association, 1985). Other authors have adapted the Houts questionnaire to specific audiences and denominational perspectives, including Ruth Towns and Elmer Towns, *Women Gifted for Ministry: How to Discover and Practice Your Spiritual Gifts* (Nashville: Thomas Nelson, 2001); David Stark, Sandra Hirsch, and Jane Kise, *LifeKeys: Discovering Who You Are* (Minneapolis, Minn.: Bethany House Publishers, 2005); Aubrey Malphurs, *Maximizing Your Effectiveness* (Grand Rapids, Mich.: Baker Books, 2006), 199–208; Larry Gilbert, *Spiritual Gifts Inventory: Discover Your Spiritual Gift in Only 20 Minutes* (Elkton, Md.: Church Growth Institute, 1999); and specifically for teens, Jane Kise and Kevin Johnson, *Find Your Fit: Dare to Act on God's Gift for You* (Minneapolis, Minn.: Bethany House, 1999).
23. Dunn, *Jesus and the Spirit*, 291–300.
24. Findley B. Edge, *The Greening of the Church* (Dallas, Tex.: Word, 1971), 141.

WAYPOINT 1

1. William James, http://thinkexist.com/quotes/william_james.
2. Ann Curry, "Rick Warren: Pastor in the Political Spotlight," *Dateline NBC*, Dec. 19, 2008.

3. Michael H. Kernis, "Toward a Conceptualization of Optimal Self-esteem," in *Psychology Inquiry: An International Journal for the Advancement of Psychological Theory*, vol. 14 (New York: Psychology Press, 2003), 1–26.

4. For the latest secular research into elements of authenticity in leadership, see Bruce J. Avolio and William L. Gardner, "Authentic Leadership Development: Getting to the Root of Positive Forms of Leadership" in *The Leadership Quarterly*, vol. 16, issue 3 (College Park, Md.: International Leadership Association, June 2005), 315–338.

5. Peter Northouse, *Introduction to Leadership: Concepts and Practice* (Thousand Oaks, Calif.: Sage Publications, 2009), 2–3.

6. Various nomenclatures exist for the three types of leadership traits. Below is a comparison of some of the most notable examples.

A Comparison of Designations for the Three Leadership Traits		
Strategic Leadership	**Tactical Leadership**	**Operational Leadership**
Visionaries (George Barna,[a] Leith Anderson,[b] and Phil Miglioratti[c]) *Role one leaders* (Phil Miglioratti[c]) *Top management* (John Wimber and Eddie Gibbs[d]) *Strong, directive pastoral leadership* (C. Peter Wagner[e]) *Upper-level management* (John Kotter[f]) *Sodality leadership* (Ralph Winter[g]) *To infect others with a vision for change* (Warren Bennis and Burt Nanus[h])	*Administrators* (Phil Miglioratti[c]) *Role two leaders* Phil Miglioratti[c]) *Planning, organizing, staffing, and controlling* (Henri Fayol[i]) *Middle-level management* (D. Martin Butler and Robert D. Herman[j]) *Middle management* (John Wimber, Eddie Gibbs,[d] and John Kotter[f]) *"Enables others to achieve goals"* (Richard Hutcheson[k]) *Problem solvers* (Gary Yukl[l]) *Modality leadership* (Raplh Winter[g]) *To accomplish change and master routines* (Warren Bennis and Burt Nanus[h])	*Workers* (Phil Miglioratti[c]) *Role three leaders* (Phil Miglioratti[c]) *Foremen* (John Wimber and Eddie Gibbs[d])
[a] George Barna, *The Power of Vision* (Ventura, Calif.: Regal Books, 1992), 38–39. [b] Leith Anderson, *Dying for Change* (Minneapolis, Minn.: Bethany House, 1990), 177–178. [c] Phil Miglioratti, "Putting Your Laymen Where They Will Do the Most Good," in *The Pastor's Church Growth Handbook* (Pasadena, Calif.: Church Growth Press, 1979), 146. [d] Eddie Gibbs, *I Believe in Church Growth* (Grand Rapids, Mich.: Eerdmans Publishing, 1981), 383–385. [e] C. Peter Wagner, *Leading Your Church to Growth* (Ventura, Calif.: Regal Books, 1984), 73–74. [f] John Kotter, *A Force for Change: How Leadership Differs from Management* (Boston: Harvard University Press, 1990). [g] Ralph Winter, cited by Wagner, *Leading Your Church to Growth*, 141–165. [h] Warren G. Bennis and Burt Nanus, *Leaders: Strategies for Taking Charge* (New York: Harper & Row, 1985), 221. *continued*		

ⁱ Henri Fayol, *General and Industrial Management* (London: Pitman, 1916). Fayol was one of the first theoriticans to clearly differentiate the tactical and strategic roles of leadership.

^jD. Martin Butler and Robert D. Herman, "Effective Ministerial Leadership," in *Nonprofit Manbagement and Leadership* (1999), 9:229–239.

^kRichard Hutcheson Jr., *The Wheel Within the Wheel: Confronting the Management Crisis of the Pluralistic Church* (Atlanta: John Knox Press, 1979), 54.

^lGary Yukl, *Managerial Practice Survey* (Albany, N.Y.: Gary Yukl and Man Associates, 1990).

7. For more on strategic, tactical, and operational leadership, including a questionnaire to see which trait you or your leaders exhibit, see my book *Preparing for Change Reaction: How to Introduce Change in Your Church* (Indianapolis, Ind.: Wesleyan Publishing House, 2007), 29–48.

8. Michael O'Brien, *Hesburgh: A Biography* (Washington, D.C.: Catholic University of America Press, 1998), 256.

9. Quoted by Gail McMeekin, *The 12 Secrets of Highly Creative Women: A Portable Mentor* (San Francisco: Red Wheel/Weiser, 2000), 207.

10. Whitesel, *Preparing for Change Reaction*, 37.

11. Bruce J. Avilio and Fred Luthans, *The High Impact Leader: Moments Matter in Accelerating Authentic Leadership Development* (New York: McGraw-Hill, 2005), 13.

12. Northouse, *Introduction to Leadership Concepts and Practice*, 2.

13. Fred Luthans and Bruce J. Avolio, "Authentic Leadership: A Positive Development Approach," in *Positive Organizational Scholarship: Foundations of a New Discipline*, K. S. Cameron, J. E. Dutton, and R. E. Quinn, eds. (San Francisco: Berrett-Koehler, 2003), 243.

14. Ibid.

15. Scott Schmieding, *Fighting Cancer with Faith* (Baton Rouge, La.: DivineRx, nd).

16. Bob Whitesel, *Inside the Organic Church: Learning from 12 Emerging Congregations* (Nashville: Abingdon Press, 2006), 133–134.

17. Luthans and Avilio, *The High Impact Leader*, 94–95.

18. Bob Whitesel, *Growth By Accident, Death By Planning: Missteps with Staff* (Nashville: Abingdon Press, 2004), 27.

19. Ibid.

20. Adrian Chan, Sean T. Hannah, and William L. Gardner "Veritable Authentic Leadership: Emergence, Functioning, and Impacts" in *Authentic Leadership Theory and Practice, Volume 3: Origins, Effects and Development*, Bruce J. Avolio, William L. Gardner and Fred O. Walumbwa, eds. (Greenwich, Conn.: JAI Press, 2005), 26.

21. Remus Ilies, Frederick P. Morgeson, and Jennifer D. Nahrgang, "Authentic Leadership and Eudaemonic Well-being: Understanding Leader–follower

Outcomes" in *The Leadership Quarterly*, vol. 16, issue 3 (College Park, Md.: International Leadership Association, June 2005), 383.

22. For a questionnaire to determine whether you have strategic, tactical, or operational leadership traits, see my book *Preparing for Change Reaction: How to Introduce Change in Your Church*, 46–47.

WAYPOINT O

1. George Bernard Shaw, commenting upon the outlook of John Bunyan's hero, Christian, as Christian looked back from the "brink of the river of death over the strife and labor of his pilgrimage," from "Man and Superman," in *Plays by George Bernard Shaw* (New York: Signet Classics, 1960), 257.

2. Alistair Davidson, *Antonio Gramsci: Towards an Intellectual Biography* (Atlantic Highlands, N.J.: Humanities Press, 1977).

3. Clinton sometimes adds an additional sixth phase called "afterglow" or "celebration," though he admits it occurs rarely and much of it overlaps with "convergence" (*The Making of a Leader: Recognizing the Lessons and Stages of Leadership Development* [Colorado Springs, Colo.: NavPress, 1988], 30). Since "afterglow" is atypical and a suitable research base to analyze it is not available, I have chosen not to reflect on "afterglow" separately, but instead to address the areas in which "afterglow" overlaps with "convergence."

4. Clinton, *The Making of a Leader*, 33.

5. Ibid.

6. Ibid.

7. Shaw, 257.

APPENDIX

1. Donald A. McGavran, *Effective Evangelism: A Theological Mandate* (Phillipsburg, N.J.: Presbyterian and Reformed Publishing Company, 1988). Eugene Nida had earlier warned of the Christian propensity to eschew assessment in *Message and Mission: The Communication of the Christian Faith* (New York: Harper & Row, 1960).

2. See John 17:3 and Romans 10:13, also James F. Engel, *Contemporary Christian Communications: Its Theory and Practice* (Nashville: Thomas Nelson, 1979), 66–68.

3. Nida and McGavran emphasized that outreach should to be evaluated and not simply assumed. See Nida's *Message and Mission* and McGavran's and Wagner's *Understanding Church Growth* (Grand Rapids, Mich.: Eerdmans Publishing, 1970), where McGavran called the church's avoidance of evaluation equivalent to creating a "universal fog" of empirical murkiness, 76–120.

4. Engel, *Contemporary Christian Communications*, 79–80.
5. This is not to say that presentations of the good news are not necessary, effective, or needed. They are. But Engel saw, as did my friend Doug, a fixation or "nearsightedness" in evangelical churches where the new birth event blinded the church to its important task in the process that leads up to the new birth waypoint and beyond. *Contemporary Christian Communications*, 86.
6. Bob Whitesel, *Inside the Organic Church: Learning from 12 Emerging Congregations* (Nashville: Abingdon Press, 2006), 108–123 and *Preparing for Change Reaction: How to Introduce Change in Your Church* (Indianapolis, Ind.: Wesleyan Publishing House, 2007), 117–131.
7. Al Tizon, *Transformation After Lausanne: Radical Evangelical Mission in Global-Local Perspective* (Eugene, Ore.: Wipf & Stock Publishers, 2008); Ron Sider, *The Scandal of Evangelical Politics: Why Are Christians Missing the Chance to Really Change the World?* (Grand Rapids, Mich.: Baker Books, 2008).
8. This can help small churches whose only option is to partner with another church to offer more waypoints on the evangelistic journey. It can increase congregational self-esteem to know that they are helping in a portion of the process. An example of a two churches that partnered two decades ago and have now grown into a "yoked mega-church" is St. Thomas's Church of Sheffield, England (Anglican Church of England), and the Philadelphia Church (Baptist Union of Great Britain). For their remarkable story, see Paddy Mallon's *Calling a City Back to God: A Sheffield Church, Over 2,000 Strong, Most Below 40 Years Old . . . What Can We Learn?* (Eastbourne, UK: Kingsway Communication, Ltd., 2003).
9. Ronald J. Sider and others, *Linking Arms, Linking Lives: How Urban-Suburban Partnerships Can Transform Communities* (Grand Rapids, Mich.: Baker Books, 2008).
10. For more on why group exits occur and preventative measures, see my book *Staying Power: Why People Leave the Church Over Change, and What You Can Do About It* (Nashville: Abingdon Press, 2003).
11. Some may wonder if expanding a church's ministry into neighboring waypoints might undermine nearby churches that are succeeding in those waypoints. However, since the majority of Americans do not attend church, there is a substantial need for more holistic and multiple-waypoint approaches to disciple the current population.
12. James F. Engel and Wilbert Norton, *What's Gone Wrong with the Harvest?: A Communication Strategy for the Church and World Evangelism* (Grand Rapids, Mich.: Zondervan, 1975), 45.

13. James F. Engel, *The Church Growth Bulletin* (Pasadena, Calif.: Fuller Evangelistic Association, 1973). Engel stressed that his decision scale emphasized how a church's "communication ministries" must change as the traveler journeys through the spiritual decision process. *What's Gone Wrong With the Harvest?*, 44–45. Unfortunately, the published designation, "Engel's Scale of Spiritual Decision," clouds Engel's emphasis upon the elastic role of the church's communication, and thus this scale's designation does not correspond to its content.

14. Engel's Scale of Spiritual Decision has been codified from several of Engel's variations. See Engel and Norton, *What's Gone Wrong with the Harvest?*, 45; Engel, *Contemporary Christian Communications*, 63–87, 225; James F. Engel and William A. Dyrness, *Changing the Mind of Missions: Where Have We Gone Wrong* (Downers Grove, Ill.: InterVarsity Press, 2000), 100–101. The current example has been adapted by the author.

15. For an explanation of each of the types of church growth found in Acts 2:42, along with measurement tools to track each, see Bob Whitesel and Kent Hunter, *A House Divided: Bridging the Generation Gaps in Your Church* (Nashville: Abingdon Press, 2000), 207–218.

16. Engel, *Contemporary Christian Communications*, 81. Scot McKnight's observations indicate that some denominations might disagree with Engel's placing baptism at +2. McKnight notes that some liturgical traditions place baptism earlier, at Engel's New Birth juncture. McKnight offers a helpful overview of when and how different denominations view baptism as corresponding to the conversionary experience. He notes that evangelicals and Pentecostals view "personal decision" as the place of conversion, while some mainline Protestants see conversion associated with a long nurturing process (McKnight calls this "conversion through socialization"). He then notes that some liturgical traditions may view conversion as attached to liturgical acts such as baptism, the sacraments, and "official rites of passage." Scot McKnight, *Turning to Jesus: The Sociology of Conversion in the Gospels* (Louisville, Ky.: Westminster John Knox Press, 2002), 1–7. Subsequently, depending on the tradition and practice, baptism may be viewed as occurring anywhere between the stages of New Birth through +2.

17. Engel, *Contemporary Christian Communications*, 82.

18. Engel sometimes talks about communion with God (+4) and Stewardship (+5) as subsets of +3 Conceptual and Behavioral Growth. Engel, *Contemporary Christian Communications*, 83; *What's Gone Wrong with the Harvest?*, 45, 52–56.

19. Engel, *Contemporary Christian Communications*, 66–68.
20. See John C. Maxwell, *The 21 Indispensable Qualities of a Leader, Becoming the Person Others Will Want to Follow* (Nashville: Thomas Nelson, 1999); Max DePree, *Leadership is an Art* (New York: Dell Publishing, 1989); Tom Rath and Barry Conchie, *Strengths-Based Leadership* (Washington, D.C.: Gallup Press, 2009); Seth Godin, *Tribes: We Need You to Lead Us* (New York: Portfolio, 2008).
21. J. Robert Clinton, *The Making of a Leader: Recognizing the Lessons and Stages of Leadership Development* (Colorado Springs, Colo.: NavPress, 1988), 30.
22. Ibid.
23. Ibid., 31.
24. Ibid.
25. While Clinton addresses the influence of personal mentoring, he does not address the influence of the Christian community to the degree of Engel. Research shows that the health of a church community is an important factor in fostering leadership development (Bob Whitesel, *Growth By Accident, Death By Planning: Missteps with Staff* [Nashville: Abingdon Press, 2004], along with parallels in the business world, Mary Jo Hatch and Majken Schultz, *The Dynamics of Organizational Identity* [Oxford, UK: Oxford University Press, 2004] and Mary Jo Hatch, Monika Kostera, and Andrzej K. Kozminski, *Three Faces of Leadership: Manager, Artist, Priest* [Malden, Mass.: Blackwell Publishing, 2005]).
26. This would be Engel's substage of "discovery and use of gifts."
27. For "A Comparison Between Institutionalization and Improvisation," see my book *Inside the Organic Church: Learning from 12 Emerging Congregations* (Nashville: Abingdon Press, 2006), 119.
28. Clinton, *The Making of a Leader*, 32.
29. Ibid.
30. Ibid.
31. While Engel emphasizes spiritual disciplines, there is no guarantee in Engel's scale that spiritual maturity will correspond with these actions. For example, just because a person is experiencing Engel's +8 Stage of stewardship of resources, or +9 stage of prayer, does not mean that person is actually growing in maturity. These are actions that should accompany maturity in faith, but do not necessarily do so. Engel emphasizes the artifacts of the journey, but Clinton emphasizes their influence.
32. For examples of the widespread use of icons in contemporary communication, see Whitesel, *Inside the Organic Church*.

33. See also my analysis of postmodern church patterns in *Inside the Organic Church* and *Preparing for Change Reaction*, noting chapter 3 on change and culture.
34. This is my version of these phases and how they relate to Engel's and Clinton's.

WAYPOINTS AND THEIR CORRELATION TO ENGEL AND CLINTON	
16	No awareness of a supreme being (Engel)
15	Awareness of a supreme being, no knowledge of the good news (Engel)
14	Initial awareness of the good news (Engel)
13	Awareness of the fundamentals of the good news (Engel)
12	Grasp of the implications of the good news (Engel)
11	Positive attitude towards the good news (Engel)
10	Personal problem recognition (Engel)
9	Decision to act (Engel)
8	Repentance and faith in Christ (Engel and Clinton)
7	NEW BIRTH (Engel and Clinton)
6	Post-decision evaluation (Engel)
5	Incorporation into the body (Engel and Clinton)
4	Spiritual foundations (Whitesel)
+3	Conceptual and behavioral growth (Engel)
+3.1	Sovereign foundations (Clinton)
3	Inner-life growth (Clinton)
+4.1	Communion with God (Engel)
+5	Stewardship (Engel)
2	Ministry emergence (Clinton)
1	Influence emergence (Whitesel)
	Life Maturation (Clinton)
0	Convergence or Afterglow (Clinton)